1988

AN INTRODUCTION TO STATISTICAL METHODS IN THE BEHAVIORAL SCIENCES

Roger E. Kirk, Consulting Editor

Exploring Statistics: An Introduction for Psychology and Education

Sarah M. Dinham
The University of Arizona

Methods in the Study of Human Behavior

Vernon Ellingstad and Norman W. Heimstra
The University of South Dakota

An Introduction to Statistical Methods in the Behavioral Sciences

Freeman F. Elzey
San Francisco State University

Experimental Design: Procedures for the Behavioral Sciences

Roger E. Kirk
Baylor University

Statistical Issues: A Reader for the Behavioral Sciences

Roger E. Kirk
Baylor University

The Practical Statistician: Simplified Handbook of Statistics

Marigold Linton
The University of Utah
Philip S. Gallo, Jr.
San Diego State University

Nonparametric and Distribution-Free Methods for the Social Sciences

Leonard A. Marascuilo
University of California, Berkeley
Maryellen McSweeney
Michigan State University

Basic Statistics: Tales of Distributions

Chris Spatz
Hendrix College
James O. Johnston
University of Arkansas at Monticello

Multivariate Analysis with Applications in Education and Psychology

Neil H. Timm
University of Pittsburgh

AN INTRODUCTION TO STATISTICAL METHODS IN THE BEHAVIORAL SCIENCES

FREEMAN F. ELZEY

San Francisco State University

Brooks/Cole Publishing Company
Monterey, California
A Division of Wadsworth Publishing Company, Inc.

ISBN: 0-8185-0194-4
L.C. Catalog Card No.: 76-9924
Printed in the United States of America

10 9 8 7 6 5 4 3

Interior & Cover Design: *John Edeen*
Typesetting and Illustrations: *TechnoLogue Corporation, Phoenix, Arizona*
Printing & Binding: *R. R. Donnelley & Sons Company, Crawfordsville, Indiana*

To Barsha and Peter

PREFACE

This book presents the fundamental statistical techniques that are generally taught in beginning courses at the undergraduate level. It represents an applied approach to the use of statistics for describing and analyzing data generated through research processes.

The focus of this book is on the major concepts and techniques covered in an introductory one-semester course; it describes commonly used statistical procedures and shows how these procedures can be used to solve problems in the behavioral sciences. Descriptive and inferential statistics are included, and fully worked-out examples are presented to illustrate each type. Methods using both numbers and graphs are employed to describe sets of data and relative placement of individual measures, formulas for estimating population parameters from sample data, and the calculation of confidence intervals. Inferential statistical methods commonly used in hypothesis-testing research involving both directional and nondirectional hypotheses are illustrated. Type I and Type II errors are covered, along with considerations of test power. The techniques discussed include t tests, one-way analysis of variance, Pearson product-moment correlation and Spearman rank-order correlation, regression, and chi square. Conventional symbolic notation has been used throughout the book.

This book is directed primarily to the student who is unfamiliar with the basic concepts of statistical techniques and the mathematics needed to apply these techniques. Only the most rudimentary algebraic skills are required, involving substitution of numbers for symbols and the solving of equations. Nothing more than addition, subtraction, multiplication, and division is needed. (A table of square roots and directions for its use are provided and should be used as needed for certain formulas.)

The book does not attempt to develop mathematical derivations or formal mathematical proofs of the various formulas; the focus is on understanding the techniques and applying them to research problems. Each technique is illustrated by a simple example, and step-by-step calculations are shown. Theoretical concepts are presented in narrative form.

All data presented in this book are fictitious and were developed specifically to illustrate the various techniques. To reduce computational drudgery, the data presented have been kept to the minimum amount necessary to illustrate the techniques. The student should be cautioned, however, that studies are seldom conducted in which the sample sizes are as small as those used in the examples and exercises in this text.

Two sets of exercises are given for each chapter; answers to problems in Group A are given at the back of the book, and answers to Group B are available to the instructor in a separate pamphlet. The two exercise sets require comparable skills, and a student who successfully completes Group A should have no difficulty completing Group B. Students may wish to work through Group A exercises and check their results with the answers provided before completing Group B exercises, which the instructor may assign as homework.

As a special feature, a supplemental text by the author, entitled *A Programmed Introduction to Statistics, Second Edition,* provides a step-by-step application of the statistical formulas using programmed instructional techniques; the programmed format allows the student to participate in the instructional process by actively responding to a sequence of finite steps and receiving immediate feedback. The programmed text is compatible with this text, since the formulas and sequence of presentation are identical in both. In the programmed book, the formulas, tables, and glossary of symbols can be removed for convenient reference while the student works with either text. Students who have difficulty with the computational aspects of statistics will find the programmed text especially helpful. The programmed sets corresponding to chapters in this text are as follows:

Text chapter	*Programmed sets*
1	—
2	1
3	2, 3, & 4
4	5
5	6 & 7
6	8 & 9 (through frame 32)
7	9 (beginning with frame 33) & 10
8	11 & 12 (through frame 21)
9	12 (beginning with frame 22) & 13
10	14
11	15 & 16
12	17
13	18 & 19
14	20 & 21
15	22
16	23
17	24 & 25

I wish to express my sincere appreciation to Professor Samuel Levine of San Francisco State University for his continual advice and encouragement during the preparation of this book. Grateful acknowledgement is also given to Jerome Podell of San Francisco State University, Arthur Roberts of California State University at Chico, and Thomas Zullo of the University of Pittsburgh for their reviews of preliminary versions of the manuscript.

My particular gratitude goes to Professor Roger Kirk of Baylor University, who meticulously edited the book at each stage of its writing. While only the author can assume responsibility for the content of a book, I am indeed appreciative of the care and concern with which Professor Kirk reviewed the manuscript. His many suggestions were quite helpful.

I am also indebted to the literary executor of the late Sir Ronald A. Fisher, F.R.S., Cambridge, and to Oliver & Boyd Limited, Edinburgh, for their permission to reprint tables from the book *Statistical Methods for Research Workers*.

Freeman F. Elzey

CONTENTS

CHAPTER 1
INTRODUCTION

A major obstacle that an instructor facing a group of students in a beginning statistics class must overcome is the apprehension and often downright fear of some students at the prospect of taking statistics. This apprehension has a number of causes. First, there is the fear of the unknown: these students do not have a clear idea of what statistics is all about, why they need to gain competence in it, and how this competence will be useful in their professional careers.

Second, because of the mathematical nature of the subject, students fear that it will demand more mathematical sophistication than they possess. Such fears are revealed in such expressions as "I was never any good in math," "I have forgotten all I ever knew about algebra," and "I managed to pass geometry and trigonometry but didn't learn a thing." Third, as the beginning student flips through the statistics text, he or she sees many unfamiliar terms, such as standard deviation, regression coefficient, and standard error of the mean, as well as an overwhelming array of symbols and formulas, and immediately despairs of mastering the content of the text in the short time of one semester.

Last, students in the behavioral sciences, including education, psychology, and anthropology, are sometimes biased against quantitative approaches to the study of people. They are skeptical about describing behavior in numerical terms, performing statistical manipulations on sets of numbers, and making sweeping statements about human behavior on the basis of statistical findings. If the instructor wants to teach statistics effectively, he must deal with these anxieties at the outset of the course.

Allaying Anxiety

Many instructors spend part of the first class session trying to calm students who feel that they are in for an unpleasant and frustrating experience. This text is designed to help the instructor dispel these fears.

Many texts that are used in beginning statistics courses include much more material than students can assimilate during a single semester. As a result, certain sections or chapters must be skipped, breaking the author's sequence of topics. This text includes only those aspects of statistics that are generally covered in a one-semester course, and it is designed so that later topics build directly from preceding ones. Therefore, it should be used in its entirety and in the sequence presented.

The language of the text has been kept as simple and direct as possible. Some students benefit by having the more difficult statistical concepts presented in several slightly different ways. Therefore, the presentation may appear to be redundant at some points. Hopefully, students who understand the concepts on first reading will not be bothered by later repetition of them.

For each technique discussed in this text, there is first a discussion of the rationale underlying its use, next a presentation of the formula or formulas used in it, and finally an illustration of the computations involved, using a simplified example. Many formulas are presented in two ways: the conceptual form shows the student what the formula is "doing" to the data, and the mathematically equivalent computational formula provides an easier format for the actual calculations.

All formulas are presented in the text, as well as in Appendix A. Appendix B contains the statistical tables needed, and Appendix C provides a glossary of symbols and abbreviations.

The features of this text are designed to reduce the anxiety of students and to make the presentation a logical, thorough, and understandable one for beginning students. For those who need or want more guidance and practice in the concepts presented in this book, a supplemental self-guiding text, *A Programmed Introduction to Statistics, Second Edition,* by Freeman F. Elzey (Monterey, Calif.: Brooks/Cole Publishing Company, 1971) will prove very helpful. A table listing the programmed sets in that book and the corresponding chapters in this text appears in the Preface (see page vii).

What Is Statistics?

The study of statistics provides us with methods for describing and summarizing research data, for specifying the probability that data obtained from a sample or samples reflect the true state of affairs in the population represented by the sample or samples, for uncovering the relationship between sets of measurements, and for making predictions.

Statistics can be divided generally into two types: descriptive and inferential. *Descriptive statistics* provide us with ways to reduce quantities of data into manageable form and to describe them precisely in terms of averages, differences, relationships, and so on. The early chapters of this text present some ways of statistically describing and graphically depicting research data. However, in research in the behavioral sciences, mere description of the data obtained from a sample or samples is of little use. The scientist is more likely to be interested in the process of making generalizations from the sample to the wider population. *Inferential statistics* provide the analytic methods for making these generalizations. For example, if two samples of students are given two different instructional methods, and the average final scores of the two groups are different, this difference may be due either to the different instructional methods or to chance factors. Inferential statistical methods permit us to determine the probability that the difference is due to chance, rather than to the effects of the instructional methods.

The basic purposes of inferential statistical methods are (1) to estimate unknown population values from the observable measurements obtained from samples and (2) to test research hypotheses, using sample data. Some of the common inferential techniques used for these two purposes are presented in this text.

Statistics as a Tool of Research

It must be stressed at the outset that statistical procedures deal with numbers. Where the numbers come from and what they represent fall in the province of the researcher. Meaningful statistical conclusions can result only from the analysis of data that have been collected through carefully controlled research studies. Where this is the case, statistics is a valuable tool in research.

Research is generally defined as a controlled inquiry used to uncover relationships among phenomena. The appropriate research design must be selected if valid conclusions are to be reached. Research projects in the behavioral sciences rely heavily on statistical procedures for data collection, organization, and analysis. In fact, assuming that the researcher has used appropriate research procedures, it is the use of statistics to present and analyze the data that provides the basis for support or nonsupport of the researcher's hypothesis. Use of proper statistical procedures is vital if the research results are to be clearly and unambiguously interpreted.

While it is true that the primary statistical functions cannot occur until the data are collected, it would be a mistake for the researcher to ignore the talents of a statistician in planning and conducting research studies. It is of utmost importance that he develop plans for organizing, summarizing, and analyzing data at the time the project is being designed. Failure to do so may lead to inappropriate and/or inefficient data collection procedures, resulting in a body of data that cannot be properly analyzed. Without statistical planning, the researcher may make costly mistakes and his conclusions may not be valid.

In summary, this text introduces a number of statistical techniques that are generally used in research studies. The tasks of stating research hypotheses, developing research designs, selecting measuring instruments, and specifying data-collection procedures are left to texts that deal with research methods.

CHAPTER 2
ORGANIZATION
OF DATA

Statistical data are the "ingredients" with which statisticians work. A *datum* is the record of a single observation. Here the term *observation* is used in the broad sense. It may be an individual's test score, a "yes" vote for a candidate, a response to an interview question, the time it takes a rat to run a maze, or the position in which a horse finishes a race. Each observation is converted to a numerical representation since, to be useful for statistical description and analysis, the outcome of an experiment or research project is usually stated in the form of numbers. A set of numerals representing records of observations is termed *statistical data*. Thus, the political preferences of a selected sample of voters, the number of runs scored by a baseball team, and the heights of sixth-grade students in San Francisco are each considered to be a set of statistical data.

The numerals constituting a set of data are quantitative representations of what we observe directly or infer from observations. These numerals can result from various types of measurement. Thus, measurement techniques provide us with a process for transforming observations or inferences into usable numerals.

In the examples given above it should be obvious that there are various kinds of measurement used for different purposes. Clearly, the number of earned baseball runs, the heights of children, and the order in which horses finish a race are determined by different measurement techniques.

Specific terms are used in research to describe the behavior or characteristic to be measured. A behavior or characteristic that takes on different values is called a *variable*. For example, if we obtain a set of spelling scores, we say that we have data on the variable of spelling ability. If we determine the sex of each member of a selected group of people, we have data on the variable of sex. Motivation, ethnic identification, social competence, age, typing ability, and so on—all are called variables. Some variables take on quantitative differences, whereas others differ in quality. Any characteristic that varies among the members of the group being measured is termed a variable.

A characteristic that does not vary is termed a *constant*. If a research study is concerned only with college freshmen, the class level is considered to be a constant. In most research studies we deal with both variables and constants; that is, we may select individuals for study who have certain known characteristics (constants) and then obtain data on other characteristics (variables) that we wish to learn about. Consider a study of the aggression levels of fourth-grade boys under two types of adult supervision. Here sex and grade level are constants, whereas level of aggression and adult supervision are variables. It should be evident that the same characteristics can be constants in some situations and variables in others.

What is measurement and how do we use it to transform observations into data? Measurement is the assignment of numbers to observations according to some preset rules. Thus, when we measure a student's arithmetic ability, we assign a number to him that reflects the pattern of his responses to a given set of arithmetic problems. The manner in which each item is judged correct or incorrect and the way in which the total score is established are determined by a set of rules of measurement; that is, the items may be valued at one point each, or items may have differential weightings according to their relative importance.

The different types of measurement used to convert observations into numerical data, are generally divided into four categories, which are called *levels of measurement*. Each of these four levels, which are described below, is uniquely useful to the statistician.

Nominal Measurement

This level of measurement involves the process of classifying objects, people, responses, and so on into categories. Thus, it is used to classify people by sex, racial affiliation, or nationality, for example. In nominal measurement we list the various category headings and then determine how many observations fall under each. For example, we can classify people according to their political affiliation, as in Table 2-1. In the table, political affiliation is the variable being considered, and each individual in the survey has been placed in one of the five categories.

Table 2-1. Political affiliations of 23 individuals.

Political affiliation	Number of individuals
Republican	7
Democrat	8
Independent	3
Socialist	3
Undecided	2

When employing nominal measurements we must follow three rules.

1. *The list of categories must be sufficient to cover all of the observations in the study.* That is, every observation must fall into one of the listed categories. (In our example, if we did not have a category titled "Undecided," we would have been unable to account for the responses of two individuals in our survey.)
2. *The categories must be mutually exclusive.* The descriptions of the categories must be such that any individual observation can be placed in only one category.
3. *No order is implied in the listing of the categories.* The headings only indicate different categories within the variable. The order in which they are listed is arbitrary and does not indicate any quantifiable differences among them. (In our example, we could just as meaningfully have listed them in any other order.)

For convenience, numerals are sometimes assigned to the categories, especially when the data are to be processed by computer. (In our example, the numeral 1 could have been assigned to Republicans, 2 to Democrats, and so on.) It is important to recognize that the numeral is assigned for identification only and does not indicate that one category is "better" than another. This procedure for grouping data into categories is frequently called "using a measurement scale," but this is actually a misnomer since no scale can be implied in the listing of the categories.

Additional examples using nominal measurement are given in Table 2-2.

Table 2-2. Frequency distributions of nominal data.

(a)			(b)		(c)	
Religious affiliation	Number of individuals	Sex	Number of individuals	Automobile type	Number of individuals
Protestant	30	Female	89	Sedan	12
Catholic	45	Male	41	Convertible	3
Jewish	60			Station Wagon	5
Other	14				

Ordinal Measurement

The ordinal level of measurement can be used in situations where we are able to detect *degrees of difference* among the observations. This scale implies that there is an "ordering" of the data. In ordinal measurement, the data are arranged in rank order and they are assigned numbers representing rankings. For example, if we line up students according to their weight, and assign 1 to the heaviest, 2 to the next heaviest, 3 to the next, and so on, these rankings constitute a set of ordinal measurements on the variable of weight. Our ordinal data might look like those presented in Table 2-3. Notice that these numbers do not indicate how much each student weighs or the amounts of weight differences among them. Ordinal measurement only indicates the placement of the individuals relative to each other. Other examples of ordinal measurement are the standings of football teams, order of finishing a task, and teacher rankings of students according to their academic potential.

Table 2-3. Rank order of weights of five students.

Name	Rank
Mary	1 (heaviest)
Peter	2
Sam	3
Sally	4
Mike	5 (lightest)

Interval Measurement

When we assume that the differences between our measurement units are the same size throughout the scale, we are using the interval level of measurement. In interval scales, the equal intervals or distances between units on the scale represent empirically equal differences in the characteristic being measured. This property of equal intervals permits us to perform arithmetic operations of addition and subtraction on data of this type. Not many measurements meet this stringent requirement. Although IQs are sometimes treated as though they were on an interval scale, equal units of IQs do not actually represent equal increments in intelligence. For example, the difference between IQs of 130 and 140 represents a much larger increase in intelligence than does the difference between IQs of 100 and 110.

A distinguishing characteristic of this scale is the fact that the zero point does not necessarily represent the total absence of the phenomenon being measured. For example, a score of zero on a statistics quiz does not mean that a person is devoid of all knowledge of statistics, and a score of zero on a college aptitude examination does not mean that the person taking the test has no aptitude for college at all! Nor is it logical to say that a person having an IQ of 120 is twice as intelligent as a person having an IQ of 60.

Generally, the test developer arbitrarily selects the numeral that is assigned to a given level of performance. (The number 400 could have been designated the average IQ just as easily as 100 was.)

A commonly cited example of interval measurement is the Fahrenheit scale for measuring temperature, in which zero does not represent the total absence of heat. It would be inaccurate to say that on this scale 100° is twice as hot as 50°.

Ratio Measurement

In contrast to the interval scale, the ratio scale does assume that there is an absolute zero point at which the scale originates. In cases where zero represents the total absence of a phenomenon and equal-sized units from this zero point represent empirically equal differences, we are using the ratio scale of measurement. Common ratio scales are those measuring weight, time, and height. On such scales it is possible to indicate that one person weighs twice as much as another or that it took one rat four times longer than its companion to run a maze. Ratios between such measurements can be meaningfully interpreted. For example, on the Kelvin scale for measuring temperature, zero indicates the total absence of heat and a temperature of 100° is considered to be twice as hot as one of 50°.

It should be noted that very few variables in educational and psychological studies lend themselves to the ratio scale of measurement. Also, many measurements, such as test scores, are commonly treated as interval-scale measurements even though the assumption of equal-sized intervals may be questionable. The ordinal and interval levels of measurement are most often used in education and psychology.

It is important that the statistician determine whether the data have been obtained by counting (nominal measurement), by ranking (ordinal measurement), or by measuring quantities (interval or ratio measurement), because different statistical approaches are used with the different types of measurement scales. In this text we will present statistical techniques that are appropriate for obtaining data using each of these scales.

At this point we need to consider one other characteristic of statistical data that affects the way in which we may analyze them. There are two types of variables—*discrete* and *continuous*. *Discrete* variables are those for which only certain values are possible. The variable of sex yields discrete measurements since it can take on only two values—male and female. Variables such as the size of a family or the number of houses on a block are also discrete since they require exact counts using integers. That is, a family may have two, three, four, or more members, but it cannot have 3.47 or 5.2 members; blocks can have 17 or 18 houses but they cannot have 17.8 houses.

Variables such as weight, length, and age, for which measurements can theoretically have *any* value, are considered *continuous* variables. For example, a person's age or weight can be represented by any one of an infinite range of values; the actual value we assign is determined by the precision of our measuring instrument. Thus, a man's weight may be 165.4124 pounds (or any other fractional value between 165 and 166 pounds), and he may be 29.6803 years old (or any other value between 29 and 30 years). Even these measurements are probably inexact; the fractional portion could be extended even further with more sensitive measuring devices. We are never able to obtain exact measurements on continuous variables; in contrast to measurements on discrete variables, which can be exact, measurements on continuous variables can only be approximate.

Psychological variables, such as intelligence, motivation, anxiety, and desire for approval, are theoretically considered continuous, even though we must settle for discrete approximations in our measurements of them. For example, if Mary obtains an IQ of 112, we must consider this an approximation of her intelligence quotient, which, barring measurement errors, we assume to be somewhere between 111.5 and 112.5.

In summary, when we use discrete variables, we are dealing with exact measurements; when we use continuous variables, we are always obtaining approximate measurements. As we shall see later, we use different statistical techniques depending upon whether the data represent continuous or discrete variables.

Summarizing Data

Our first task when we are confronted with data is that of summarizing and organizing them into a form suitable for display and analysis. For example, suppose we ask 40 elementary schoolchildren which animal they would choose as a pet and receive the following responses:

Dog	Rabbit	Cat	Turtle	Dog
Cat	Dog	Dog	Dog	Cat
Turtle	Dog	Cat	Rabbit	Cat
Rabbit	Cat	Dog	Rabbit	Dog
Cat	Cat	Cat	Cat	Turtle
Rabbit	Dog	Cat	Dog	Rabbit
Cat	Turtle	Rabbit	Dog	Dog
Rabbit	Dog	Dog	Rabbit	Dog

It is difficult to determine the children's preference pattern from this set of data. We need to organize the data to get a clear picture of the trend of the children's responses. The first step is to determine the frequency with which each animal has been chosen. In this example, "dog" was selected by 15 children. In statistical terms we say that the category "dog" has a frequency of 15. We can determine the frequency of choice for each of the other animals and list them in a *frequency distribution,* as shown in

Table 2-4. Here we have introduced our first two statistical symbols: f, meaning frequency, and N, meaning the total number of responses. In this example, the data collected represent nominal measurements, since there is no hierarchical "scale" implied in the arrangement of the animal choices presented to the children. In preparing the frequency distribution given in Table 2-4, we could just as meaningfully list the four animals in any order, but for ease of presentation we generally list the categories in the order of the frequency with which they were chosen, as we did here.

Table 2-4. Frequency distribution of pet choices of 40 children.

Animal	f
Dog	15
Cat	12
Rabbit	9
Turtle	4
	$N = 40$

In Table 2-4, a child chose only one from a limited number of alternatives. The children's choices represent measurements on a *discrete* variable; that is, we can consider this an example of exact measurement, since there is no possibility of a choice falling between any two alternatives.

Having collected these data, we can now *rank* the animals according to the children's preferences, thus converting our original nominal measurements to ordinal measurements. By assigning a rank of 1 to the most preferred animal, we can obtain the ordinal measurements given in Table 2-5. Note that we could not have ranked the animals before collecting the data. The distinction here is that the list of animals represents the nominal level of measurements, whereas the order of the children's preferences for the animals represents the ordinal level.

Table 2-5. Rank order of pet preferences of 40 children.

Animal	Rank
Dog	1
Cat	2
Rabbit	3
Turtle	4

Now we shall look at another set of data. Thirty-five college students were given a test designed to assess their anxiety at the prospect of taking a course in advanced calculus. Their anxiety-test scores are presented in Table 2-6.

Table 2-6. Anxiety-test scores for 35 students.

71	68	69	68	70
69	69	70	68	69
70	68	72	69	70
66	71	68	70	68
69	68	69	66	69
69	69	70	70	68
70	70	69	71	69

To get an overall picture of how the students scored on this test, we can prepare a frequency distribution of the scores. In statistics a score value is generally represented by the symbol X. The frequency with which a score value occurs in a set of data is listed in the f column of the frequency distribution. The frequency distribution of the anxiety-test scores is presented in Table 2-7. (In preparing a frequency distribution, it is customary to place the lowest value at the bottom of the distribution.)

Table 2-7. Frequency distribution of anxiety-test scores for 35 students.

X	f
72	1
71	3
70	9
69	12
68	8
67	0
66	2
	$N = 35$

In statistics, X generally represents a *known* value, whereas in algebra the symbol X is commonly considered an unknown quantity. In Table 2-7, each individual has a known score that can be called his or her X score.

Scores on psychological tests such as this one usually represent measurements that fall between the ordinal and interval scales. Furthermore, the variable of anxiety is theoretically considered a continuous variable; thus it is conceivable that an individual could score at any point along the continuum. Therefore, the fact that all the reported scores on this test are integers merely reflects the inability of our test to detect small differences in levels of anxiety.

The scores we obtain on a continuous variable such as anxiety are the results of a "rounding off" process. The *real* limits of each score value lie .5 above and .5 below the integer value; thus, each score value represents an interval within which the "true" score lies. For example, the *real* score of a student obtaining an anxiety-test score of 69 lies somewhere between 68.5 and 69.5. If we need to be precise in describing the distribution in Table 2-7, we can say that 12 students have anxiety-test scores falling in the interval between 68.5 and 69.5. In dealing with continuous variables, we will find the lower limit of a score value useful in some future calculations. This lower limit is represented by the symbol $\ell\ell$. For example, the $\ell\ell$ for the score value 71 is 70.5; for the score value 70, the $\ell\ell$ is 69.5.

When we prepare a frequency distribution of interval measurements, we list each value from the highest to the lowest in the X column whether or not it was obtained by any individual. (In Table 2-7 the score value of 67 is listed although no one received that particular value.)

When data are not grouped, a frequency distribution presents the f for each separate score. It is more convenient to group data with a wide range of scores into categories called *class intervals*. Table 2-8 presents a frequency distribution of scores in which two score values have been grouped to form each class interval.

Table 2-8. Grouped frequency distribution of scores.

Interval	f
20–21	1
18–19	0
16–17	8
14–15	8
12–13	5
10–11	2
8–9	1
	N = 25

When grouping the scores into class intervals, we "lose" some of our definitive information. We can see from Table 2-8 that five individuals received scores of 12 or 13, but we do not know whether all five individuals received a score of 12, all received a score of 13, or there was a mixture of the two scores. The larger the class intervals we form when we prepare a frequency distribution, the greater the loss of definitiveness.

The symbol i represents the size or the width of each class interval in a grouped frequency distribution. When the intervals are formed so that each one encompasses, say, two values, then $i = 2$, as in Table 2-8. If the width of each interval is three score values (as in intervals of 1–3, 4–6, 7–9, and so on), then $i = 3$. You should be aware of the distinction in meaning between i and f. The symbol i indicates the width of each interval; the symbol f represents the number of individuals whose scores lie within each of the intervals.

If the data in Table 2-8 represent measurement on a continuous variable, then each class interval has a real upper and lower limit, just as the individual score values discussed earlier had. The lower limit of a class interval is .5 below the lowest score value in the interval, and the upper limit is .5 above the highest score value in the interval. Thus the interval

10–11 actually ranges from 9.5 to 11.5. Its $\ell\ell$ is 9.5. In Table 2-8, the real lower and upper limits of the entire distribution are 7.5 and 21.5.

This consideration of upper and lower limits for continuous variables also pertains to distributions where fractions are used in forming class intervals. If we have a class interval of 102.59–102.60, the real lower limit of the interval would be 102.585 and its real upper limit would be 102.605.

It is important to remember that this concern with real upper and lower limits applies only to data that have been obtained from theoretically continuous variables. If the values in Figure 2-8 had represented the number of days students were tardy for school (a discrete variable, since students are considered either tardy or not tardy), we would not need to be concerned with upper and lower limits of the obtained data.

There are few hard and fast procedures for preparing frequency distributions. One practice that is generally followed is to make all of the intervals the same size. This is necessary when formulas are employed that require the use of i.

Frequency distributions that must summarize a large number of data usually have anywhere from 12 to 20 class intervals. In Table 2-7, where N was only 35, we formed only seven class intervals. Also, we usually choose a multiple of i to be the lowest value in a class interval. The lower value of each of the intervals in Table 2-8 is an even number; thus it is divisible by i, which in this case is 2.

In cases where the data must undergo further statistical treatment, the computational work can be reduced by making the interval size (i) an odd number. Then the midpoint of each interval becomes an integer rather than a fraction. For example, the midpoint of interval 108–110 is 109, whereas the midpoint of interval 90–93 is 91.5.

Exercises: Group A

1. A group of children gave the following responses when asked to name their favorite ice-cream flavor. Prepare a frequency distribution of these data.

Chocolate	Vanilla	Chocolate	Vanilla	Chocolate
Vanilla	Chocolate	Vanilla	Chocolate	Chocolate
Vanilla	Vanilla	Vanilla	Chocolate	Strawberry
Strawberry	Vanilla	Rocky road	Rocky road	Strawberry
Rocky road	Strawberry	Strawberry	Vanilla	Rocky road

2. Using the data in Exercise 1, what is the rank order of the children's preferences for ice-cream flavors?

3. Prepare an ungrouped frequency distribution of the following spelling-test scores.

18	24	19	15
13	27	15	23
19	17	22	19
22	20	28	16
21	14	21	20
9	26	14	

4. Prepare a grouped frequency distribution of the spelling achievement-test scores in Exercise 3, using an interval size of 3 points.
5. What is the $\ell\ell$ of each of the following? 12, 20, 17–19, 100–104

Exercises: Group B

6. A group of home decorators were asked to specify the color that was predominant in their own homes. Prepare a frequency distribution of the following responses.

Green	Yellow	Blue	Beige	Yellow
Beige	Beige	Green	Yellow	Beige
Yellow	Beige	Green	Green	Beige
Green	Brown	Yellow	Beige	Brown
Blue	Red	Beige	Blue	Green

7. Using the data in Exercise 6, what is the rank order of color preferences?
8. Prepare an ungrouped frequency distribution of the following IQ scores.

106	97	103	99	105
100	102	95	105	100
96	110	100	95	
94	100	109	90	
102	93	88	99	

9. Using the IQ scores in Exercise 8, prepare a grouped frequency distribution with an interval size of 4 IQ points.
10. What is the $\ell\ell$ of each of the following: 74, 90, 21–29, 300–309?

CHAPTER 3

MEASURES OF CENTRAL TENDENCY AND PERCENTILES

Data that have been collected and organized into a frequency distribution are ready for further statistical treatment. Our first concern in describing a set of statistical data may be to determine the one score value that best characterizes the entire frequency distribution. When there are many scores in a frequency distribution, they generally tend to group at some central or representative value; this value is called *a measure of central tendency*. In statistics there are several central values that are of interest. We shall examine three measures of central tendency—the mode, the median, and the mean.

The Mode

The mode is defined as the most frequently occurring score value in a frequency distribution; it is the value that has the greatest frequency. In column (a) in Table 3-1 the value 38 is the mode of the frequency distribution because that score was obtained by more individuals than was any other score. The mode of the distribution in column (b) of Table 3-1 is score value 99, because it is the value that was received by the most individuals. A frequency distribution may have more than one mode; the distribution in column (c) of Table 3-1 is called *bimodal* because it has two values, 59 and 55, that have highest frequencies of occurrence. A distribution that has many modes is called *multi-modal*.

Table 3-1. Three frequency distributions of ungrouped data.

(a)		(b)		(c)	
X	f	X	f	X	f
41	1	100	7	60	9
40	4	99	10	59	12
39	5	98	9	58	10
38	9	97	8	57	11
37	2	96	6	56	8
36	1	95	6	55	12
		94	2	54	9
		93	0	53	6
		92	1	52	2

The mode is not necessarily a value near the center of a frequency distribution, as Table 3-1 illustrates. It can be a high or a low score value. The mode of a distribution tells us nothing about the range of scores or their variability in the distribution. It only tells us which score value or values occurred most frequently.

In a frequency distribution of grouped data, the interval that occurs most frequently is called the *modal interval* of the distribution. In Table 3-2 the interval 61–63 is the modal interval.

Table 3-2. Frequency distribution of grouped data.

Interval	f
70–72	7
67–69	12
64–66	12
61–63	14
58–60	11
55–57	9
52–54	8
49–51	4

Since the mode need not be centrally located in the distribution, it is not a very useful measure of central tendency. The mode also tends to vary more from one sample to another than do the other measures of central tendency that will be discussed.

The Median

The median is the value in a frequency distribution that divides the *frequency* of scores in half; that is, 50% of the scores are above the median and 50% are below it. The median of each of the frequency distributions in Table 3-3 is 13, because 5 people in each distribution have scores above 13 and 5 people have scores below 13. Obviously, these three distributions are quite different. The scores in (a) are scattered, whereas in (c) they are very close together. These distributions illustrate the point that, although the median is a measure of central tendency, to determine it we need not take into account the values of the scores above or below it. It is determined only by how many scores are on either side of it.

It is easy to determine the median for the distributions in Table 3-3 by inspection. But how can we determine the median of the distribution in Table 3-4? If we assume that this frequency distribution represents measurements on a continuous variable, then each X value must have a lower and an upper limit. In Table 3-5 we have reconstructed the distribution in Table 3-4 to reflect these limits for each X value. Because the distribution in Table 3-5 has $N = 35$, we know that 17.5 (50%) of the scores must lie above the median and 17.5 (50%) of them must lie below it. We learn from the f

column in Table 3-5 that the value we are looking for, the 17.5th score, lies somewhere in the interval 68.5–69.5. We shall call this our *target interval*. We can now say that the median is a value that lies somewhere between 68.5 and 69.5. But which value is it?

Table 3-3. Three frequency distributions of ungrouped data.

(a)		(b)		(c)	
X	f	X	f	X	f
17	1				
16	0	16	1		
15	3	15	1	15	3
14	1	14	3	14	2
13	1	13	1	13	1
12	2	12	2	12	5
11	1	11	2		
10	0	10	1		
9	1				
8	1				

Table 3-4. Frequency distribution of ungrouped data.

X	f
72	1
71	3
70	9
69	12
68	8
67	0
66	2
	N = 35

Table 3-5. Frequency distribution of ungrouped data with each value represented by its limits.

Interval	f
71.5–72.5	1
70.5–71.5	3
69.5–70.5	9
68.5–69.5	12
67.5–68.5	8
66.5–67.5	0
65.5–66.5	2
	N = 35

To calculate the exact value of the median, we must now introduce our first statistical formula.

Formula 1. Calculation of the median.

$$Mdn = \ell\ell + \left(\frac{.5N - \Sigma f_b}{f_w}\right) i$$

in which $\Sigma = the\ sum\ of$
f_b = frequency below the interval which contains the Mdn
f_w = frequency within the interval which contains the Mdn

In Formula 1, the formula for the calculation of the median, Mdn is the symbol for the median. Formula 1 also introduces some other new symbols. One is the capital Greek letter Σ, which is pronounced "sigma" and means "the sum of." The expression Σf_b, indicates that we are to sum the frequencies occurring below the target interval. In this example, $\Sigma f_b = 8 + 0 + 2 = 10$. The frequency of the target interval (f_w) is 12. Its $\ell\ell$ is 68.5. The width of the interval (i) is 1, and $N = 35$. Substituting these values for the symbols in Formula 1, we obtain:

$$Mdn = 68.5 + \left(\frac{.5(35) - 10}{12}\right) 1 = 69.125$$

We have determined that the median for the distribution in Table 3-5 is 69.125. This is the point on the continuous scale above which and below which 50% of the scores lie.

To calculate the median for grouped data, as in Table 3-6, we determine by observation that $N = 24$. Therefore, the $Mdn,$ the point above which and below which 50% of the scores lie, must lie within the interval 64–66. The $\ell\ell$ of this interval is 63.5, $\Sigma f_b = 9$, and $f_w = 5$. Since these are grouped data, with three score values in each interval, $i = 3$.

Using Formula 1: $Mdn = 63.5 + \left(\dfrac{.5(24) - 9}{5}\right) 3 = 63.5 + 1.8 = 65.3$

The median of the distribution in Table 3-6 is 65.3.

Table 3-6. Frequency distribution for grouped data.

Interval	f
70–72	4
67–69	6
64–66	5
61–63	4
58–60	2
55–57	1
52–54	1
49–51	1
	$N = 24$

As we shall see later, the *Mdn* represents the 50th percentile. The median generally gives us more information about the nature of the distribution of scores than does the mode, because it gives us the score that divides the frequencies into two halves, whereas the mode tells us nothing about the other scores in the distribution. For example, if you are told that the modal score on a midterm examination is 97, you know nothing about the distribution of scores. If you are told that the median score is 75, you know that 50% of the students scored above that score and that 50% scored below it, but you still do not know how the scores were "spread" around 75.

The Mean

A measure of central tendency that takes into account the *value* of each score is called the *arithmetic mean*. The arithmetic mean of a distribution is what is commonly called the *arithmetic average* of all the scores. We shall refer to it simply as the *mean*. It is obtained as you ordinarily obtain an average; that is, by adding all the scores together and dividing this total by the number of scores in the distribution. Formula 2 is the formula for the calculation of the mean.

Formula 2. Calculation of the mean.

$$\bar{X} = \frac{\Sigma fX}{N}$$

This formula introduces the symbol for the sample mean, $\bar{X}$ (read as "X bar"). The symbol ΣfX indicates that we multiply each score value by its f and then sum all of the products. This sum is then divided by N to obtain the mean. The fX column in Table 3-7 gives each score value times its frequency. ΣfX is given at the bottom of the column. To determine the mean of this distribution, we substitute the values for the symbols in Formula 2 and solve for $\bar{X}$.

$$\bar{X} = \frac{2208}{30} = 73.6$$

The mean of the distribution in Table 3-7 is 73.6. What does the mean of a distribution really represent? The mean is the unique point in a distribution that represents the "balance point" of the data. If we think of the data in Table 3-7 as weights on a calibrated teeter-totter, we might picture them distributed as in Figure 3-1.

Table 3-7. Frequency distribution of ungrouped data.

X	f	fX
78	1	78
77	2	154
76	0	0
75	4	300
74	7	518
73	9	657
72	4	288
71	3	213
	N = 30	ΣfX = 2208

Figure 3-1. Graphic display of frequency distribution in Table 3-7.

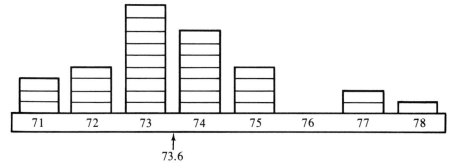

The point at which the teeter-totter would balance is 73.6. This figure illustrates an important property of the mean: the sum of the deviations of the smaller scores from the mean is equal to the sum of the deviations of the larger scores from the mean. For the distribution in Table 3-7, we can compute the sum of the deviations from $\bar{X}$ as follows:

X values larger than $\bar{X}$	$\bar{X}$	Deviation of X from $\bar{X}$	f	Deviation values
78	73.6	4.4	1	4.4
77	73.6	3.4	2	6.8
76	73.6	2.4	0	0
75	73.6	1.4	4	5.6
74	73.6	.4	7	2.8
			Sum of deviations =	19.6

X values smaller than $\bar{X}$	$\bar{X}$	Deviation of X from $\bar{X}$	f	Deviation values
73	73.6	−0.6	9	−5.4
72	73.6	−1.6	4	−6.4
71	73.6	−2.6	3	−7.8
			Sum of deviations =	−19.6

Here we have shown that the sum of the deviations for scores larger than the mean is the same as the sum of the deviations for scores smaller than the mean. If we add all of the deviations we get $-19.6 + 19.6 = 0$. This is probably the most important property of the mean: that the sum of all the deviations from it is zero.

In contrast to the mode and the median, the mean is sensitive to the value of each score in the distribution. For example, if the individual in Table 3-7 who received a score of 78 had received a score of 90, neither the mode nor the median of the distribution would have been affected, but the mean certainly would have been higher!

To compute the mean from data in a grouped frequency distribution, we also use Formula 2. However, we must first make an assumption about the scores in each interval. Suppose, in a distribution, an interval of 101–105 has a frequency of 7. Not knowing precisely what score value each of the seven individuals received, we must assume that the mean of their scores is at the midpoint of the interval 101–105, which is the value 103. Therefore, for further calculations, we must treat these seven individuals as if all of them had scored 103. This introduces the possibility of error in our calculations (all seven individuals could really have scored 101); but this possibility exists whenever we group data. Our "best guess" is always the midpoint of the interval.

When we calculate the mean for grouped data, we use the midpoint of each interval as an X value and proceed as before. Table 3-8 presents a grouped frequency distribution and shows the calculation of its mean.

Table 3-8. Frequency distribution of grouped data and calculation of the mean.

Interval	Midpoint (X)	f	fX
64–66	65	2	130
61–63	62	3	186
58–60	59	6	354
55–57	56	10	560
52–54	53	12	636
49–51	50	9	450
46–48	47	4	188
43–45	44	0	0
40–42	41	4	164
		$N = 50$	$\Sigma fX = 2668$

$$\bar{X} = \frac{2668}{50} = 53.36$$

When we are faced with a large array of scores in a frequency distribution, and when a calculator or computer is not available, we may simplify the laborious computations by merely subtracting a constant from each X value, computing the mean on these reduced values, and then adding the constant to the obtained mean to get the mean of the original distribution.

The computation of the mean of the distribution in Table 3-7 can be simplified by reducing each X by 70. This procedure is illustrated in Table 3-9. Note that the mean obtained by this process is exactly the same as the mean that we obtained when we used the original score values. In Table 3-9, the mean of the reduced scores is 3.6. Since we subtracted a constant of 70 from each X, we must now add 70 to the obtained mean of 3.6 to get the true mean of 73.6.

Table 3-9. Calculation of the mean by reducing each value by a constant.

X	(X − 70)	f	f(X − 70)
78	8	1	8
77	7	2	14
76	6	0	0
75	5	4	20
74	4	7	28
73	3	9	27
72	2	4	8
71	1	3	3
		$N = 30$	$\Sigma f(X - 70) = 108$

$$\text{Obtained } \bar{X} = \frac{108}{30} = 3.6$$

$$\text{True } \bar{X} = 3.6 + 70 = 73.6$$

In a similar fashion, the procedure for obtaining the frequency distribution of grouped data can be simplified by reducing the midpoint of each interval by a constant amount. The computation of the mean of the data in Table 3-8 can be greatly simplified by subtracting a constant of 40 from the midpoint of each interval. This process is illustrated in Table 3-10.

This same arithmetical property applies to adding a constant to each score; in this case, the obtained mean of the distribution should be increased by the amount of the constant. If each score in a distribution is multiplied or divided by a constant, the obtained mean is multiplied or divided by the same amount.

In summary, we have learned how to determine three measures of central tendency:

Mode. The most frequently occurring score in a frequency distribution.
Median. The point in a frequency distribution above which half of the scores lie and below which half of them lie.
Mean. The arithmetic average of the scores in a frequency distribution.

Table 3-10. Calculation of the mean by reducing each midpoint by a constant.

Interval	Midpoint (X)	X − 40	f	f(X − 40)
64–66	65	25	2	50
61–63	62	22	3	66
58–60	59	19	6	114
55–57	56	16	10	160
52–54	53	13	12	156
49–51	50	10	9	90
46–48	47	7	4	28
43–45	44	4	0	0
40–42	41	1	4	4
			$N = 50$	$\Sigma f(X - 40) = 668$

$$\text{Obtained } \overline{X} = \frac{668}{50} = 13.36$$

$$\text{True } \overline{X} = 13.36 + 40 = 53.36$$

Whereas the mean is computed by using the *value* of each score in the distribution, this is true of neither the mode nor the median: the mode is based solely on the frequency of the scores and the median is based on the relative positions of the scores, without regard to their values. Ordinarily, the mean is the most useful and stable measure of central tendency, and for most sets of data, it is the most representative score. Furthermore, as we shall see, the mean lends itself to a wide variety of statistical manipulations; the other two measures do not.

Percentile Equivalents

When a set of data contains many scores, it is sometimes desirable to express a given individual's position in the distribution as a *percentile rank*. A percentile rank is a percentage that tells where an individual score lies in relation to the other scores in a frequency distribution. Specifically, the percentile equivalent of a score tells us the percentage of scores falling *below* that particular score. We have shown earlier that the score at the 50th percentile is the median of a distribution, because 50% of the scores fall below it. We used Formula 1 to calculate the value of the median; therefore, this is the formula that is used to calculate the value at the 50th percentile. With little modification, Formula 1 can be used to determine the value corresponding to any percentile rank.

Suppose we wish to determine the value of the score at the 20th percentile of the distribution of continuous data presented in Table 3-11. We are looking for the value below which 20% of the scores fall. Since $N = 40$, we are looking for 20% of 40 or $.20 \times 40 = 8$. Therefore, we wish to determine the value of the eighth score from the bottom of the distribution.

Table 3-11. Frequency distribution of grouped data.

Interval	f
31–35	4
26–30	8
21–25	9
16–20	10
11–15	6
6–10	1
1–5	2
	N = 40

Counting up the frequencies of scores from the bottom, we see that the eighth score from the bottom is located in interval 11–15. This, then, is the target interval for our calculations. Since these are continuous data, we need a method for specifying which value within the interval represents the 20th percentile—in this case, the eighth score from the bottom.

To adapt Formula 1 for use in computing the 20th percentile, we determine values using our target interval of 11–15. Thus, $\ell\ell = 10.5$, $\Sigma f_b = 3$, $f_w = 6$, and $i = 5$. In Formula 1, the value .5 is the decimal equivalent of 50%, because this is the formula for the median. In computing other percentiles we must change this number to the decimal equivalent of the percentile we are seeking. Thus, for the 20th percentile, this number is .2.

We can now substitute the values for the symbols in the modified Formula 1 and solve for the value at the 20th percentile.

$$20\text{th percentile} = \ell\ell + \left(\frac{.2N - \Sigma f_b}{f_w}\right) i$$

$$= 10.5 + \left(\frac{.2(40) - 3}{6}\right) 5$$

$$= 10.5 + 4.17 = 14.67$$

We have determined that the value of the score at the 20th percentile in Table 3-11 is 14.67. This means that 20% of the individuals received scores lower than 14.67 (and 80% received higher scores).

In summary, the following are the steps for determining the value of a score at a given percentile rank in a frequency distribution.

1. Determine how many scores from the bottom of the distribution the target value lies by multiplying N by the percentile expressed in decimal form.
2. Locate the target interval containing the value by counting up the frequency column from the bottom.

3. Determine $\ell\ell$, Σf_b, f_w, and i for the target interval.
4. Modify Formula 1 by substituting the decimal equivalent of the given percentile for .5.
5. Substitute the values for the symbols in the modified Formula 1 and solve for the score value.

To determine the value of the score at the 80th percentile in Table 3-11, the calculations are as follows:

.80(40) = 32nd score from the bottom of the distribution
Target interval is 26–30

$$80\text{th percentile} = 25.5 + \left(\frac{.8(40) - 28}{8} \right) 5 = 28$$

The score value 28 lies at the 80th percentile of the distribution; that is, 80% of the individuals scored lower than 28 and 20% scored higher.

Percentiles may be described as *quartiles* and given the symbol Q. The score at the 25th percentile is known as the 1st quartile and is symbolized Q_1, because one quarter of the scores lie below it. The 2nd quartile, Q_2, is the value below which 50% of the scores lie and is also called the 50th percentile or the median. The third quartile, Q_3, falls at the 75th percentile.

In addition to quartiles, percentiles are sometimes referred to in terms of *deciles*. Since the term "decimal" refers to the number ten, the 1st decile, D_1, is at the 10th percentile; the 2nd decile, D_2, is at the 20th percentile; and so forth.

Sometimes it is necessary to determine the percentile equivalent of a given score value. For this computation we use Formula 3, which yields the percentile in decimal form for any selected X value in the distribution.

Formula 3. Calculation of the percentile.

$$\text{Percentile in decimal form} = \frac{\left(\dfrac{X - \ell\ell}{i} \right) f_w + \Sigma f_b}{N}$$

in which X = score value for which the percentile is to be computed
f_b = frequency below the i which contains the score
f_w = frequency within the i which contains the score

Multiply the decimal form of the percentile by 100 in order to determine the percentile.

If we wish to determine the percentile equivalent for score 22 in Table 3-11, we determine $\ell\ell$, i, f_w, and Σf_b, using the interval 21–25, which contains $X = 22$. Substituting these values in Formula 3, we obtain:

$$\frac{\left(\dfrac{22 - 20.5}{5}\right)9 + 19}{40} = .5425$$

Multiplying .5425 by 100, we determine that the score of 22 is at the 54.25th percentile.

The description of an individual's position in a distribution as a percentile tells us more than the score value alone does. If we are told that Joe's score is 41 on a mathematics-achievement test, we have no way of telling whether this is a high or a low score in relation to the scores of the other students tested. But if we are told that he scored at the 90th percentile, we know that he did quite well, since 90% of the students scored below him. If we have only Joe's percentile rank, however, we still do not have any of the other actual scores in the distribution. They could be widely spaced or they could all be grouped very close to Joe's score. The percentile rank of a score only describes the position of that score in a distribution, not how different it is from other scores.

Exercises: Group A

1. A group of 22 Boy Scouts were tested on their ability to read a map. The following frequency distribution of their map-reading test scores was obtained. Determine the mode, median, and mean of these data.

X	f
30	1
29	2
28	7
27	6
26	2
25	2
24	0
23	2

2. Simplify the calculation of the mean of the frequency distribution in Exercise 1 by subtracting a constant of 20 points from each score. Check the answer with your answer to Exercise 1.

3. If Tenderfoot Scout Tom is at the 40th percentile in map reading, calculate his score, using the data in Exercise 1. If Eagle Scout Sam is at the 75th percentile, what is his score?

4. Scout Charlie earned a map-reading score of 29. Using the data in Exercise 1, determine the percentile equivalent of his score. Scout Danny earned a score of 25. What is the percentile rank of his score?

5. A second-grade teacher tested a group of children to determine their comprehension of a story. He obtained the following frequency distribution of

comprehension scores. Determine the mode, median, and mean of this distribution.

Interval	f
88–91	3
84–87	6
80–83	4
76–79	3
72–75	0
68–71	2

6. Simplify the calculation of the mean of the frequency distribution in Exercise 5 by subtracting a constant of 60 points from each interval. Check the answer with your answer to Exercise 5.
7. Susan is at the 82nd percentile in reading comprehension. Determine her score, using the data in Exercise 5. Janice is at the 35th percentile. What is her score?
8. Sally obtained a reading-comprehension score of 84. Calculate the percentile equivalent of her score, using the data given in Exercise 5. Judy obtained a reading-comprehension score of 77. What is the percentile rank of her score?

Exercises: Group B

9. The visual acuity of the employees in the Able Manufacturing Company was tested and the following frequency distribution of visual-acuity scores was obtained. Determine the mode, median, and mean of these data.

X	f
63	3
62	3
61	7
60	5
59	3
58	2
57	1

10. Simplify the calculation of the mean of the frequency distribution in Exercise 9 by subtracting a constant of 50 points from each score. Check the answer with your answer to Exercise 9.
11. James Long is at the 95th percentile in the visual-acuity test described in Exercise 9. What is his score? Louise Lotus is at the 20th percentile. What is her score?
12. Marie Souza received a visual-acuity test score of 62. Using the data in Exercise 9, calculate the percentile equivalent of her score? Fred Fisher received a score of 60. What is the percentile equivalent of his score?

13. After a period of instruction, a group of chimpanzees was given a problem-solving test. The following problem-solving test scores were obtained. Determine the mode, median, and mean of this distribution.

Interval	f
48–50	2
45–47	0
42–44	9
39–41	8
36–38	3
33–35	2
30–32	1

14. Simplify the calculation of the mean of the frequency distribution in Exercise 13 by subtracting a constant of 30 points from each interval. Check the answer with your answer to Exercise 13.

15. Chimpanzee X scored at the 18th percentile on the problem-solving test described in Exercise 13. What is her score? Chimpanzee Y scored at the 44th percentile. What is his score?

16. Chimpanzee P obtained a problem-solving test score of 34. Using the data in Exercise 13, determine the percentile equivalent of her score? Chimpanzee Q obtained a score of 44. What is the percentile equivalent of his score?

CHAPTER 4
DISPLAY OF DATA

The score value representing a measure of central tendency and the percentile equivalents of score values tell us nothing about the *spread* of the scores in a frequency distribution. Even when a distribution of scores is drawn up in tabular form, it is difficult to see the "shape" of the distribution. It is often easier to see how the scores are spread within a distribution when they are presented in graphic form.

Many types of graphs can be prepared to display statistical data. The particular type that is appropriate for a given set of data depends upon the level of measurement involved and upon whether the data represent discrete or continuous variables.

Pie Charts

For nominal data, a simple frequency distribution presented in tabular form will generally give a clear "picture" of how the data are distributed. For example, the distribution in Table 4-1 presents the data in a way that can be easily interpreted. If a graph is desired, a common technique for depicting nominal data is the preparation of a "pie chart," in which the percentage of N representing each category's frequency is used to determine the size of its corresponding segment. Figure 4-1 shows the pie chart for the data presented in Table 4-1.

Table 4-1. Frequency distribution of nominal data.

Religious affiliation	f	%
Protestant	211	38.3
Catholic	194	35.3
Jewish	89	16.2
Other	56	10.2
	$N = 550$	

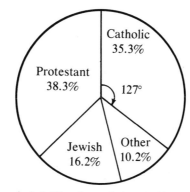

Figure 4-1. Pie chart of data in Table 4-1.

The area of each segment in the pie chart represents the percentage of frequencies for the corresponding category in the frequency distribution. To determine how large to make each segment, we determine the percentage of the circle (360°) that corresponds to the percentage of each frequency. In our example, 35.3% of the people in the sample are Catholic. Therefore, we take 35.3% of 360°, which is 127.08°. Using a protractor, we draw a pie segment with an angle of 127.08° to represent the portion of the sample which is Catholic. The angles of the other segments of the circle are determined similarly.

In Figure 4-1, the segment for Catholics extends from 0° clockwise to 127.08°. Of course, this segment, as well as any of the others, could be placed anywhere in the circle. In a pie chart, it is customary to label each segment, and to show the percentage represented by each segment rather than the degrees of their angles.

Bar Graphs

Another appropriate method for graphically depicting nominal measurements, such as colors, ethnic group affiliations, geographical areas, and so forth, is the bar graph. The data presented in Table 4-1 are depicted in bar-graph form in Figure 4-2. Notice that the heights of the bars correspond to the amounts of the frequencies of the various categories, and that there are spaces between the bars in this graph. This spacing of the bars indicates that there is no continuum underlying the nominal categories. In a bar graph, the spaces between the bars should be about one-half the widths of the bars. The bars are generally arranged in the order of their magnitude, with the largest at the extreme left side of the graph and the smallest at the extreme right.

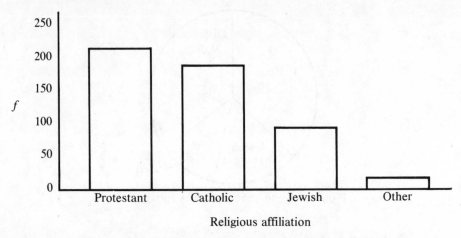

Figure 4-2. Bar graph of data in Table 4-1.

Bar Histograms

A special type of bar graph, called a *bar histogram,* is used when measurements are to be depicted on the interval or ratio scale. A bar histogram resembles a bar graph, except that in it the bars are adjacent to each other; this indicates that the data depicted form a continuum. Figure 4-3 presents a frequency distribution for ungrouped discrete measurements of absences per student and its bar histogram. Notice that the horizontal axis in the bar histogram in Figure 4-3 gives the discrete values for these data, and the height of each bar represents the frequency with which each discrete value occurs.

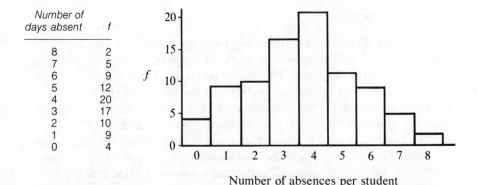

Number of days absent	f
8	2
7	5
6	9
5	12
4	20
3	17
2	10
1	9
0	4

Figure 4-3. Frequency distribution and bar histogram of absentee rate.

In a bar histogram depicting data from a continuous variable, the horizontal axis shows the real lower and upper limits of each interval. The grouped frequency distribution and the bar histogram showing the intelligence quotients for 110 students are given in Figure 4-4. Notice that in the bar histogram, the boundaries of each bar on the horizontal axis represent the real limits of the corresponding intervals in the frequency distribution. In Figure 4-4, we see how much easier it is to get an idea of the shape of the distribution from the bar histogram than it is from the frequency distribution.

The following are conventions that are generally followed in the preparation of histograms:

1. The frequencies of the observations should appear along the vertical axis, with the zero point at the bottom of the axis.
2. Values of the variable being depicted should appear along the horizontal axis, with the lowest value at the left of the axis.
3. Both axes must be uniformly calibrated. Even where an interval has zero frequency, space must be left in the histogram representing zero frequency.
4. The widths of the bars must all be the same.

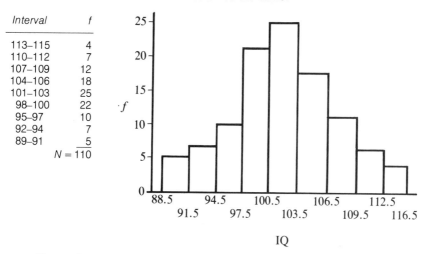

Interval	f
113–115	4
110–112	7
107–109	12
104–106	18
101–103	25
98–100	22
95–97	10
92–94	7
89–91	5
	N = 110

Figure 4-4. Frequency distribution and bar histogram of intelligence quotients.

Frequency Polygons

The bar histogram is used to display graphically a set of interval or ratio data. Another type of graph, called the *frequency polygon,* can be used instead, if we wish to emphasize further the continuous nature of the measurement scale. In preparing a frequency polygon, we can use the same calibrations on the vertical and horizontal axes as we used for the bar histogram; instead of representing each interval by a bar, however, we can place a dot over the midpoint of the interval and then connect all of the dots to form the polygon. The heights of the dots indicate the frequencies of the intervals. Figure 4-5 presents the frequency polygon for the data given in Figure 4-4.

In Figure 4-5, the midpoint of each interval in the frequency distribution is represented by a dot at the height that corresponds to that interval's frequency. As an illustration, the bar for interval 95–97 in the histogram is given in dotted outline. The midpoint of the interval is shown as a dot at the center of the top of the bar, directly over the IQ value of 96, which is the midpoint of the interval. In similar fashion, each dot on the frequency polygon corresponds to the center of the top of a bar from the histogram.

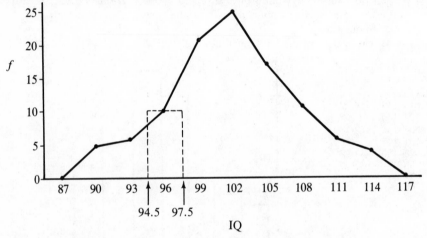

Figure 4-5. Frequency polygon for data in Figure 4-4.

Usually the ends of a frequency polygon are "tied down" to the horizontal axis by extending the distribution to include intervals at each end that have zero frequencies. In the frequency polygon in Figure 4-5 the frequency of zero is shown for midpoints 87 and 117.

As is shown in Figure 4-6, when many score values and many frequencies are depicted in a frequency polygon, the trend of the data, or the shape of the distribution, becomes quite apparent. In these cases, a smooth curve can be drawn through the frequency polygon. Such a curve is superimposed on the frequency polygon in Figure 4-6. This curve, sometimes called a smoothed polygon, represents the best-fitting curved line that can be drawn through the many points, as opposed to a straight line connecting each adjacent pair of dots.

This curve is an approximation of the frequency polygon; it has smoothed out the jagged edges, leaving only the trend. However, much of the jaggedness in a frequency polygon may be due to random error in the data, so that the smoothed curve may well be a more accurate depiction of the distribution of the "true" measurements than the frequency polygon is.

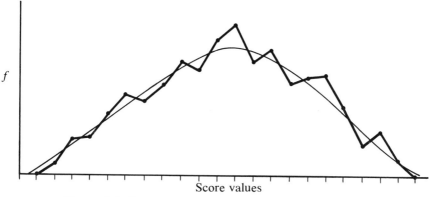

Figure 4-6. Frequency polygon and smoothed curve.

Types of Distribution Curves

The shape of a distribution curve depends upon the way in which the data are distributed. Figure 4-7 gives four typical curves.

The negatively-skewed curve in Figure 4-7(a) represents a frequency distribution in which the frequency of large values is much greater that the frequency of small values. This curve is skewed to the left, because the slope of the curve trails off toward the left end of the graph, where the lower values lie.

Figure 4-7(b) is called a positively-skewed curve, since the slope of this curve trails off to the right, where the higher values lie. A test that is very difficult would probably result in a positively-skewed curve, since few students would obtain high scores. In frequency distributions where there are two modes, the smoothed curve, which might look like Figure 4-7(c), is called a bimodal curve.

A symmetrical distribution curve, as is shown in Figure 4-7(d), has some distinctive properties that are of interest to statisticians. Since the curve is symmetrical, its left side is a mirror image of its right side. The mode of the curve, which is at its center, divides the distribution exactly in half. Thus, the mode is also the median, since half of the frequencies lie below it and half of them lie above it. If we compute the mean of a symmetrical distribution, we would find that it also coincides with the mode.

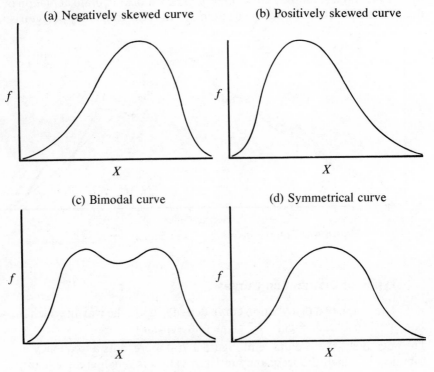

Figure 4-7. Four types of distribution curves.

As Figure 4-8(a) shows, the mode, median, and mean all coincide in a symmetrical distribution. This is not the case with skewed curves. In positively-skewed curves, such as Figure 4-8(b), the median falls to the right of the mode and the mean lies even farther to the right. The order of these three measures of central tendency is reversed in negatively-skewed curves, as is shown in Figure 4-8(c). These differences show that the value of the mean is more affected by the shape of the distribution than is the value of either the mode or the median.

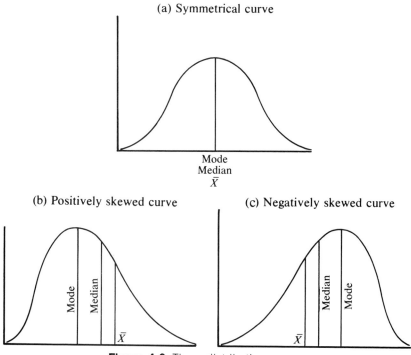

Figure 4-8. Three distribution curves.

Exercises: Group A

1. A survey researcher asked 182 individuals what type of transportation they used to get to their place of employment. Prepare either a pie chart or a bar histogram, whichever is appropriate, for the following responses.

Type	f
Private auto	80
Bus	35
Train	21
Car pool	46

2. For the responses in Exercise 1, prepare a bar graph or a frequency polygon, whichever is appropriate.

3. The frequency distribution below shows the number of trials a group of college freshmen took to recall a list of nonsense syllables accurately. Prepare either a pie chart or a bar histogram, whichever is appropriate, for these data.

Number of trials	f
6	3
5	8
4	6
3	4
2	2
1	1

4. Prepare a bar graph or a frequency polygon, whichever is appropriate, for the data in Exercise 3.

5. A group of high school graduates were given a scholastic-aptitude test. The following test scores were obtained. Prepare either a bar graph or a bar histogram, whichever is appropriate, for these data.

Interval	f
125–129	6
120–124	10
115–119	29
110–114	15
105–109	11
100–104	7

6. For the frequency distribution in Exercise 5, prepare a pie chart or a frequency polygon, whichever is appropriate.

Exercises: Group B

7. The following frequency distribution shows the number of pairs of track shoes competing teams wore out during a cross-country run. Prepare either a pie chart or a bar histogram, whichever is appropriate, depicting these data.

Number of pairs	f
9	4
8	7
7	8
6	4
5	2
4	1

8. Prepare either a bar graph or a frequency polygon, whichever is appropriate, for the data in Exercise 7.

9. A sensitivity group is composed of the following ethnic groups. Prepare either a pie chart or a bar histogram, whichever is appropriate, to depict the composition of the group.

Ethnic group	f
Black	14
Caucasian	12
Spanish	8
Oriental	6
Other	2

10. For the data in Exercise 9, prepare either a bar graph or a frequency polygon, whichever is appropriate.

11. A group of fourth-grade children were given an arithmetic test, and the following frequency distribution was obtained. Prepare either a bar graph or a bar histogram, whichever is appropriate, for these data.

Interval	f
96–98	2
93–95	4
90–92	7
87–89	9
84–86	6
81–83	2

12. For the data in Exercise 11, prepare a pie chart or a frequency polygon, whichever is appropriate.

CHAPTER 5
MEASURES OF VARIABILITY

If we know that a set of data has a mean of 40 or a median of 64, we have representative values for these data, but we still know nothing about the spread of the scores or the extent to which they vary. Bar histograms, frequency polygons, and "smoothed" curves give us graphic representations of the shape of a frequency distribution, but they do not provide us with a statistical way of describing the variability of the scores. To describe a set of data adequately, we need both a measure of central tendency (the mean, the median, or the mode) and a measure of variability. In this chapter, we will explore several ways to describe statistically the variation or dispersion of data.

The Range

The simplest way to represent the spread of the scores in a frequency distribution is to determine the *range*. Formula 4 is the formula for calculating the range of scores in a distribution. It merely determines the difference between the highest score value and the lowest.

Formula 4. Calculation of the range.

$$\text{Range} = H - L$$

in which H = highest score in frequency distribution
L = lowest score in frequency distribution

In the frequency distribution shown in Table 5-1, the range of scores is $40 - 32 = 8$. Obviously, the range gives us the span of score values in a distribution but tells us nothing about the nature of the distribution of the scores within the limits of the range. The magnitude of the range is affected by only the two extreme values in the distribution.

Table 5-1. A frequency distribution of continuous data.

X	f
40	2
39	0
38	3
37	9
36	12
35	9
34	8
33	5
32	2
	N = 50

The Interquartile and Semi-interquartile Ranges

A more useful measure of variability is the *interquartile range*. It is determined by taking the difference between Q_1 (the 25th percentile) and Q_3 (the 75th percentile) in a distribution; that is, the interquartile range encompasses the middle 50% of the scores. The *semi-interquartile range,* symbolized by Q, is half of the interquartile range. It is calculated by Formula 5. The semi-interquartile range is the *average* of the range between Q_1 and the median and the range between Q_3 and the median.

Formula 5. Calculation of the semi-interquartile range.

$$Q = \frac{Q_3 - Q_1}{2}$$

To calculate the interquartile and semi-interquartile ranges for the data in Table 5-1, we use Formula 1 to compute $Q_1 = 34.19$ and $Q_3 = 36.67$. The interquartile range is $36.67 - 34.19 = 2.48$. Using Formula 5, we calculate the semi-interquartile range:

$$Q = \frac{36.67 - 34.19}{2} = 1.24$$

These calculations indicate that the average range of score values within the two inner quartiles is slightly less than 1¼ points. Unlike the range, the interquartile range and the semi-interquartile range are not affected by the values of the extreme scores in the distribution; therefore, they provide more stable measures of variability than the range does.

The Average Deviation

The *average deviation,* or *mean absolute deviation,* although rarely used, is a more refined measure of variability than either the range or the semi-interquartile range since it is computed by using the actual value of each of the scores rather than just its relative position in the distribution. The average deviation is determined by calculating the average of the amounts that the scores deviate from the mean, regardless of the signs of the deviations. To determine the *average deviation* of the scores from the mean, we must first determine how much each score deviates from the mean. In Formula 6, the symbol x represents the amount of deviation of a score from the mean. It is important here and in future calculations to distinguish between X, which is a "raw" score, and x, which is a deviation score.

Formula 6. Calculation of a deviation score.

$$x = X - \bar{X}$$

Formula 7 shows the calculation of the average deviation.

Formula 7. Calculation of the average deviation.

$$\text{A.D.} = \frac{\Sigma f|x|}{N}$$

in which $|x|$ =the absolute deviation of a raw score from the mean

---

The expression *absolute deviation* means that we are concerned only with how *much* a score deviates from its mean, not with whether it is above or below the mean. Therefore, in determining an absolute deviation score, we ignore the sign of the deviation.

Table 5-2 shows the calculation of the average deviation for the data given in Table 5-1. The mean of these data is $\bar{X} = 35.5$. The deviation of each score value has been determined by Formula 6. The absolute deviation-score values are given in the column headed $|x|$. The average deviation of this distribution is 1.44. This tells us that the average number of score points that the scores in the distribution deviate from the mean is slightly less than 1½ points. Thus, unlike the range and the semi-interquartile range, the average deviation takes into account the numerical values of the raw scores. However, the average deviation is rarely used in statistical work, because it does not lend itself to further statistical analysis. It is merely a descriptive statistic.

Table 5-2. Calculation of the average deviation.

X	f	fX	x	|x|	f|x|
40	2	80	4.5	4.5	9.0
39	0	0	3.5	3.5	0
38	3	114	2.5	2.5	7.5
37	9	333	1.5	1.5	13.5
36	12	432	.5	.5	6.0
35	9	315	−.5	.5	4.5
34	8	272	−1.5	1.5	12.0
33	5	165	−2.5	2.5	12.5
32	2	64	−3.5	3.5	7.0
	N = 50	ΣfX = 1775			Σf|x| = 72.0

Using Formula 2: $\bar{X} = \dfrac{\Sigma fX}{N} = \dfrac{1775}{50} = 35.5$

Using Formula 7: A.D. $= \dfrac{\Sigma f|x|}{N} = \dfrac{72}{50} = 1.44$

The Variance and the Standard Deviation

Probably the two most important measures of variability are the *variance* and the *standard deviation,* because they provide measures that are used in making statistical inferences. These two measures will be discussed and used throughout most of the remainder of this text, so it is important to learn how they are computed. To calculate the average deviation, we used the absolute deviation scores. The *variance,* which is a mathematically more useful measure of variability than the average deviation, requires the squaring of the deviation scores; therefore, in calculating it, we can take into account the sign of each deviation score. Formula 8a shows the calculation of the variance using the deviation-score method.

Formula 8a. Calculation of the sample variance (deviation-score method).

$$s'^2 = \frac{\Sigma fx^2}{N}$$

The symbol s'^2 (pronounced s prime squared) represents a variance calculated from the data in a sample. A discussion of the term *sample* is given in the next chapter. (We are reserving the symbol s for an important use later.)

Again using the frequency distribution given in Table 5-1 that we have used for calculations, Table 5-3 illustrates the calculation of the variance by the deviation-score method. The variance of the distribution in this table is $s'^2 = 3.17$. Each deviation score used in Formula 8a must be squared before it is multiplied by f. A common computational error is to multiply by f and then square the product.

Table 5-3. Calculation of the variance by the deviation-score method.

X	f	x	x²	fx²
40	2	4.5	20.25	40.5
39	0	3.5	12.25	0
38	3	2.5	6.25	18.75
37	9	1.5	2.25	20.25
36	12	.5	.25	3.0
35	9	− .5	.25	2.25
34	8	−1.5	2.25	18.0
33	5	−2.5	6.25	31.25
32	2	−3.5	12.25	24.5
	$N = 50$			$\Sigma fx^2 = 158.5$

$$\text{Using Formula 8a: } s'^2 = \frac{\Sigma fx^2}{N} = \frac{158.5}{50} = 3.17$$

The numerator in Formula 8a, Σfx^2, represents the sum of squared deviations from the mean. This term is usually shortened to the *sum of squares* for convenience. As we proceed with our study of statistics, we shall find that this quantity has important uses.

Computing the variance by the deviation-score method is laborious when the N of a distribution is large and there are many score values involved. In a case of this sort, it is easier to use the mathematically-equivalent raw-score method, which is presented in Formula 8b. This formula does not require that we determine the deviation scores; instead, we can work directly with the "raw" data.

Formula 8b. Calculation of the sample variance (raw-score method).

$$s'^2 = \frac{\Sigma fX^2}{N} - \bar{X}^2$$

Table 5-4 presents the calculation of s'^2 using Formula 8b for the data that were presented in Table 5-3. Again, notice that each X has been squared before is has been multiplied by its f; the results appear in the right-hand column. Both the deviation-score method (Formula 8a) and the raw-score method (Formula 8b) yield the same value for the variance, $s'^2 = 3.17$.

Table 5-4. Calculation of the variance by the raw-score method.

X	f	fX	X^2	fX^2
40	2	80	1,600	3,200
39	0	0	1,521	0
38	3	114	1,444	4,332
37	9	333	1,369	12,321
36	12	432	1,296	15,552
35	9	315	1,225	11,025
34	8	272	1,156	9,248
33	5	165	1,089	5,445
32	2	64	1,024	2,048
	$N = 50$	$\Sigma fX = 1775$		$\Sigma fX^2 = 63,171$

Using Formula 2: $\bar{X} = \dfrac{\Sigma fX}{N} = \dfrac{1775}{50} = 35.5$

Using Formula 8b: $s'^2 = \dfrac{\Sigma fX^2}{N} - \bar{X}^2 = \dfrac{63,171}{50} - (35.5)^2 = 3.17$

Besides the variance, the most useful measure of variability is the *standard deviation*. Formula 9 calculates the standard deviation by taking the square root of the variance.

Formula 9. Calculation of the sample standard deviation.

$$s' = \sqrt{s'^2}$$

Since the variance, s'^2, for the data in Table 5-4 is 3.17, then the standard deviation, s', for the same set of data is $\sqrt{3.17}$ or 1.78. The standard deviation is usually considered the standard unit for describing the deviation of a score from its mean. The interpretation of the standard deviation is discussed in the next chapter.

Up to this point, we have found three ways to describe a person's score. It can be expressed as a raw score (X), as a percentile, and as a deviation score (x). Another useful measure of a score's position in the distribution, the *z score*, determines how far a raw score deviates from the mean in standard-deviation units. A score expressed in this way is called a *relative deviate*. Formula 10 shows the method for determining the z score corresponding to a particular X.

Formula 10. Calculation of a relative deviate.

$$z = \frac{x}{s'}$$

Using the $\overline{X} = 35.5$ and $s' = 1.78$ that we have already determined, we can calculate the z score for a person who received a raw score of 38 by first finding the deviation score, $x = 38 - 35.5 = 2.5$, and then substituting these values in Formula 10 as follows:

$$z = \frac{2.5}{1.78} = 1.40$$

This procedure could be followed for each X score in the distribution. Then each person's score would be expressed in terms of its distance from the mean in standard-deviation units. For X scores that are larger than the mean, the corresponding z scores will be positive. X scores that are smaller than the mean will have negative corresponding z scores. For example, for $X = 34$, $x = -1.5$, and $z = -1.5/1.78 = -.84$.

At this point you may wonder why we have converted the raw scores to deviation scores and then to relative deviates. The reasons will become clear when we explore the important properties of the standard deviation in connection with a particular form of distribution called the *normal distribution*. In later chapters, we will see that converting a score to a relative deviate will allow us to make statistical interpretations that would not otherwise be possible. This ability will be particularly valuable when we begin the study of statistical inference.

Exercises: Group A

1. An anxiety test was given to a group of seniors just before they took their comprehensive final examination. Compute the range of the following distribution of anxiety scores.

Anxiety scores	f
54	3
53	3
52	3
51	5
50	7
49	4
48	1

2. Compute the semi-interquartile range of the distribution in Exercise 1.

3. Compute the average deviation of the scores in Exercise 1.

4. Compute the variance of the scores in Exercise 1, using the deviation-score method.

5. Compute the variance of the scores in Exercise 1, using the raw-score method.

6. Compute the standard deviation of the scores in Exercise 1.

7. Compute the relative deviate for score 53, using the frequency distribution in Exercise 1.

8. Compute the relative deviate for score 50, using the frequency distribution in Exercise 1.

Exercises: Group B

9. A frequency distribution of geology midterm-examination scores is given below. Compute the range of this distribution.

X	f
30	1
29	2
28	7
27	6
26	2
25	2
24	0
23	2

10. Compute the semi-interquartile range of the data in Exercise 9.

11. Compute the average deviation of the data in Exercise 9.

12. Compute the variance of the data in Exercise 9, using the deviation-score method.

13. Compute the variance of the data in Exercise 9, using the raw-score method.

14. Compute the standard deviation of the data in Exercise 9.

15. Compute the relative deviate for score 30, using the distribution in Exercise 9.

16. Compute the relative deviate for score 25, using the distribution in Exercise 9.

CHAPTER 6
INTRODUCTION TO STATISTICAL INFERENCE— THE NORMAL CURVE

If we wished to determine the mean height of all students currently enrolled in physical-education classes at Terrence University, we might be able to arrange to measure all of them on the same day. We could then compute the mean height of this group. In this example, we would have measured the *population* defined as "Terrence University students currently enrolled in physical-education classes." Having measured every student, we would know the value of the population mean height, and we would not have to make any inferences about its value. On the other hand, if it were not feasible for us to measure every student fitting the description, we could select a *sample* of the population, measure them, and compute the mean height of the sample. (Methods for selecting samples will be discussed later.) We could then infer that the mean height of the sample was "very similar" to the mean height of the population. We would know that the obtained sample mean was probably not exactly equal to the population mean, because samples are seldom perfect representations of their populations: there is always some *sampling error* involved when a sample is selected from a population.

One of the important concerns of the statistician is the study of the relationship between a population and samples drawn from it. This relationship can take one of two forms:

1. The relationship between obtained sample values and the unknown population value. In this case, we must make an inference about the mean height of the population, for example, from the measurements obtained from a sample or samples. This type of statistical inference is diagrammed in Figure 6-1.

2. The relationship between a known population value and values of samples taken from it. If we know that the mean height of the population is 70 inches, we can then make inferences about the mean heights of a sample or samples taken from it. This kind of statistical inference can be diagrammed as shown in Figure 6-2.

In our study of *statistical inference*, we will be concerned with both types of relationship. Making educated estimates about the relationship between a population and its samples is a major adventure in statistics.

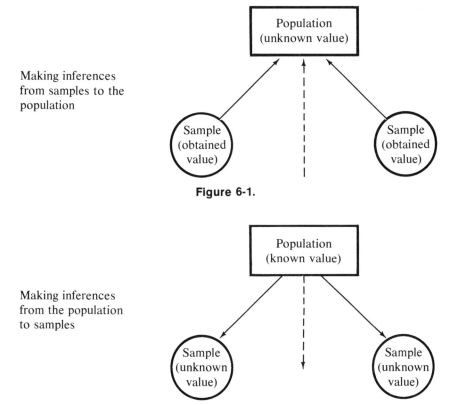

Making inferences
from samples to the
population

Figure 6-1.

Making inferences
from the population
to samples

Figure 6-2.

Before embarking upon this adventure, we need to define some terms and processes.

Population

Usually we think of a population as a large number of people. The term *population* has a specific meaning to statisticians. Examples of statistical populations are the weights of all 6-year-old males in the U.S., the daily calorie intake rates of all 8-day-old rats, the number of rooms in all single-family dwellings in Chicago, the arithmetic-achievement scores of all sixth-grade students in the Halifax school district. The key word in the above examples is *all*. It is important for research purposes that the terms defining a population be clear and specific, so that there is no confusion regarding its composition.

Technically, a statistical population does not include the individuals or objects in a defined group, but rather their measurements on a given variable. Thus, in the first example given under this heading, the statistical population is not all 6-year-old males in the U.S., but rather their weights.

Using this definition, we are not limited to describing populations in terms of numbers of people, animals or objects. We can speak of a population of reaction times for Tom Smith (here only one person is involved) or populations of arithmetic-test scores and manual-dexterity ratings of third-grade pupils (thus, the same group can yield two statistical populations).

Sample

A sample is any selected subset of a population. Samples vary in size from one up to one less than the size of the population. The basic function of statistical inference is to analyze data drawn from a sample or samples in order to generalize to the population from which the samples were drawn. Therefore, the researcher must select samples that are likely to be representative of the population. Of course, there is no way to insure selection of a perfectly representative sample, but statistical analysis can provide an estimate of error in sampling.

The most important assumption underlying statistical-inference procedures is that the sample or samples have been randomly selected from the population. A *random sample* is defined as one in which every sample of the same size has an equal chance of being selected from a given population.

For studies in the behavioral sciences, this process is not as simple as it sounds. First, it assumes that we can identify every sample of a population and afford each sample an equal opportunity for selection. When we are dealing with very large populations, it is difficult or impossible to meet this requirement. (Consider the task of specifying each member of the population of kindergarten children in American schools.) Secondly, assuming that we can identify the members of a specified population, we must have a method that ensures a random selection of its members to serve as a representative sample. One way is to place each member's name or code number in a barrel, stir them thoroughly, and blindly draw out a sample. Another method is to assign each member of the population a code number, and select code numbers for the sample by using a table of random numbers in which a large collection of numbers have been prerandomized.

In most cases, neither of the above processes can be used to select samples for studies in the behavioral sciences. Usually we must settle for some pre-existing group to serve as a sample—such as when we study Mr. Johnson's first-grade class and assume that it is representative of all first-grade pupils. This may or may not be a warranted assumption. On the other hand, in studies where two or more samples are selected to compare the effects of treatment, we may not be able to select the samples randomly from the population, but at least we can assign subjects randomly to the groups receiving different treatment conditions.

The measurements obtained from random samples have certain characteristics that affect the inferences we make about population values. First, since members have been randomly selected for the samples, they undoubtedly differ from sample to sample; therefore, the measurements (data) obtained for different samples from the same population will also differ.

Second, large samples tend to be more representative of a population than small samples. Therefore, measurements obtained from large samples are more likely to correspond to the values in the population than are small sample measurements. The rest of our study of statistics will be concerned with examining ways of dealing with these two characteristics of measurements from random samples.

We need a way to distinguish between sample and population characteristics. A sample characteristic is called a *statistic;* a population characteristic is called a *parameter*. Thus, the mean of a sample is a statistic, whereas the mean of a population is a parameter. There is a symbol system that always tells us whether we are dealing with statistics or parameters. Up to now, we have considered the small quantities of measurements in our examples to be sample data. Generally, Roman letters are used to denote sample statistics. We have used $\bar{X}$ for the sample mean, s'^2 for the sample variance, and s' for the sample standard deviation.

When we refer to population parameters, we use Greek letters. The symbol for the population mean is μ (pronounced mew). The symbol for the population variance is σ^2 (pronounced sigma squared). This is the lower-case Greek letter. (Recall that Σ, the symbol meaning "the sum of," is the upper-case sigma.) The symbol for the population standard deviation is σ.

The Normal Distribution

Frequency distributions come in all shapes and sizes. In Chapter 4, we showed curves representing various "shapes" of frequency distributions. Most important for inferential statistics is the normal probability distribution, generally referred to as the *normal distribution*.

The normal distribution is a mathematical construct; that is, it is derived from mathematical theory and thus does not depict a *real* set of data. However, it is extremely useful as a theoretical model that approximates many distributions found in nature. It is particularly valuable in the study of sampling error, which is covered extensively in the next chapter. A curve representing a normal distribution is called a *normal curve*.

The normal curve is represented, not by one specific shape, but by a family of normal curves, each of which has the same properties. Figure 6-3 shows three normal curves. These curves could represent the IQ scores of eighth-grade females, the heights of all 44-year-old men, or the racing times of all runners in the 100-yard dash. Since we are presently interested only in the properties of this curve, the actual frequencies and score values it represents are of no concern to us.

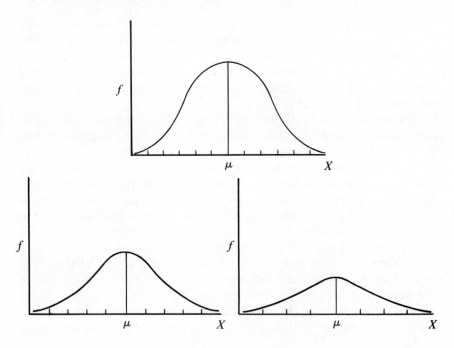

Figure 6-3. Three normal curves.

For each curve, the values (X) lie along the horizontal axis, and the frequencies of the values (f) lie along the vertical axis. The exact shapes of these normal curves differ, depending on the distances between values along the horizontal axis and/or the distances between frequencies along the vertical axis, but we can consider the characteristics of these normal curves to be identical. For convenience, we shall refer to the family of normal curves simply as the normal curve.

Several characteristics of the theoretical normal curve are of considerable value to the statistician. One such characteristic is *symmetry;* the curve is bell-shaped; that is, it has the same shape on either side of the center point, with the largest frequency of values located near the center and the smaller frequencies occurring at the two tails of the curve.

Another important characteristic of this curve is that it is *unimodal,* with its mean, median, and mode all coinciding at the same value. This means that the mean (arithmetic average) is also the most frequently occurring value (the mode), and it lies at the point that divides the curve exactly in half, with 50% of the population lying above the mean and 50% lying below it (the median).

The curve is also *asymptotic,* in that it extends from the mean toward infinity in both directions. Notice that the tails of the curve do not ever actually touch the horizontal axis.

Because it is a theoretical model, the curve is continuous; thus, the distribution of discrete measurements on it only approximates a normal distribution. Conversely, since our actual measurements of continuous variables are always necessarily discrete, they also only approximate this theoretical curve.

Because the theoretical normal curve represents the distribution of an infinite population of measurements, we will designate its mean as μ and its standard deviation as σ. The mean is located at the exact center of this curve, as it is in all symmetrical curves. In Chapter 5, we introduced the concept of variability, using the standard deviation as a measure of dispersion within a set of data. The standard deviation is even more important in statistical work when it is used as a measure of variability of normally-distributed data.

We will use the set of normally distributed data that are represented by the curve in Figure 6-4 to illustrate the properties of the normal curve. If we wish to show graphically where the standard deviation is located on a normal curve, we find the point on the curve at which the curve starts growing faster horizontally than it is growing vertically—the *point of inflection* of the curve—and we draw a perpendicular line from this point to

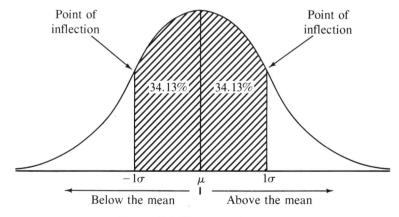

Figure 6-4. The normal curve.

the horizontal axis, as we have done in Figure 6-4. If we were to calculate the value of the standard deviation from the data in this normal distribution, we would find that it does indeed lie at the value on the horizontal axis where the vertical line touches.

Since the curve is symmetrical, what is true of the curve on one side of the mean is also true of it on the other side. Therefore, Figure 6-4 shows two points of inflection and two vertical lines dropping to the horizontal axis from these points. The point designated 1σ is said to be one standard deviation above the mean, because it is located on the right of μ, where the values are larger than μ. The same point to the left of μ is designated -1σ and is said to be one standard deviation below the μ.

The entire area under the normal curve, or under any other, is taken as representing 100% of the scores in the distribution; thus, it can be divided into parts representing percentages of the whole. We have already noted that the area to the right of the mean represents 50% of the total area. It is a characteristic of the normal curve that areas containing specific percentages of the total can be determined by using the mean as a point of departure. For example, in Figure 6-4, 34.13% of the total area under the curve lies between the mean and the vertical line we have drawn at 1σ. The distance along the horizontal axis from the mean to the intersection with this line is, by definition, the *standard deviation* of the distribution.

This designation of the standard deviation holds true for both sides of the mean. Thus, we have a point on the horizontal axis to the right of μ that is termed one standard deviation above the mean, or simply 1σ, and also a point to the left of μ that is termed one standard deviation below the mean, or -1σ. Both of these points are shown in Figure 6-4. We can see that 68.26%, or about ⅔, of the scores in the distribution lie between 1σ and -1σ.

If we measure the distance along the horizontal axis from μ to 1σ and then measure the same distance starting at 1σ and moving toward the tail of the curve, we locate the point that represents the second standard deviation, or 2σ. Although the distances along the axis from the mean to 1σ and from 1σ to 2σ are exactly the same, the areas under the curve are different for these two segments. Again, this holds true on both sides of the mean, so we can locate 2σ and -2σ as shown in Figure 6-5. We recall that 34.13% of the area under the curve lies between μ and 1σ. However, it is evident from Figure 6-5 that a much smaller percentage of the area lies between 1σ and 2σ—only 13.60%.

We can now locate a point along the axis that is three times as far from μ as 1σ is; we call this point 3σ. This distance, too, can be measured to the right and to the left of μ, giving us 3σ and -3σ, as shown in Figure 6-6. The figure shows that only a very small percentage of the area under the curve lies between 2σ and 3σ—2.16%, in fact. As we said earlier, since the

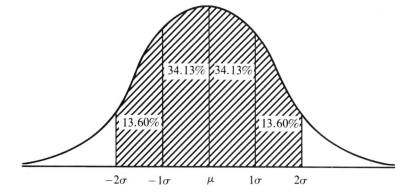

Figure 6-5. The normal curve.

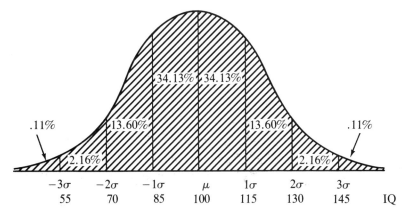

Figure 6-6. The normal curve.

normal curve is a theoretical curve, it extends to infinity in both directions. The curve virtually touches the horizontal axis, however, at 3σ and -3σ. Indeed, as Figure 6-6 indicates, only .11% of the scores lie above 3σ or below -3σ. We can also see in Figure 6-6 that the total area under the curve accounts for 100% of the scores in the distribution (the sum of all the percentages shown).

Now let's examine how we can interpret any particular score if we know only how far it is, in standard deviation units, from the mean. To do this, we shall use a concrete example of IQ scores and assume that they are normally distributed in the population. The curve in Figure 6-6 depicts IQ scores along the horizontal axis. The mean IQ score is 100 and the standard deviation is 15 IQ points; that is, the value of the IQ that lies at 1σ is 15 points larger than the value of μ, or 115. We now have a measure of central tendency, a measure of variability, and the assumption of normality. These characteristics are all we need to obtain a complete picture of the distribution. We know that 50% of the IQ scores are above 100, and 50% are below 100. With $\sigma = 15$, we know that at 1σ the IQ score is 115, and that at -1σ the IQ score is 85. In similar fashion, we can compute the IQ scores at the other σ points shown in Figure 6-6.

Using the percentages associated with the various areas under the curve, we can determine any person's position in relation to the total population by computing how far his IQ score is, in standard deviation units, from the mean of the distribution. For example, suppose a person has an IQ of 130. This is 30 points larger than the mean, or two standard deviations above the mean, and thus falls at the point designated 2σ. We can easily tell that 97.73% of the population have IQs lower than his and that 2.27% have higher IQs.

In statistical work, percentages are less convenient to work with than their decimal equivalents; thus, 34.13% is expressed as .3413 and 13.59% is expressed as .1359.

Figure 6-7 presents the normal curve, and indicates both standard deviations and the proportions of the data that are located within each area. The sum of all the proportions under the curve is 1.0. Notice that the horizontal axis is now labelled z, indicating what we learned in Chapter 5, that z scores can be used to express raw scores in standard-deviation units. When we analyze a distribution of raw scores, we can convert each raw score into a z score using Formula 10, thereby transforming the original distribution into a distribution of z scores. A z score is a standard score, since its mean and standard deviation always have constant values. The mean of a distribution of z scores is always zero and the standard deviation is always 1; z scores are measures of deviation above and below the mean of zero. Therefore, instead of saying "Jane scored two standard deviations below the mean," we can simply say "Jane's $z = -2.00$." By examining Figure 6-7, we can immediately tell that .0227 of the population scored below Jane and .9773 scored above her. This illustrates how helpful z scores are when we are dealing with normally distributed data.

Up to now, we have been dealing with areas bounded at specific standard deviation points, or z scores. We need a method for computing the proportions of areas with boundaries falling *between* any two z scores, even when these are fractional values. Table 1, at the end of the book, presents the proportions of the area under the curve associated with different z scores. Using this table, we can determine the proportion of the area under the normal curve corresponding to any interval for which the boundaries are expressed as z scores. The first column in Table 1 presents z-score values, and the second column shows the proportion of the total area under the curve that lies between μ and any particular z score.

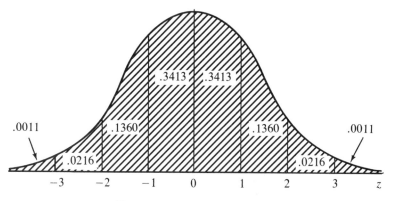

Figure 6-7. The normal curve.

In order to use this table we must first convert the raw scores to z scores. In our example using IQ scores, we would use Formula 6 to determine the deviation score for a person with an IQ of 125. (Here μ is substituted for $\overline{X}$, since we are dealing with a population parameter rather than a sample statistic.)

$$x = X - \mu = 125 - 100 = 25$$

Then, using Formula 10 (with σ instead of s'), we determine the z score:

$$z = \frac{x}{\sigma} = \frac{25}{15} = 1.67$$

Therefore, a person with an IQ of 125 has a z score of 1.67. Notice that the value of the z score represents the distance expressed in the number of standard deviations the raw score lies away from the mean. If the z score is positive, it represents a value above the mean; if it is negative, it indicates a value below the mean. Table 1 shows that the proportion of the total area under the curve that lies between μ and $z = 1.67$ is .4525.

In another example using Table 1, suppose we wish to find the proportion of the population with IQs between 80 and 90. The z score equivalents for these two IQs are $z = -1.33$ and $z = -.67$, respectively. (Remember, the sign of the z score tells us whether it is located above or below the mean. Table 1 is used for both positive and negative z scores, since the areas under the curve remain the same in both cases.) Table 1 tells us that the proportion of the total area from μ to $z = -1.33$ is .4082 and from μ to $z = -.67$ is .2486. The proportion lying between these two z scores, or between IQs 80 and 90, is .4082 − .2486 = .1596. This is shown graphically in Figure 6-8.

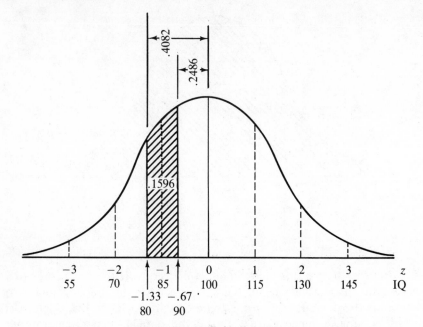

Figure 6-8. The normal curve.

In summary, the total area under the normal curve is considered 1.0. The proportion of this area that lies between any two raw-score values can be determined by converting the raw scores to z scores, and then using Table 1 to determine the proportions of the total area that lie between the mean and the respective z score values.

Exercises: Group A

1. A group of elementary-school children were given a test designed to measure divergent-thinking ability. The children's scores had a mean of 30 points and a standard deviation of 4 points. Assuming that their scores were normally distributed, what proportion of the children received scores of 24 or less?

2. What proportion received scores of 37 or greater?

3. What proportion received scores from 25 through 32?

4. What proportion received scores from 31 through 33?

5. What proportion received scores from 26 through 28?

Exercises: Group B

6. A group of graduates from a business college were given a clerical-aptitude test. Their scores were normally distributed, with a mean of 108 and a standard

deviation of 20. What proportion of the students received a score of 129 or more?

7. What proportion received a score of 109 or less?
8. What proportion received scores from 70 through 130?
9. What proportion received scores from 110 through 120?
10. What proportion received scores from 55 through 75?

CHAPTER 7
PROBABILITY

The concept of probability is the basis upon which all statistical decisions are made. If we were not blessed with probability theory, statistics would be limited to the rather mundane function of mere description. But through the application of statistical formulas, we can specify the probability that events will occur by chance, and thereby make intelligent judgments about experimental results. The processes underlying statistical inference are based entirely on considerations of probability.

Probabilities range from 0 to 1.00. If we roll a standard pair of dice, the probability that we will roll a 13 on a given roll is 0. The probability that our pet rooster will lay an egg tomorrow is also 0. When it is impossible for an event to occur, its probability is 0.

If we toss a coin, the probability that it will land either heads or tails is 1.00. If I release my pencil, the probability that it will fall to the desk is also 1.00. When it is certain that an event will occur, its probability is 1.00.

These examples are unequivocal. When we make statistical inferences in the behavioral sciences, however, we are never in a position to enjoy the luxury of these extremes. We are forced to make interpretations of data in spite of some degree of uncertainty. Therefore, we must understand how probability is determined so that we can make judicious use of it.

When we are able to specify all of the possible events that may happen, and to determine the relative frequency with which unique events may occur on the basis of chance alone, we can determine the *probability* that an event will occur. (The term *relative frequency* refers to the proportion of times each event occurs relative to the total number of possible events.) This probability is stated as a proportion of 1.00.

For example, consider a die with 6 sides, each of which shows a number from 1 through 6. There are six possible events that can occur on one roll of this die. If we rolled it an infinite number of times, the relative frequency of occurrence of each number would be 1/6. That is, the probability of rolling a 5 on any one roll would be 1/6 or .167. The relative frequency of occurrence for each number on the die is shown graphically in Figure 7-1. This figure depicts a rectangular distribution, because each possible event has an equal probability (.167) of happening.

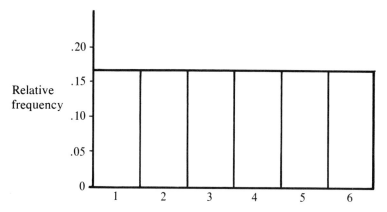

Figure 7-1. Relative frequency distribution for one die.

We call the relative frequency distribution in Figure 7-1 a *probability distribution*. From this distribution, we can see that the probability of rolling either a 1 or a 2 on a particular roll is .333, and the probability of rolling a number larger than 3 is .500. Of course, the probability of rolling a number from 1 through 6 is 1.000. In statistics we use the symbol P for probability. Therefore, the probability of rolling a 2, 4, 5, or 6 on one roll of the die is $P = .667$.

If a pair of dice is rolled an infinite number of times, then there are 36 possible combinations of dice surfaces, each of which yields 11 possible events—that is, total points. The relative frequency of occurrence for each of these possible events is shown in Table 7-1. This probability distribution of throws of a pair of dice is diagrammed as a frequency polygon in Figure 7-2.

Table 7-1. Relative frequency of occurrence

Total points	Possible ways of occurring	Relative frequency
2	1	.028
3	2	.056
4	3	.083
5	4	.111
6	5	.139
7	6	.167
8	5	.139
9	4	.111
10	3	.083
11	2	.056
12	1	.028
	36	

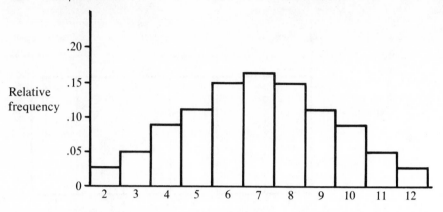

Figure 7-2. Relative frequency distribution for two dice.

Two of the points just made should be emphasized. First, we must note that probability distributions occur as a result of chance; that is, they come about when randomness is free to have its way over an infinite number of events. Second, we have used the expression *will occur* in connection with the concept of probability. This expression refers to a speculation about the relative frequency with which a specific event will take place, based upon a given probability distribution. In inferential statistics we can also reverse this process; when we obtain a sample statistic, we can use an appropriate probability distribution to answer the question "What is the probability that the statistic we obtained could have happened by chance?" Answering this question is one of the major functions of statistical analysis.

The probability distributions given in Figures 7-1 and 7-2 depict relative frequencies for discrete data. (A pair of dice can come up totaling only 11 discrete numbers.) In such cases, it is possible to specify the probability of each occurrence. This is not so when continuous variables are involved. This is because when we work with continuous variables, we are theoretically dealing with an infinite number of different values under the curve. It would be impossible to divide the total area, which is considered to be 1.00, by an infinite number of possible values. However, we can compute probabilities for areas between any two values under the curve. Thus, probabilities in continuous probability distributions are defined in terms of intervals under the curve rather than in terms of individual values.

Let's apply this discussion of probability to the normal curve. We may consider the normal curve to be a probability distribution that has been derived from mathematical theory. This is one of the most useful probability distributions in the study of statistics. Since it is a distribution of a continuous variable, we can only specify probabilities for areas under it.

The probability of randomly selecting a score from a given area under the curve is equal to the proportion of the total number of scores that is contained in the area. Therefore, when the normal curve represents a probability distribution, the probability that a score will be randomly selected from a particular area can be determined through the use of z scores and reference to Table 1. This means that the proportions that we calculated in Chapter 6 can be considered probability statements and the values given in Table 1 can be interpreted as probabilities.

We can answer the question "What is the probability that a randomly selected individual represented in Figure 6-6 will have an IQ between 80 and 90?" in the following manner. We merely convert the proportion of .1596 into a probability statement: "The probability that we would select at random from this population an individual who has an IQ between 80 and 90 is $P = .1596$." In other words, about 16 times out of 100 (or about 16% of the time), we would randomly select an individual who has an IQ within this range.

We can also state that the probability of randomly selecting an individual with an IQ below 70 is $P = .0227$; therefore, it is a rather unlikely occurrence.

By using Table 1, we can determine the probability of selecting at random a person who has a z score of, for example, -1.34 or lower. Table 1 shows the probability of obtaining a score lying between μ and $z = -1.34$ to be $P = .4099$. We know that for values below μ, $P = .5000$. Therefore, the probability of obtaining a z score of -1.34 or lower is $P = .5000 - .4099 = .0901$.

Let's look at one more example of the procedure for determining probabilities using Table 1. Suppose we know that the population of completion times for a test of dexterity is normally distributed, with $\mu = 45$ minutes and $\sigma = 5$ minutes. What is the probability that a randomly selected individual will complete the test in from 38 to 47 minutes? Because time is considered a continuous variable, we must use the limits of 38 and 47 in our calculations. The limits of 38 are 37.5–38.5; the limits of 47 are 46.5–47.5. Therefore, we are interested in the interval from 37.5 to 47.5.

We must first determine the z scores for these two values and their associated probabilities from Table 1.

For $X = 38$: $z = \dfrac{x}{\sigma} = \dfrac{37.5 - 45}{5} = -1.5$. P between μ and $z = .4332$

For $X = 47$: $z = \dfrac{x}{\sigma} = \dfrac{47.5 - 45}{5} = 0.5$. P between μ and $z = .1915$

The probability of selecting an individual with a test time that falls between these two z scores is $P = .4332 + .1915 = .6247$. This example is diagrammed in Figure 7-3.

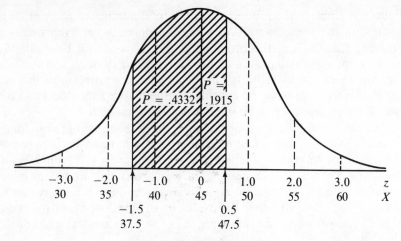

Figure 7-3. The normal curve.

The important point to remember when using Table 1 is that the probabilities given in the table are for the area between the mean and the z scores, whether the z scores are positive or negative.

The Distribution of Sample Means

We have by now interpreted the area under the normal curve in terms of percentages, proportions, and probabilities. In our previous examples, the curve has represented the distribution of the individual measures comprising the population. We shall now extend this use of the curve to the calculation of means of samples.

When we randomly select samples from a population, it is highly unlikely that the value of each sample mean will equal the value of the population mean, since very few samples are exact microcosms of the population. Completely by chance, some of the samples will have $\bar{X}$s larger than μ, and some will have $\bar{X}$s smaller than μ. Many of them will have $\bar{X}$s close to μ, and few will deviate greatly from μ on either side. We need to know how the means of randomly selected samples are distributed.

The following three theorems, which are derived from the Central Limit Theorem, are the foundations upon which lies much of our ability to draw inferences from sample data.

Theorem 1
The means of a multitude of equal-sized samples drawn from a normally-distributed population are themselves normally distributed.

Theorem 2
The means of a multitude of equal-sized samples, regardless of the shape of the population distribution, approach a normal distribution as the sample size increases.

Theorem 3
The mean of a multitude of normally distributed sample means is the population mean.

Theorem 1 holds true regardless of the number of observations in each sample. Theorem 2 is important because, in the behavioral sciences, we are generally concerned with variables for which little or nothing is known about the form of the population distribution. In general, a sample size of 30 or more is considered large enough for us to use the normal curve as a close approximation of the distribution of sample means. Theorem 3 tells us that the value of the mean of all the sample means is equal to the value of the mean of the population from which the samples were drawn. The probability distribution of the sample means is called a *sampling distribution of means,* with the population mean at the center of the distribution.

Of what practical value is it to know that the distribution of means of samples, each based on 30 or more observations, closely resembles the normal curve? It signifies that we can compute the standard deviation of the sample means, and then use Table 1 to determine probabilities for the means, just as we did for individual scores. To do this, we must compute the variance and standard deviation of the sample means just as we did earlier, using Formulas 8 and 9. The standard deviation of the means of a multitude of equal-sized samples is called the *standard error of the mean,* and the symbol for this parameter is $\sigma_{\bar{X}}$.

Figure 7-4 presents a distribution of sample means of reading scores, where each sample has $N = 50$. Theorems 2 and 3 hold for this example. (It is important to remember that this is a distribution of mean scores of a large number of samples, not a distribution of individual scores.)

The curve depicted in Figure 7-4 is a normal curve, and all of the properties we have attributed to it in connection with the distribution of individual scores are also valid for the distribution of sample means. We can see from Figure 7-4 that the mean of all the sample means is μ. Remember that these samples are all of the same size.

In Figure 7-4, the σ units are designated as $\sigma_{\bar{X}}$ because this is a distribution of sample means. In this example, we know that the population mean reading score is 70, and we can determine the $\sigma_{\bar{X}}$ from the distribution of sample means around μ by computing the standard deviation of the sample means. An alternate way to calculate $\sigma_{\bar{X}}$ is to use the formula, $\sigma_{\bar{X}} = \sigma/\sqrt{N}$, where N is the number of sample means. Let's suppose that our

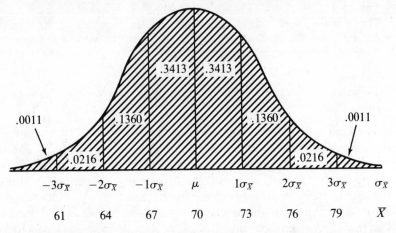

Figure 7-4. Sampling distribution of mean reading scores.

calculations yield $\sigma_{\bar{X}} = 3$. This tells us that the standard error of the mean is three points. Knowing this, and using Table 1, we can then determine the probability of selecting a sample with a mean within any particular interval of mean scores. In this example, the probability of obtaining a sample with a mean between 68 and 75 is determined as follows:

> Since reading achievement is considered a continuous variable, the real limits of this interval are 67.5 and 75.5.
>
> For $\bar{X} = 67.5$: $z = \dfrac{67.5 - 70}{3} = -0.83$. From μ to z, $P = .2967$.
>
> For $\bar{X} = 75.5$: $z = \dfrac{75.5 - 70}{3} = 1.83$. From μ to z, $P = .4664$.

Therefore, the probability of obtaining from this population a sample of 50 individuals that has a mean reading score between 68 and 75 is .2967 + .4664 = .7631.

This use of the normal curve as an approximation of the sampling distribution of means forms the basis for some of the major statistical-inference procedures.

Exercises: Group A

1. Suppose that a multitude of same-sized samples were randomly selected from a population, where $\mu = 70$ and the standard error of the mean is computed to be $\sigma_{\bar{X}} = 9$. What is the probability of randomly selecting from this population a sample that has a mean of 74 or greater?

2. What is the probability of randomly selecting a sample that has a mean of 67 or less?

3. What is the probability of randomly selecting a sample that has a mean that falls between 58 and 62?

4. What is the probability of randomly selecting a sample that has a mean that falls between 72 and 84?

5. What is the probability of randomly selecting a sample that has a mean that falls between 60 and 81?

Exercises: Group B

6. Suppose that a multitude of same-sized samples were randomly selected from a population where $\mu = 120$ and the standard error of the mean is computed to be $\sigma_{\overline{X}} = 12$. What is the probability of randomly selecting a sample that has a mean of 100 or greater?

7. What is the probability of selecting a sample having a mean of 110 or less?

8. What is the probability of selecting a sample with a mean that falls between 133 and 143?

9. What is the probability of selecting a sample with a mean that falls between 95 and 135?

10. What is the probability of selecting a sample with a mean that falls between 94 and 114?

CHAPTER 8
ESTIMATING POPULATION PARAMETERS

In Chapters 6 and 7, we indulged in the "conceptual luxuries" of dealing with populations in which parameters were known; of taking infinite numbers of samples from such populations and examining the distributions of their means; and of determining probabilities in selecting samples, given a known sampling distribution. These examples helped to show how data "behave" in populations and samples.

Now we must turn to more practical applications of our statistical knowledge. Very seldom do we have access to the values of population parameters. Our efforts, for the most part, are directed toward making estimates of parameters such as the population mean, variance, standard deviation, and standard error of the mean, where we have only sample data at hand.

This chapter will be concerned with methods used to analyze data obtained from only one sample in order to estimate the values of certain parameters of the population from which the sample was randomly selected. Specifically, we will look at methods for estimating σ^2 and $\sigma_{\bar{X}}$. Chapter 9 will present methods used to make inferences about the value of the population mean from sample data.

Estimating the Population Variance and the Standard Deviation

When we deal with the relationship between a population and its samples, we must be aware of two statistical facts: (1) A population has parameters with specific values (these are usually not known)—that is, in a given population, the mean has one value which does not vary. The variance of all measurements in a population is also a specific value. (2) Sample statistics, such as $\bar{X}$ and s'^2, vary from sample to sample because of *sampling error*.

These two facts lead us to our first problem in statistical inference. Given the data in a sample, what is our best estimate of the parameters of the population from which it was selected?

In estimating the value of the population variance, σ^2, from sample data, our first inclination is to compute the sample variance, s'^2, using Formula 8, and to let this serve as our best estimate of the value of the population variance. However, mathematicians have determined that s'^2 is a biased estimate of σ^2, since it tends to underestimate the value of σ^2.

Our desire, of course, is to make an unbiased estimate of σ^2. What is an unbiased estimate? Basically, we obtain an unbiased estimate of a parameter when the mean of the estimates made from all possible samples of the same size equals the parameter. If we take an infinite number of samples of the same size from a population, however, the mean of all their variances will be slightly smaller than the population variance. For this reason, we say that s'^2 provides a biased estimate of σ^2; that is, the value of s'^2, when it is calculated from the data in one sample, will tend to underestimate the population variance.

The reason for this is that we calculate s'^2 by using $\bar{X}$, rather than μ (which is, of course, unknown), as the point of origin for deviation scores. Since $\bar{X}$ undoubtedly is not exactly equal to μ, we have calculated the deviation scores, and hence the variance, from the mean of the sample distribution which yields the smallest possible sum of squares, rather than from μ, which would have given us a larger sum of squares and, consequently, a larger variance estimate. (Incidentally, if we know the value of μ and take the sample deviations from it, the s'^2 computed by Formula 8 will give us an unbiased estimate of σ^2.)

The question confronting us is "How do we make an unbiased estimate of σ^2 when we have only sample data?" We can calculate it by using Formula 11 to compute the "sum of squares" and using Formula 12 to compute the variance estimate.

Formula 11. Calculation of the sum of squared deviations ("sum of squares"). (Formulas 11a and 11b are equivalent.)

Deviation-Score Method	$\Sigma x^2 = \Sigma(X - \bar{X})^2$	(Formula 11a)
Raw-Score Method	$\Sigma x^2 = \Sigma X^2 - \dfrac{(\Sigma X)^2}{N}$	(Formula 11b)

Formula 11 presents two ways to calculate the sum of squares. These formulas use Σx^2 instead of Σfx^2, which is used in Formula 8a. The f was included in Formula 8a only for the purpose of illustrating the method of computation. The two expressions Σx^2 and Σfx^2 represent exactly the same thing: the sum of the squared deviation scores. For simplicity, we will no longer include f in formulas.

Formula 11a gives the deviation-score method for calculating the sum of squares, and Formula 11b gives the raw-score method. These two formulas are algebraically equivalent and they yield identical values. The raw-score formula is easier to use when values are to be computed directly from the data.

Formula 12. Estimate of the population variance from sample data. (Formulas 12a and 12b are equivalent.)

Deviation-Score Method $s^2 = \dfrac{\Sigma x^2}{N - 1}$ (Formula 12a)

Raw-Score Method $s^2 = \dfrac{N\Sigma X^2 - (\Sigma X)^2}{N(N - 1)}$ (Formula 12b)

Formula 12 shows two methods for estimating the population variance from sample data: the deviation-score method and the raw-score method. Notice that the denominator in Formula 12a is $N - 1$ rather than N, as it is in Formula 8a. This reduction in the denominator compensates for the "biasedness" that would occur if we used Formula 8a to estimate σ^2.

So that we do not become confused about the symbols for variance and variance estimates that have been used thus far, we shall review them.

s'^2 is the variance of a set of sample measurements.
σ^2 is the variance of a population of measurements.
s^2 is an unbiased estimate of the population variance derived from sample data.

Let us now apply what we have discussed to a set of sample data. Table 8-1 presents the music-aptitude scores of a random sample of 30 music students. Notice that the f has been dropped from the sums. The sample mean for these data is $\bar{X} = 1104/30 = 36.8$. Using Formula 8b, we find the sample variance to be $s'^2 = 40{,}692/30 - (36.8)^2 = 2.16$. Using Formula 11b, we determine that the sum of squares is $\Sigma x^2 = 40{,}692 - (1104)^2/30 = 64.8$. The unbiased estimate of the population variance, according to Formula 12a, is $s^2 = 64.8/(30 - 1) = 2.23$. If we use Formula 12b, the raw-score method, instead, we obtain the same variance estimate,

$$s^2 = \frac{30 \, (40{,}692) - (1104)^2}{30 \, (30 - 1)} = 2.23.$$

Notice that the sample variance, s'^2, is somewhat smaller than the unbiased variance estimate, s^2. (As an exercise to illustrate the effect on the population variance estimate if μ is a value other than the obtained sample $\bar{X}$, try computing the variance of the data in Table 8-1 by the deviation-score method, designating any value other than 36.8 to be the mean. You will see that all other calculated values of s^2 are larger than 2.23.)

Table 8-1. Music-aptitude scores for 30 students.

X	f	fX	X^2	fX^2
40	1	40	1600	1600
39	3	117	1521	4563
38	5	190	1444	7220
37	9	333	1369	12321
36	6	216	1296	7776
35	4	140	1225	4900
34	2	68	1156	2312
	$N = 30$	$\Sigma X = 1104$		$\Sigma X^2 = 40{,}692$

Degrees of Freedom

In Formula 12, the algebraic expression $N - 1$ is called the number of *degrees of freedom*. The important concept of degrees of freedom pervades much of the remainder of our study of statistics. The degrees of freedom, symbolized as *df,* are determined by the number of scores in a sample that are "free to vary" when we estimate a population parameter. To comprehend thoroughly the meaning of *df,* we need to understand advanced statistical theory, which is beyond the scope of this text. For our purposes, we shall concentrate on how the *df* are determined, not on their theoretical underpinnings.

In general, the *df* refer to the number of independent scores that are used in estimating a population parameter. The word independent is significant. In the denominator of Formula 12a, which is used to estimate the population variance, the degrees of freedom are one less than the sample size. This is because, for a given value of $\overline{X}$, if the sum of the deviation scores is to equal zero (which it must), all of the sample values are "free to vary" except one. In a sample of 20 scores, therefore, with a given mean, 19 scores can be *any* values—that is, they are free to vary—but the 20th score must be a certain value so that the sum of deviation scores will equal zero. Thus, the 20th score is not free to vary; it is fixed. In this example, the number of degrees of freedom is $df = N - 1$ or 19.

In Table 8-1, where $\overline{X} = 36.8$, 29 of the 30 scores could have been any values (they were independent of each other, or free to vary), but once they were established, the 30th score had to be a certain value (it was not independent of the other scores) for Σx to equal zero.

We now have some new terminology to describe the method used in calculating the variance estimate. Instead of reading Formula 12a as "The population variance is estimated by dividing the sum of squared deviations from the sample mean by the number of observations in the sample minus one" we can now say "The population variance is estimated by dividing the sum of squares by the degrees of freedom." The latter expression will be of value to us when we reach Chapter 13, which covers analysis of variance.

The number of degrees of freedom is not always determined by $N - 1$. The *df* depend on the number of restrictions that are placed on sample values when a population parameter is estimated. However, the principle is always the same; the *df* of a statistic that is used as an estimate of a parameter are determined by the number of independent values that are used in making the estimate. We shall see many uses of the concept of degrees of freedom as we explore various statistical tests.

If we take the square root of our estimate of the population variance, we have a very good approximation of the population's standard deviation, which is represented by the symbol s. Using the data given in Table 8-1, we can estimate the standard deviation of the population to be $s = \sqrt{s^2} = \sqrt{2.23} = 1.49$. In this case, the Roman symbols s^2 and s are used, because they represent estimates based on sample data.

Estimating the Standard Error of the Mean

In Chapter 7, we learned that a sampling distribution of sample means can be developed around μ by computing the standard deviation of a multitude of sample means of like-sized samples; this standard deviation is called the standard error of the mean and is symbolized by $\sigma_{\bar{X}}$. But how can we develop such a sampling distribution when we cannot obtain a multitude of samples? Fortunately, statisticians have developed a formula for estimating the value of the standard error of the mean using only the data in one sample. This estimate is symbolized by $s_{\bar{X}}$, because it is derived from sample data. The method used to calculate it is presented in Formula 13.

Formula 13. Estimate of the standard error of the mean.

$$s_{\bar{X}} = \frac{s}{\sqrt{N}}$$

This formula shows that dividing the estimate of the population's standard deviation by the square root of the sample size yields an estimate of the standard deviation of sample means, which is called the *estimate of the standard error of the mean*. This formula is extremely valuable because it allows us to estimate from the data in a single sample how a multitude of sample means would vary around the population mean.

We determined that, for the data in Table 8-1, $s = 1.49$. By applying Formula 13, we can estimate that the standard error of the mean is

$$s_{\bar{X}} = \frac{1.49}{\sqrt{30}} = \frac{1.49}{5.477} = .272$$

(A table of squares and square roots, with directions for its use, is presented as Table 7 at the end of the book.) This tells us that the standard deviation of a multitude of sample means (the standard error of the mean), for samples of 30 observations each, is estimated to be .272 points.

Examination of Formula 13 reveals that the size of $s_{\bar{X}}$ is a function of two values, s and N. For samples of the same size, the larger the s is, the larger $s_{\bar{X}}$ will be. This is logical because the means of random samples would be expected to vary more in populations with widely varying scores than in populations with relatively homogeneous scores.

On the other hand, for a population with a given s, the larger the sample is, the smaller will be the $s_{\bar{X}}$. This also stands to reason because we would expect the means of large samples to vary less from μ (have less error) than the means of small samples. We always wish to reduce error, and now we have discovered that one way to accomplish this is to obtain large samples.

Table 8-2 gives concise examples of the methods of calculation introduced in this chapter. This example shows the computation of the standard error of the mean from the data in one sample, using both the raw-score method and the deviation-score method.

Table 8-2. Calculation of the estimate of the standard error of the mean.

X	f	fX	X²	fX²	x	x²	fx²
14	1	14	196	196	4	16	16
13	3	39	169	507	3	9	27
12	2	24	144	288	2	4	8
11	8	88	121	968	1	1	8
10	7	70	100	700	0	0	0
9	6	54	81	486	−1	1	6
8	3	24	64	192	−2	4	12
7	3	21	49	147	−3	9	27
6	1	6	36	36	−4	16	16
	$N = 34$	$\Sigma X = 340$		$\Sigma X^2 = 3520$			$\Sigma x^2 = 120$

$$\bar{X} = \frac{340}{34} = 10$$

Calculation of sum of squares:

Formula 11a: $\Sigma x^2 = \Sigma(X - \bar{X})^2 = 120$ (right-hand column)

Formula 11b: $\Sigma x^2 = \Sigma X^2 - \dfrac{(\Sigma X)^2}{N} = 3520 - \dfrac{(340)^2}{34} = 120$

Calculation of estimate of population variance:

Formula 12a: $s^2 = \dfrac{\Sigma x^2}{N-1} = \dfrac{120}{34-1} = 3.64$

Formula 12b: $s^2 = \dfrac{N\Sigma X^2 - (\Sigma X)^2}{N(N-1)} = \dfrac{34(3520) - (340)^2}{34(34-1)} = 3.64$

Calculation of estimate of population standard deviation:

Formula 9 (adapted): $s = \sqrt{s^2} = \sqrt{3.64} = 1.91$

Calculation of estimate of the standard error of the mean:

Formula 13: $s_{\bar{x}} = \dfrac{s}{\sqrt{N}} = \dfrac{1.91}{\sqrt{34}} = .33$

Having estimated the standard error of the mean from sample data, we could develop a sampling distribution of sample means around the population mean. But, alas, we seldom know the value of the population mean. However, we can put the estimate of the standard error of the mean to good use in establishing *confidence intervals* for the value of the population mean. This method is given in the next chapter.

Exercises: Group A

1. A random sample of 14 prisoners was selected from a prison population and the following frequency distribution of their adjustment scores was obtained. Compute the sum of squares for these adjustment scores, using the deviation-score method and the raw-score method. Check to see that your two answers are identical.

Adjustment scores	f
32	2
31	0
30	3
29	4
28	2
27	2
26	1

2. How many degrees of freedom are associated with the frequency distribution in Exercise 1?

3. Calculate the unbiased estimate of the population variance for the distribution in Exercise 1, using the deviation-score method and the raw-score method. Check to see that your two answers are identical.

4. Calculate the estimate of the population standard deviation for the distribution in Exercise 1.

5. Calculate the estimate of the standard error of the mean, using the data in Exercise 1.

6. The superintendent of the local school district wished to obtain data on the level of writing skills of the high-school students in his district. He randomly selected 20 students from the enrollments of the high schools and obtained the following writing-proficiency scores.

Interval	f
18–20	2
15–17	2
12–14	3
9–11	5
6–8	4
3–5	3
0–2	1

Compute the sum of squares for these writing-proficiency scores, using the deviation-score method and the raw-score method. Make sure that your two answers are identical.

7. How many degrees of freedom are associated with the frequency distribution in Exercise 6?

8. Calculate the unbiased estimate of the population variance for the distribution in Exercise 6, using the deviation-score method and the raw-score method. Check to see that your two answers are identical.

9. Calculate the estimate of the standard deviation of the population for the distribution in Exercise 6.

10. Calculate the estimate of the standard error of the mean, using the data in Exercise 6.

Exercises: Group B

11. A randomly selected sample of 18 enlistees in the U.S. Army was administered a physical-agility test. The following distribution of agility scores was obtained.

X	f
48	2
47	2
46	3
45	4
44	3
43	3
42	0
41	1

Compute the sum of squares for these agility scores, using the deviation-score method and the raw-score method. Check to make certain that your two answers are identical.

12. How many degrees of freedom are associated with the frequency distribution in Exercise 11?

13. Calculate the unbiased estimate of the population variance for the distribution in Exercise 11, using the deviation-score method and the raw-score method. Check to see that your two answers are identical.

14. Calculate the estimate of the population standard deviation for the distribution in Exercise 11.

15. Calculate the estimate of the standard error of the mean, using the data in Exercise 11.

16. A randomly selected sample of 24 rats was administered a depressant; then each was tested to measure its reaction to an electric shock. The following distribution of reaction scores was obtained.

Interval	f
24–27	2
20–23	3
16–19	8
12–15	3
8–11	5
4–7	3

Compute the sum of squares for these reaction scores, using the deviation-score method and the raw-score method. Make sure that your two answers are identical.

17. How many degrees of freedom are associated with the frequency distribution in Exercise 16?

18. Calculate the unbiased estimate of the population variance for the distribution in Exercise 16, using the deviation-score method and the raw-score method. Check to see that your two answers are identical.

19. Calculate the estimate of the population standard deviation for the distribution in Exercise 16.

20. Calculate the estimate of the standard error of the mean, using the data in Exercise 16.

CHAPTER 9
ESTABLISHING CONFIDENCE INTERVALS

One of the common statistical problems we face when we are confronted with a set of sample data is how to make an "educated guess" concerning how accurately the value of the sample mean represents the value of the unknown population mean. In other words, we wish to use the sample values to provide a basis for an inference about the value of the parameter, μ.

As background for this problem in statistical inference, let us first consider a population from which we can select an infinite number of samples of 50 cases each. As we saw in Chapter 7, we can prepare a distribution of sample means. The mean of such a distribution will be the mean of the population, and the standard deviation of the sample means is the standard error of the mean. Since the means of samples are normally distributed, we can use our knowledge of the probabilities associated with the areas under the normal curve as it applies to a distribution of sample means.

Suppose we now wish to determine the interval, centering on μ, within which .95 of the sample means lie. To establish this interval we need to specify, in $\sigma_{\bar{X}}$ units (or z-score units), the points above and below μ between which .95 of the sample means are contained. Since Table 1 shows the proportions of the area under the normal curve located between the mean and each z score, we need to find the z score that demarks .4750 of the total area above μ and .4750 of the total area below μ. From the "μ to z" column of Table 1, we find that .4750 is associated with the z score 1.96. Therefore, the boundaries of the interval containing .95 of the sample means are located at $z = -1.96$ and $z = 1.96$.

The interval bounded by these two points and the relevant probability areas are shown in Figure 9-1. This figure shows that .95 of the sample means lie between $-1.96\sigma_{\bar{X}}$ and $1.96\sigma_{\bar{X}}$. We already know that this proportion can be considered a probability. Therefore, if we select one sample from this distribution at random, the probability is .025 that its mean lies below $-1.96\sigma_{\bar{X}}$ and .025 that it lies above $1.96\sigma_{\bar{X}}$. On the other hand, the probability of our selecting a sample with a mean that lies within the interval bounded by $-1.96\sigma_{\bar{X}}$ and $1.96\sigma_{\bar{X}}$ is $P = .95$.

For example, suppose we know that the mean of a population is 35 and $\sigma_{\bar{X}}$ is 1.5. To determine the interval containing .95 of the $\bar{X}$s, we must determine the values of the sample means at $-1.96\sigma_{\bar{X}}$ and $1.96\sigma_{\bar{X}}$. For $-1.96\sigma_{\bar{X}}$, this value lies at 1.96×1.5 below the mean, which is $35 - 2.94$, or 32.06. For $1.96\sigma_{\bar{X}}$, this value lies at 1.96×1.5 above the mean, which is $35 + 2.94$, or 37.94. This interval is shown in Figure 9-1.

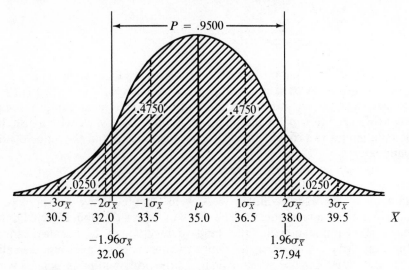

Figure 9-1. Interval containing 95% of the sample means.

We can say that there is a probability of .95 that the mean of one sample randomly selected from this distribution will lie between 32.06 and 37.94. We can also say that the probability that its mean will have a value outside (either above or below) this interval is .05.

The logic used in these examples will help us to understand how the properties of the normal curve can be used to establish an interval within which there is a specified probability of an $\bar{X}$ occurring. However, since we are rarely in a position to take an infinite number of samples from a population, let us now return to a more typical case, in which we have only one sample and must use the data obtained from it to make inferences about the population mean. For example, suppose we wish to estimate the mean height of males in the United States. If we could measure all men in the nation, and calculate their mean height to be 69 inches, we could state with certainty, barring measurement errors, that this represents the mean height of American males. But if we can take only one random sample of males and compute the mean height of this sample, we cannot state with complete confidence that the mean of the sample is identical with the population mean. This is true because, as we have seen, the means of samples vary around the population mean; few samples are likely to yield means that are identical with the population mean.

Of course, the sample mean is the one value that is our best estimate of the population mean, in cases where we have data from only one sample. Suppose we randomly select a sample of males and calculate their mean height to be 68 inches. Then, our best guess for the population mean has to be 68 inches. However, we will have little confidence that our guess is correct, since we know that a sample mean is likely to be located either above or below the unknown population mean. When we use the sample mean as an estimate of the population mean, we are making a *point estimate* of the population value. It is difficult to know how much confidence to place in this point estimate, because we have no information by which to gauge its accuracy.

We need a procedure that will enable us to state the degree of confidence we have in an estimate. One such procedure entails establishing a *range* of values for estimating the population mean, instead of just taking the sample mean as a point estimate of it. If we make an *interval estimate* using sample data, we can determine the degree of confidence we have that our interval contains the population mean. Our procedure, then, is to establish a *confidence interval* from sample data from which we can make inferences about the population mean.

The 95% Confidence Interval

One commonly used method for making statements about the value of the population mean is to determine the 95% confidence interval. By using this procedure, we shall determine an interval such that, if we repeated the procedure for a large number of samples, 95% of them would encompass the population mean.

Our method for establishing the 95% confidence interval follows: We have shown that the probability is .95 that a randomly selected z score lies between -1.96 and 1.96. This can be shown as

$$P(-1.96 \leq z \leq 1.96) = .95$$

This expression is read "The probability that a z score is equal to or greater than -1.96, or equal to or less than 1.96, is .95." In addition, we have defined z as $(\bar{X} - \mu)/s_{\bar{x}}$. Substituting this in the above expression, we have

$$P(-1.96 \leq \frac{\bar{X} - \mu}{s_{\bar{x}}} \leq 1.96) = .95$$

Now, multiplying through by $s_{\bar{x}}$, this expression becomes

$$P(-1.96s_{\bar{x}} \leq \bar{X} - \mu \leq 1.96s_{\bar{x}}) = .95$$

If we subtract $\bar{X}$ from each member of the expression, we have

$$P(-\bar{X} - 1.96s_{\bar{x}} \leq -\mu \leq -\bar{X} + 1.96s_{\bar{x}}) = .95$$

Now, by changing signs throughout the expression, which also reverses the sign of the inequalities, we have

$$P(\bar{X} + 1.96s_{\bar{x}} \geq \mu \geq \bar{X} - 1.96s_{\bar{x}}) = .95$$

Rearranging the terms gives

$$P(\bar{X} - 1.96s_{\bar{x}} \leq \mu \leq \bar{X} + 1.96s_{\bar{x}}) = .95$$

This last expression gives us the specification of the 95% confidence interval. It is read as "The probability is .95 that the interval bounded by $\bar{X}$ + 1.96$s_{\bar{x}}$ and $\bar{X}$ − 1.96$s_{\bar{x}}$ encompasses the population mean." This method for establishing a confidence interval will work quite well for relatively large samples, those with $N = 30$ or more. A method that can be used for small samples will be presented later.

To illustrate how the confidence interval is established, we will randomly select a sample of 100 U.S. males and measure their heights. Assume that in the sample, $\bar{X} = 68$ inches, and $s^2 = 36$. The point estimate of μ would then be 68 inches. We know, however, that this is a more or less inaccurate estimate; a confidence interval will give us more accurate information. Therefore, using Formula 13, we estimate that $s_{\bar{x}} = .6$ inches.

We have shown that the 95% confidence interval is determined by the value that lies at −1.96$s_{\bar{x}}$ and the value that lies at 1.96$s_{\bar{x}}$. If $\bar{X} = 68$ and $s_{\bar{x}} = .6$, then the value that lies at −1.96$s_{\bar{x}}$ must be −1.96 × .6, or −1.18 inches from the mean. This value, which represents the lower boundary of the 95% confidence interval, is 66.82 inches.

The upper boundary of the interval is 1.96 × .6 or 1.18 inches from the mean, which is 69.18 inches. Therefore, the 95% confidence interval developed from the data in this sample is from 66.82 to 69.18 inches.

We reason that if we could obtain a large number of samples, each with $N = 100$, and determine an interval from each of them using this method, then 95% of these intervals would encompass the population mean. Since we have the data from only one sample, we conclude that the probability is .95 that our interval ranging from 66.82 to 69.18 inches is one of those that encompasses the mean height of the male population.

Of course, it is obvious that the μ must have a specific value, although it is not known to us. Either the value of μ falls within our established 95% confidence interval, or it does not. It is an all-or-nothing situation, so the concept of probability is not involved. Thus, it is actually incorrect to state that the probability that μ lies within the interval is .95.

How do we interpret the confidence interval? If we took a multitude of samples and calculated the 95% confidence interval for each sample, we would find that, because of sampling error, the limits of the intervals would vary from sample to sample. Some of these intervals, 95% of them, in fact, would contain μ and some would not. This provides a basis for interpreting the meaning of a confidence interval. But in this case, we do not have a multitude of samples; we have only one sample, from which we have developed one 95% confidence interval. We cannot say that the probability is .95 that μ lies within our interval. We can say, however, that if this process of establishing intervals is applied to many samples, it will yield intervals that contain the population mean 95 times out of 100. We must therefore conclude that the probability is .95 that our interval is one of those that encompasses μ.

The 99% Confidence Interval

If we need an interval that will have an even greater probability of containing μ, we can calculate the 99% confidence interval. We can then state that, in the long run, 99% of the intervals determined by this method will encompass μ.

The method used to determine the 99% confidence interval is similar to the procedure for calculating the 95% confidence interval. As we would expect, the 99% confidence interval will be wider than the 95% confidence interval for the same data. But we will have a higher degree of confidence that the 99% interval encompasses μ.

The first step is to determine the two points on the horizontal axis of the normal curve that designate the boundaries of the central .99 of the area under the curve. Table 1 shows that .4951 of the area lies between μ and $z = 2.58$. Since we are indicating variability in terms of $s_{\bar{x}}$, we can say that .99 of the area is contained within the interval $-2.58s_{\bar{x}}$ to $2.58s_{\bar{x}}$.

In the example used earlier, in which $\bar{X} = 68$ inches and $s_{\bar{x}} = .6$ inches, the boundaries of the 99% confidence interval are determined as follows. The value at $-2.58s_{\bar{x}}$ lies at $-2.58 \times .6$ from the mean, which is $68 - 1.55$, or 66.45 inches. The value at $2.58s_{\bar{x}}$ lies at $2.58 \times .6$, from the mean, or 69.55 inches. Notice that the 99% confidence interval is wider than the 95% confidence interval, which covered the area from 66.82 to 69.18. Intervals formed in this manner for a multitude of samples would encompass the μ 99% of the time. Thus, probability that our interval based upon one sample is one of these encompassing μ is $P = .99$.

In summary, the probability expressed in a confidence interval refers to the likelihood that it is one of the many possible intervals that can be determined for one population that contain the population mean. It does not state the likelihood that the population mean will fall within a given interval. There is only one population mean with a specific value (although it is unknown to us), but there are as many possible intervals as there are possible samples. Each sample yields its own interval, and these intervals differ from sample to sample. In computing a confidence interval for a given sample, we are attempting to determine the probability that it is one of those intervals that encompass the population mean, rather than one of those that do not.

We could, of course, determine any other confidence interval for the data in our sample. For example, using Table 1, we could compute the 50% confidence interval or the 80% confidence interval. We have used the 95% and 99% confidence intervals here because they are the ones most commonly used in making inferences about the population mean.

The t Distribution

Up to this point, we have considered two situations in which the population values were assumed to be normally distributed:

1. In cases where the parameter σ was known, we determined $\sigma_{\bar{X}}$ by $\sigma/\sqrt{N}$ and found that the z scores calculated by $(\bar{X} - \mu)/\sigma_{\bar{X}}$ were normally distributed, with a mean of 0 and a standard deviation of 1, regardless of the sample size.
2. In cases where σ was unknown, we estimated it by using $s_{\bar{X}} = s/\sqrt{N}$. We found that the ratio $(\bar{X} - \mu)/s_{\bar{X}}$ was approximately normally distributed for large-sized samples.

The first procedure can be used with both large- and small-sized samples. However, its usefulness is limited since we seldom know the value of σ. The second procedure is useful when we have relatively large samples (those with an N of 30 or more), but as the sample size becomes smaller, the distribution of the ratio, $(\bar{X} - \mu)/s_{\bar{X}}$, becomes increasingly dissimilar to the normal curve.

We must now learn how to establish the sampling distribution of means for small samples when the value of $\sigma_{\bar{X}}$ is unknown. In such instances, we estimate the standard error of the mean using Formula 13. Since $s_{\bar{X}}$ is calculated from the data in a sample, we know that its value will vary from sample to sample. We also know that there will be less variability in the values of $s_{\bar{X}}$ when we use a multitude of large-sized samples than there will be when we use small-sized samples—that is, the smaller the sample size, the more variability there will be in $s_{\bar{X}}$ from sample to sample. Thus, we must conclude that the $s_{\bar{X}}$ derived from a large sample is a closer approximation of $\sigma_{\bar{X}}$ than is one derived from a small sample.

Let's examine more closely what this means. We have stated that z scores computed from the ratio $(\bar{X} - \mu)/\sigma_{\bar{X}}$ are normally distributed, regardless of sample size. This is because where σ is known, $\sigma_{\bar{X}}$ can be calculated and it is a fixed value. The μ is also a fixed value. Thus, in the ratio $(\bar{X} - \mu)/\sigma_{\bar{X}}$ there is only one statistic, $\bar{X}$, that varies from sample to sample. Since for normally distributed populations $\bar{X}$s are normally distributed, the z scores computed from this ratio are also normally distributed.

For large samples, $s_{\bar{x}}$ provides a close approximation of $\sigma_{\bar{x}}$, and may be taken as a substitute for $\sigma_{\bar{x}}$, and the distribution of values computed from the ratio $(\bar{X} - \mu)/s_{\bar{x}}$ closely resembles the normal distribution.

For small samples, there are two statistics in the ratio $(\bar{X} - \mu)/s_{\bar{x}}$ that vary, $\bar{X}$ and $s_{\bar{x}}$. Because the denominator, $s_{\bar{x}}$, is not a fixed value but varies from sample to sample, the ratios are not exactly normally distributed; they are more widely dispersed than they would be in a normal distribution. This dispersion becomes more pronounced as the sample size becomes smaller.

Therefore, we cannot use the normal curve to represent the sampling distribution of small samples when $s_{\bar{x}}$ is used as an estimate of $\sigma_{\bar{x}}$. The distributions that are appropriate in this situation are called t distributions. They were developed by William S. Gossett in the early part of this century. Gossett wrote under the pseudonym "Student"; the distributions he developed have been assigned the symbol t. Thus, they are referred to as *Student's distributions of t* or, more simply, as *t distributions*.

The probabilities associated with differences between μ and $\bar{X}$, using $s_{\bar{x}}$, are derived from t distributions. The shape of the t distribution varies according to the number of degrees of freedom for a sample. Thus, instead of only one t distribution, there is a family of them, one for each sample based on its size. Figure 9-2 presents the t distributions for three different dfs, and compares them to the normal curve. This figure shows that t distributions for large samples, such as those in which $df = 25$, more nearly correspond to the normal curve than do t distributions based upon small

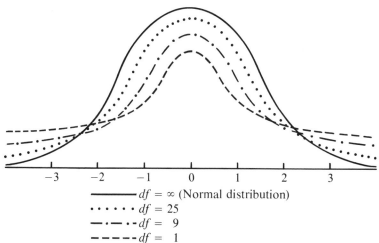

$df = \infty$ (Normal distribution)
· · · · · · $df = 25$
— · — · · $df = 9$
— — — — $df = 1$

Figure 9-2. The t distributions for three different dfs compared with the normal curve.

samples, such as those in which $df = 9$ or $df = 1$. For small samples, the ratio $(\bar{X} - \mu)/s_{\bar{x}}$ is designated t rather than z, since z is reserved for use only with the normal curve.

The distributions of t and z are similar in that both have a mean of zero, are symmetrical, and are bell-shaped. They differ in that less of the t distribution's area is clustered close to the mean and more of its area is located in the tails.

What does all of this mean in terms of the area under the t-distribution curve? It means that, whereas we used z scores of -1.96 and 1.96 to specify the 95% confidence interval for the normal curve, we must go farther away from the mean toward the tails of a t-distribution curve to delineate the same area. To determine the t values associated with areas under the t-distribution curve, we first need to determine the df for the statistic. We have seen that the df is $N - 1$ for statistics based upon the data in one sample.

Tables could be prepared giving the area under each t-distribution curve just as Table 1 was prepared for the normal curve. But this would be impractical, since we would need a separate table for each df. Instead, Table 2 in the back of the book gives the four most commonly used probability levels for each df. As was the case with z scores, t values can be positive or negative depending upon whether they are above or below the mean. The values given in Table 2 represent both positive and negative t values. Since t-distribution curves are symmetrical, the area above a positive t is the same as the area below a negative t of the same value. Table 2 gives us the t values that cut off .10, .05, .02, and .01 of the area contained in *both* tails of each t distribution. This is sometimes called a table of two-tail values of t.

As an example of how to interpret Table 2, for $df = 21$, in the column headed $P = .05$, we find the t value of 2.080. This means that .05 of the area under the t-distribution curve based on 21 degrees of freedom lies outside of the area bounded by $t = -2.080$ and $t = 2.080$. Thus, to the left of $t = -2.080$ lies .025 of the area, and to the right of $t = 2.080$ lies .025 of the area. Between $t = -2.080$ and $t = 2.080$ lies .95 of the area under this particular curve.

Table 2 shows that t values are larger for small dfs than for large ones. We must go farther out on t-distribution curves based upon small dfs than on the curves based on larger dfs to cut off the same area. The bottom row of this table gives t values for a sample with an infinite df. For $P = .05$, $t = 1.96$; this is exactly the value of z we used in determining the 95% confidence interval for a normally distributed sampling distribution. This illustrates the point made earlier, that the larger the sample size, the more nearly the t distribution follows the normal distribution. At infinity, they coincide.

Let's illustrate the use of the t distributions given in Table 2 to determine the 95% confidence interval for μ, based on data in a sample of ten individuals. Here $df = N - 1 = 9$. Since the 95% confidence interval cuts off $P = .05$ of the area, with this proportion equally divided between the two tails of the distribution, this is the value we use in computing the boundaries of the interval. For $df = 9$ and $P = .05$, Table 2 indicates that $t = 2.262$. (Note that this is much larger than the $z = 1.96$ that we used with the normally distributed data.) Suppose that our sample has $\bar{X} = 30$ and $s_{\bar{x}} = 3$. The 95% confidence interval is determined by the values that lie at $-2.262 s_{\bar{x}}$ and $2.262 s_{\bar{x}}$.

The lower boundary lies at -2.262×3 from the mean of 30. This is $30 - 6.786 = 23.214$. The upper boundary lies at 2.262×3 from the mean. This is $30 + 6.786 = 36.786$. If we wish to determine the 99% confidence interval for the same data, Table 2 indicates that for $P = .01$, we should use a t value of 3.25. This will give us lower and upper boundaries of 20.25 and 39.75.

Earlier we said that a sample of approximately 30 cases is generally considered a "large sample." This arbitrary size was selected because statistics for a sample with $df = 29$ "behave" almost as though the sample had $df = \infty$. As is shown in Table 2, for $df = 29$, at $P = .05$, $t = 2.045$. This is not very different from $t = 1.96$ for $df = \infty$. However, this difference increases markedly as the dfs become smaller. To be perfectly accurate, we should always use the t distribution when we are dealing with sample means where $\sigma_{\bar{x}}$ is unknown, even though the t distributions for large dfs are almost identical with the normal distribution.

We shall have more opportunity to use Table 2 as we explore other statistical techniques that involve sample means.

Exercises: Group A

1. A college professor randomly selected 30 sophomore girls and gave each of them a social-development self-test. Using their test scores, he computed $\bar{X} = 60$ and $s = 6$. What is the 95% confidence interval for the population mean?

2. Using the data in Exercise 1, what is the 99% confidence interval for the population mean?

3. A researcher wished to estimate the mean length of time it takes fourth-grade children to read a short story. He randomly selected 15 children and measured their reaction times. He calculated $\bar{X} = 18$ and $s = 1.3$. What is the 95% confidence interval for the population mean?

4. Using the data in Exercise 3, what is the 99% confidence interval for the population mean?

5. A randomly selected group of 200 residents was asked to rate the quality of the schools in their city, giving a score of 100 for excellent and of 0 for poor. Their

ratings yielded $\bar{X}$ = 75 and s = 9. What is the 95% confidence interval for the population mean?

6. Using the data in Exercise 5, what is the 99% confidence interval for the population mean?

Exercises: Group B

7. A high-school counselor determined that a randomly selected sample of 18 students who were referred to him for counselling had a mean language-ability score of 72 and an s of 11. What is the 95% confidence interval for the population mean?

8. Using the data in Exercise 7, what is the 99% confidence interval for the population mean?

9. A school psychologist randomly selected a sample of 61 delinquent boys and tested them on their self-concepts. He obtained a mean self-concept score of 142 and an s of 18. What is the 95% confidence interval for the population mean?

10. Using the data in Exercise 9, what is the 99% confidence interval for the population mean?

11. A random sample of 29 cocker spaniels was fed a special diet for three months. At the conclusion of the feeding period, the dogs were tested on their ability to react to a loud stimulus. They obtained a mean reaction time of .6 seconds, with an s of .02. What is the 95% confidence interval for the population mean?

12. Using the data in Exercise 11, what is the 99% confidence interval for the population mean?

CHAPTER 10
INTRODUCTION TO
HYPOTHESIS TESTING

The statistician engages in two forms of statistical inference—estimating population parameters and testing hypotheses. In forming confidence intervals, we were involved in estimating the parameter μ from sample data. In this chapter, we will introduce the other major function of statistics, that of providing a basis upon which to make a decision about the tenability of a hypothesis.

Up to this point, we have been considering data for only one sample. In practical research, however, where we are constantly testing hypotheses, we usually wish to compare two or more samples. For example, we may wish to determine whether there is a difference in achievement between students who are taught by the lecture method and those who are taught by the discussion method, or whether boys can jump farther than girls. Sometimes we may want to make comparisons among more than two groups; but first, let's consider the situation in which only two groups are to be compared.

Suppose we randomly select two samples of fourth-grade children, with 50 children in each sample, and teach them music appreciation by two different methods. For convenience, we will designate these Method A and Method B. At the end of the school year, we administer a music-appreciation test to both groups and obtain scores for both samples. We compute the mean and standard deviation for both samples and obtain the following data:

	Method A	Method B
N	50	50
$\overline{X}$	75	79
s	7	8

From these data, we can tell that the group of students taught by Method B (we will call this group Sample B) received a higher mean score than the group taught by Method A (called Sample A). If we knew that these sample means were identical to the population means for the two methods, we could then say that Method B was superior to Method A. But from our previous discussion, we know that sampling error is always involved when we select a sample from a population. (In this case, the population is all fourth-grade children who might be taught music appreciation by Method A or Method B.) Even if we take two random samples from the same population, the means will be different, because of sampling error. Therefore, we need to know by how much the means must differ before we can assume that they are derived from different populations. In other words, the question that we, as statisticians, ask is "What is the probability that the difference between the two sample means is due to sampling error?" Can the difference between the sample means for Sample A and Sample B be attributed to random error in our sampling, or do children taught by one method actually learn more than those taught by the other method? In effect, are we dealing with two different populations?

Before we examine the procedure used to answer this question, we must consider how a researcher states a research hypothesis and how a statistician deals with it. In our example, the research question to be answered is:

Research question: Is there a difference in effectiveness between Method A and Method B for teaching music appreciation to fourth-grade students?

Restated as a research hypothesis, this question becomes:

Research hypothesis: There is a difference between the effectiveness of Method A and the effectiveness of Method B for teaching music appreciation to fourth-grade students.

To make a statistical analysis of the data, we must state the research hypothesis in statistical terms. The hypothesis might then read:

Research hypothesis: The mean music-appreciation score for the population of fourth-grade students taught by Method A is different from the mean score of those taught by Method B.

We run into an interesting problem when we attempt to test the validity of this hypothesis by applying statistical techniques to data obtained from two samples given different methods. The problem is that the research hypothesis is nonspecific in that it does not state the size of the difference in effectiveness. We need a hypothesis that is explicit enough to be testable. The research hypothesis can be restated to make it specific by converting it into a *null hypothesis*. It might then read as follows:

Null hypothesis: There is no difference in effectiveness between Method A and Method B for teaching music appreciation to fourth-grade students.

To a statistician, this is the same as saying that the scores obtained by Group A and the scores obtained by Group B came from the same population of scores, and that the difference between the means of the two samples is due to nothing more than sampling error.

Although most null hypotheses state that the difference between population means is zero, other kinds of statements can also be tested. A null hypothesis can specify, for example, that a difference between population means is 10 points. In this case, the research hypothesis might be that the difference between population means is not 10 points. In this text, we will be testing only the null hypothesis of no difference, but you should be aware that the statement of a null hypothesis can also take other forms.

Returning to our example, we have made the null hypothesis of no difference in effectiveness between Method A and Method B. Our task is to decide whether or not to reject the null hypothesis. To help us in this decision, we apply statistical techniques to the data in the two samples; this will enable us to determine the probability that the null hypothesis is false. We will decide not to reject the null hypothesis if there is a high probability that the difference between the two sample means could have resulted from sampling error; we will decide to reject the null hypothesis if there is a low probability that the difference between the two sample means could have resulted from sampling error. A decision to reject the null hypothesis will be tantamount to deciding that the two sample means did come from sampling distributions that have different means, and that a real difference exists between the test scores of children taught by Method A and those taught by Method B. Whether the difference in scores is the result of the difference in effectiveness of the two teaching methods or of other factors, such as teacher motivation or environmental differences in the classrooms, will be the concern of the researcher as he interprets the statistical findings. The statistical test only determines the probability that the findings occurred by chance.

Decisions Regarding the Null Hypothesis

Notice that the decision is whether or not to reject the null hypothesis. Deciding to not reject the null hypothesis is not the same as deciding to accept it. Why do we make this seemingly minute semantic distinction between "not rejecting" and "accepting" the null hypothesis? We need to remember that the null hypothesis states that there is no difference between the groups. This is an exact statement about the difference between the groups. If the results of our project are inconsistent with this null hypothesis, we can legitimately reject it. However, if our results are consistent with the null hypothesis, they cannot be interpreted as grounds for accepting it, because a finding consistent with the null hypothesis can also be consistent with a number of other hypotheses. For example, if we find that students receiving Method B far outscore the students receiving

Method A, we can correctly decide to reject the null hypothesis. On the other hand, if we find that they do not score significantly higher, we cannot legitimately conclude that there is no difference (which would mean accepting the null hypothesis). It may be, in fact, that Method B is a little more effective than Method A (or that Method A is a little better), but that our research project failed to detect this difference. Our decision not to reject the null hypothesis means only that the data obtained in our samples were not sufficiently different to let us conclude that the difference didn't occur by chance.

In summary, we should never "accept" the null hypothesis; we should only "reject" or "not reject" it. If a statistical test does not indicate that the two samples came from different populations, we can only conclude that we failed to detect a significant difference. It does not mean that, in fact, no difference exists. Therefore we can only "not reject" the hypothesis that there is no difference. We are not justified in concluding that there is no difference.

Testing the Null Hypothesis

When we test the null hypothesis, we are concerned with the difference between a pair of sample means. By stating the null hypothesis, we make an explicit assumption that the difference between the two sample means is due to sampling error. The next step is to determine the sampling distribution of differences between pairs of sample means.

To show how we decide whether to reject the null hypothesis, we must once again create a hypothetical situation. Suppose we have unlimited time and resources at our disposal and can take many, many samples from the same population. Let's assume that the number of scores in each sample is 50. Earlier, we learned that a distribution of these sample means would provide us with the standard error of the mean ($\sigma_{\bar{x}}$). Now we are interested in learning about the sampling distribution of differences between pairs of sample means. To do this, we can imagine that we are able to form every conceivable combination of two sample means in a given population. This will give us an array of pairs of sample means. We then determine the difference between the mean scores for each pair, always subtracting the mean of the second sample from the mean of the first. If we make a distribution of these differences between paired sample means, we will get a sampling distribution that is in the form of a normal distribution. Figure 10-1 shows this sampling distribution of differences between sample means selected from the same population.

An important feature of this distribution of differences is that the mean difference score is always equal to zero. It is evident that the differences between pairs of sample means selected from the same population would vary around zero.

The Standard Error of the Difference between Means

After computing the differences between the means of a multitude of pairs of samples, we can compute the standard deviation of these differences. The special term used to describe the standard deviation of differences between means is called the *standard error of the difference*, and its symbol is $\sigma_{\bar{X}_1-\bar{X}_2}$. In Figure 10-1, the $\sigma_{\bar{X}_1-\bar{X}_2}$ values are shown along the horizontal axis, exactly as $\sigma_{\bar{X}}$ was in earlier examples. The major distinction between these two measures is that the $\sigma_{\bar{X}}$ is a measure of the dispersion of sample means around the population mean, whereas the $\sigma_{\bar{X}_1-\bar{X}_2}$ is a measure of the dispersion of differences between paired sample means around a mean of zero.

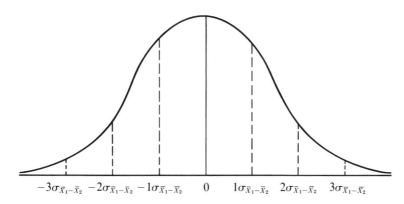

Figure 10-1. Sampling distribution of differences between pairs of sample means selected from the same population.

The probability functions of the normal curve apply to this particular sampling distribution of mean differences, because the $\sigma_{\bar{X}_1-\bar{X}_2}$ is assumed to have been computed from the differences between the means of all possible pairs—that is, the population—of samples. Thus, the standard error of the difference is considered a population parameter, and it is assigned the Greek symbol, $\sigma_{\bar{X}_1-\bar{X}_2}$.

How do we use this sampling distribution in deciding whether or not to reject the null hypothesis? Using sample data, we can never know for certain whether the null hypothesis is false. Our task is to make an intelligent decision in the face of uncertainty. We can only state the risk we are willing to run of rejecting the null hypothesis when it is really true. Naturally, we would like the probability of our making the wrong decision to be quite low.

It is up to the individual researcher to determine how much risk of error he is willing to run if he decides to reject the null hypothesis. Of course, he or she must set this risk level before conducting the experiment. Researchers usually set this risk level at $P = .05$ or $P = .01$.

In our example, suppose we have set $P = .05$ as the probability level. In so doing, we are saying that if we decide to reject the null hypothesis, the probability is $P = .05$ that we are making the wrong decision. Since $P = .05$ represents a very small probability of incorrectly rejecting the null hypothesis, we have decided that we are willing to run that much risk. By examining the data in our two samples, we can determine the probability that they came from the same population. If this probability is less than $P = .05$, we will reject the null hypothesis that they came from the same population. On the other hand, if the probability of obtaining a difference between the sample means is greater than .05, we will not reject the null hypothesis, and we will conclude that the difference between the means could be due to sampling error.

From the properties of the normal curve, we know that .95 of the differences between sample means lie between $-1.96\sigma_{\bar{X}_1-\bar{X}_2}$ and $1.96\sigma_{\bar{X}_1-\bar{X}_2}$. Therefore, the probability that the difference between a given pair of sample means lies between these two points is $P = .95$, and the probability that the difference between a pair of means lies outside these two points is $P = .05$ ($P = .025$ below $-1.96\sigma_{\bar{X}_1-\bar{X}_2}$ and $P = .025$ above $1.96\sigma_{\bar{X}_1-\bar{X}_2}$).

After we have distributed all of the differences between the paired sample means in our hypothetical situation, suppose we determine that the $\sigma_{\bar{X}_1-\bar{X}_2}$ of this distribution is 3 points. To determine the two values that correspond to $-1.96\sigma_{\bar{X}_1-\bar{X}_2}$ and $1.96\sigma_{\bar{X}_1-\bar{X}_2}$, we calculate as follows:

$$\text{For } -1.96 \ \sigma_{\bar{X}_1-\bar{X}_2}: \quad -1.96 \times 3 = -5.88$$
$$\text{For } 1.96 \ \sigma_{\bar{X}_1-\bar{X}_2}: \quad \ \ 1.96 \times 3 = \ \ 5.88$$

Figure 10-2 presents the sampling distribution of differences between sample means, with these two values shown as cutoff points for $P = .95$. Notice that, for these data, the mean of the distribution is zero, with the differences between the means distributed on either side of this midpoint. (The negative differences are results of our method of pairing sample means, because in some pairs we are subtracting a larger mean from a smaller one. This occurs in 50% of the pairs, so that half of the distribution of differences consists of negative differences and half consists of positive differences.)

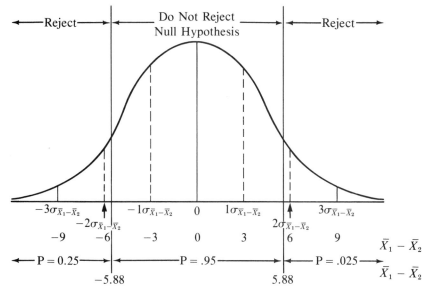

Figure 10-2. Sampling distribution of differences between pairs of sample means selected from the same population.

Since we originally decided to set $P = .05$ as our probability level, Figure 10-2 indicates the area under the curve where an obtained difference between a pair of sample means must lie if we are to reject the null hypothesis. We can state that the probability, due to sampling error only, of obtaining two samples whose means differ by 5.88 points or less (regardless of whether the difference is negative or positive) is $P = .95$. The probability of obtaining two samples whose means differ by more than 5.88 points is $P = .05$. Looking back at the data in our two samples, we find that the mean score of the students given Method B was 4 points higher than the mean score of the students given Method A. The sampling distribution in Figure 10-2 reveals that a mean difference of 4 points falls within the $P = .95$ area, indicating that such a difference has a high probability of occurring by chance. Since the probability is not less than .05 that the obtained difference between means occurred by chance, we cannot reject the null hypothesis that there is no difference in the effectiveness between Method A and Method B for teaching music appreciation to fourth-grade students. We must conclude that the difference between the means of our two samples could have been due to sampling error. On the other hand, if the difference between our sample means had been 8 points, for instance, we would have rejected the null hypothesis, because the probability of our obtaining such a large difference solely due to sampling error is less than .05.

We have shown in Figure 10-2 the sampling distribution of differences between a multitude of pairs of sample means to illustrate how we can make probability statements about their occurrence and how we can reach decisions regarding the null hypothesis based on the probability that a pair of sample means will differ because of sampling error. In actuality, we never have the luxury of many pairs of samples; research studies usually deal with only two samples. The statistical problem in such situations is to use the values of the samples themselves to estimate the amount of variability in the distribution of differences between sample means. From this estimate we can form a sampling distribution and determine the probability that the two sample means are from the same population.

Fortunately, there is a method for estimating the standard error of the difference. An estimate of this value is obtained by applying a statistical formula to the data in the two samples. The process by which we estimate the standard error of the mean and develop sampling distributions from this estimate is discussed in the next chapter.

Exercises: Group A

1. A researcher wishes to determine whether the variable method and the constant method of training chickens to peck at a red circle differ in effectiveness. What is the research hypothesis he or she wishes to test?

2. State the null hypothesis that is to be tested for the research hypothesis in Exercise 1.

3. Suppose a multitude of pairs of samples have been randomly selected, where each sample in a pair has been given a different method of training. Suppose that $\sigma_{\bar{X}_1-\bar{X}_2} = 4$. If the researcher set $P = .05$ as the probability level and if he obtained a mean of 40 for the sample given the variable method and a mean of 50 for the sample given the constant method, would he reject the null hypothesis?

4. Given the data in Exercise 3, would the researcher reject the null hypothesis if he obtained a mean of 48 for the variable-method sample and a mean of 42 for the constant-method sample?

5. A statistics instructor has a hunch that the Exercises in Group A and Group B are not of equal difficulty. What is the research hypothesis he wishes to examine?

6. State the null hypothesis that is to be tested for the research hypothesis given in Exercise 5.

7. Suppose a multitude of pairs of samples have been randomly selected, where each sample in a pair has been given a different set of exercises. Suppose $\sigma_{\bar{X}_1-\bar{X}_2}$ = 2.5 points. If the instructor sets $P = .05$ as the probability level and if he obtains a sample mean for Group A Exercises of 12 points and a sample mean for Group B Exercises of 8 points, would he reject the null hypothesis?

8. Given the data in Exercise 7, would the instructor reject the null hypothesis if he obtains a sample mean for Group A Exercises of 7 points and a sample mean for Group B Exercises of 14 points?

Exercises: Group B

9. A university historian feels that freshmen and seniors in the university differ in their feelings about academic freedom. He desires to use the Academic-Opinion Questionnaire to examine this question. What is the research hypothesis he wishes to examine?

10. State the null hypothesis that the historian in Exercise 9 wishes to test.

11. Suppose a multitude of pairs of samples have been selected, with each pair having a freshman and a senior sample. Each sample is given the Academic-Opinion Questionnaire. Suppose $\sigma_{\bar{X}_1 - \bar{X}_2} = 1.7$ points. If the historian sets $P = .05$ as the probability level and if he obtains a freshman mean of 20 and a senior mean of 17, would he reject the null hypothesis?

12. Given the data in Exercise 11, would he reject the null hypothesis if he obtains a freshman mean of 15 and a senior mean of 20?

13. A publisher of elementary-level arithmetic textbooks publishes books in both Type Style A and Type Style B. He wishes to determine if there is a difference in the effectiveness of the two type styles for children's arithmetic achievement. What is the research hypothesis he wishes to examine?

14. State the null hypothesis that the publisher in Exercise 13 wishes to test.

15. Suppose a multitude of pairs of samples of elementary schoolchildren have been randomly selected, where each sample in a pair has been given a different type style. Suppose that $\sigma_{\bar{X}_1 - \bar{X}_2} = 4.6$ points. If the publisher set $P = .05$ as the probability level and if he obtained a Type A mean of 30 and a Type B mean of 40, would he reject the null hypothesis?

16. Given the data in Exercise 15, would the publisher reject the null hypothesis if he obtained a Type A mean of 39 and a Type B mean of 36?

CHAPTER 11
TESTING FOR THE DIFFERENCE BETWEEN POPULATION MEANS

A typical research situation is one in which we wish to decide whether or not to reject the null hypothesis when we have only the data in two samples. Since we do not have an infinite number of pairs of samples that will enable us to form a sampling distribution of differences, we must employ statistical methods to estimate the value of the standard error of the difference. Using this estimate, we can then specify a sampling distribution to use in examining the null hypothesis.

This chapter will present two methods for estimating the standard error of the difference based upon the data in two samples. Both methods assume that the scores in the samples come from a normally distributed population. The symbol for an estimate of the population standard error of the difference, calculated from sample data, is $s_{\bar{X}_1 - \bar{X}_2}$. The statistical test used to analyze the difference between a pair of sample means, when $s_{\bar{X}_1 - \bar{X}_2}$ is used to specify the sampling distribution, is commonly called a t test, because distributions of this sort belong to the family of t distributions. The first method involves calculating $s_{\bar{X}_1 - \bar{X}_2}$ when the data are obtained from two independent samples. The second method will use data obtained from two nonindependent samples.

Two samples are considered independent if members have been randomly assigned to the two groups. When this procedure is followed, the scores obtained by members of one sample are not in any way related to or influenced by the scores obtained by members of the other sample. Thus, the scores in the two samples are independent of one another, and the means of the two samples are said to be *independent sample means*. The example in Chapter 10, in which fourth-grade children were randomly assigned to the two methods of teaching music appreciation, involved independent samples because the assignment of one child to a particular sample did not influence the assignment of other children to the samples. Therefore, the means of these two sets of scores represent independent sample means.

However, the means are not independent if the scores in the two samples are obtained from the same sample of individuals. This occurs, for example, when the individuals in one sample receive both a pretest and a posttest. Since in this case the same individuals produced both sets of scores, we cannot say that the posttest scores are unrelated to, or are independent of, the pretest scores. Therefore, we say that the means of these two sets of data represent *nonindependent sample means.*

Samples also cannot be considered independent if the individuals in the two samples have been paired in any way. For example, if a researcher suspects that the intelligence levels of pupils will affect their performance on a test of manual dexterity, he may decide to group pupils into pairs on the basis of their IQs, and then randomly divide each pair between the two samples. The mean manual-dexterity scores he obtains from these two samples will be nonindependent because the individuals in the samples have been assigned to groups on the basis of their IQs, with the assignment of one member of a pair to one group dictating the assignment of the other member to the second group. Thus, in this case the study involves non-independent sample means, even though the two samples are made up of different individuals.

We use different statistical formulas to calculate $s_{\overline{X}_1 - \overline{X}_2}$ depending on whether we are dealing with independent or nonindependent sample means. First we shall examine methods for testing the null hypothesis when the data represent independent sample means; later, we shall present methods for analyzing nonindependent means.

Testing the Difference between Independent Means

Mathematical statisticians have given us a set of formulas that permits us to calculate an estimate of the standard error of the difference when we are given only the data in two independent samples. For example, suppose we wish to determine whether or not to reject the null hypothesis that Method 1 and Method 2 are equally effective for teaching reading. If we assume that the null hypothesis is true, we are saying that the reading scores in the two samples all come from the same population of reading scores. Under this assumption, our best estimate of the population variance should be obtained by pooling the sums of squares and the degrees of freedom that we obtain from both samples. Formula 14 gives us two equivalent methods for estimating the population variance, s^2, by pooling the data in the two samples.

Formula 14a uses the sums of squares in both samples; Formula 14b uses variance estimates derived from each of the samples. Both formulas yield identical estimates of the population variance. With the estimate of s^2 obtained from Formula 14, we can use Formula 15 to estimate the standard error of the difference.

Formula 14. Estimation of the common population variance (pooled variance) from the data in two samples. (Formulas 14a and 14b are equivalent).

$$s^2 = \frac{\Sigma x_1{}^2 + \Sigma x_2{}^2}{N_1 + N_2 - 2} \qquad \textit{(Formula 14a)}$$

$$s^2 = \frac{(N_1 - 1)s_1{}^2 + (N_2 - 1)s_2{}^2}{N_1 + N_2 - 2} \qquad \textit{(Formula 14b)}$$

Formula 15. Estimate of the standard error of the difference between means (pooled-variance method).

$$s_{\bar{X}_1 - \bar{X}_2} = \sqrt{\frac{s^2}{N_1} + \frac{s^2}{N_2}}$$

Formula 16. Calculation of the t ratio for independent means.

$$t = \frac{\bar{X}_1 - \bar{X}_2}{s_{\bar{X}_1 - \bar{X}_2}}$$

Degrees of Freedom: $N_1 + N_2 - 2$

We can now employ $s_{\bar{X}_1 - \bar{X}_2}$ to develop a sampling distribution of differences between pairs of sample means for use in determining the probability that the obtained difference between the two sample means occurred by chance. Since this sampling distribution is derived from an estimate of the standard error of the difference ($s_{\bar{X}_1 - \bar{X}_2}$) rather than from a known population parameter ($\sigma_{\bar{X}_1 - \bar{X}_2}$), it follows the appropriate t distribution rather than the normal distribution as was the case in Chapter 10. The t distribution that is appropriate to represent the sampling distribution depends on the degrees of freedom associated with the two sample means. For Sample No. 1 the df is $N_1 - 1$, and for Sample No. 2 the df is $N_2 - 1$. Thus, the pooled df of the samples is $(N_1 - 1) + (N_2 - 1)$ or $N_1 + N_2 - 2$.

Once we have calculated $s_{\bar{X}_1 - \bar{X}_2}$ and have identified the appropriate t distribution based upon the pooled df, we are in a position to develop the sampling distribution and to evaluate the difference between the two obtained sample means.

Formula 16 gives the method for calculating the t ratio for independent means.

Formula 16 shows that we compute a *t* ratio based on the ratio of the difference between sample means to the estimate of the standard error of the difference. If this obtained *t* ratio is larger than we expect, based on our preset level for significance, we reject the null hypothesis. If the *t* ratio is smaller, we do not reject the null hypothesis.

Figure 11-1 depicts the sampling-distribution curve in the form of a *t* distribution. The curve of the distribution is indicated by a dotted line because the shape of the particular *t* distribution depends upon the degrees of freedom associated with it. Likewise, the vertical lines indicating the .95 area under the curve are dotted because their placement depends on the particular *t* distribution. For *t* distributions with small *dfs*, these lines will be located farther out on the horizontal axis—that is, farther apart—than they will be for *t* distributions with large *dfs*. For example, Table 2 indicates that for $df = 17$, at $P = .05$, these vertical lines would be located at $t = -2.11$ and $t = 2.11$. For $df = 5$, at $P = .05$, they would be located at $t = -2.571$ and $t = 2.571$. For an infinite df, the *t* distribution is identical with the normal distribution, and the vertical lines for $P = .05$ are located at $t = -1.96$ and $t = 1.96$; these values are the same as the *z* scores delineating the same area, as we learned when examining the properties of the normal curve.

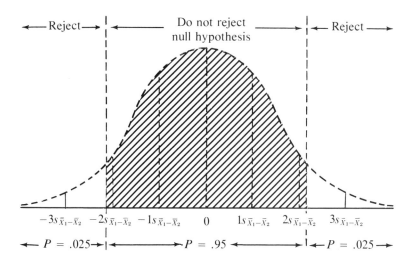

Figure 11-1. The sampling distribution of differences between sample means (*t* distribution).

To illustrate how this procedure works, we will perform the calculations using Example 11-1.

Example 11-1

An educator wanted to find out if different methods of driver training resulted in different driver-proficiency levels. He randomly assigned students to two groups and taught one group using videotape demonstrations (Method 1) and the other using live demonstrations (Method 2). He set $P = .01$ as his level of significance. At the conclusion of the training, he obtained the following driver-proficiency scores for the students in the two groups.

Method 1		Method 2	
27	19	24	31
28	25	28	29
20	31	31	26
27	24	27	33
30	23	28	29
28	27	23	28
		29	26

The information given in Example 11-1 indicates that the educator is interested only in detecting a difference, regardless of whether the difference favors Method 1 or Method 2. By setting $P = .01$ as his significance level, he has decided that he will not reject the null hypothesis if the difference between his two sample means lies in the probability area $P = .99$ of the appropriate sampling distribution. On the other hand, he will reject the null hypothesis if the difference between the means has a probability of occurring by chance as low as $P = .01$. Since he is willing to reject the null hypothesis regardless of the direction of the difference, he is interested in differences that fall in either tail of the sampling distribution. This means that his significance level of $P = .01$ must be divided between the two tails, with $P = .005$ in either tail. This is called a two-tail test. The distinction between one-tail and two-tail tests is examined in depth in Chapter 12.

To test the null hypothesis that there is no difference between the driver-proficiency scores of students taught by Method 1 and by Method 2, he must determine the means of the two samples, calculate the sum of squares for each sample, estimate the population variance from the data in the two samples, and estimate the standard error of the difference. These calculations are presented below.

Method 1	Method 2
$N_1 = 12$	$N_2 = 14$
$\Sigma X_1 = 309$	$\Sigma X_2 = 392$
$\Sigma X_1^2 = 8,107$	$\Sigma X_2^2 = 11,072$
$\bar{X}_1 = \dfrac{309}{12} = 25.75$	$\bar{X}_2 = \dfrac{392}{14} = 28.0$

Using Formula 11b: $\Sigma x_1{}^2 = \Sigma X_1{}^2 - \dfrac{(\Sigma X_1)^2}{N_1} = 8,107 - \dfrac{(309)^2}{12} = 150.25$

$\Sigma x_2{}^2 = \Sigma X_2{}^2 - \dfrac{(\Sigma X_2)^2}{N_2} = 11,072 - \dfrac{(392)^2}{14} = 96.0$

Using Formula 14a: $s^2 = \dfrac{\Sigma x_1{}^2 + \Sigma x_2{}^2}{N_1 + N_2 - 2} = \dfrac{150.25. + 96.0}{12 + 14 - 2} = 10.26$

Using Formula 15: $s_{\bar{X}_1 - \bar{X}_2} = \sqrt{\dfrac{s^2}{N_1} + \dfrac{s^2}{N_2}} = \sqrt{\dfrac{10.26}{12} + \dfrac{10.26}{14}} = 1.26$

The degrees of freedom associated with the two independent sample means are $N_1 + N_2 - 2 = 24$. Using this value and Table 2, he can form the appropriate sampling distribution. Table 2 shows that for $df = 24$, the t values that cut off $P = .01$ of the area ($P = .005$ in each tail) are $t = -2.797$ and $t = 2.797$. The appropriate sampling distribution for these data is shown in Figure 11-2.

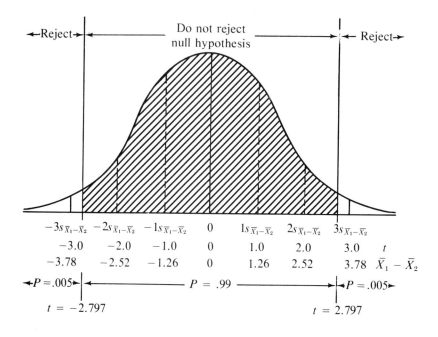

Figure 11-2. The sampling distribution of differences for data in Example 11-1 (t distribution for $df = 24$).

He must now determine where the difference between the two sample means lies, in relation to the regions representing rejection of the null hypothesis. For this, he needs to compute the t ratio, using Formula 16.

$$t = \frac{\bar{X}_1 - \bar{X}_2}{s_{\bar{X}_1 - \bar{X}_2}} = \frac{25.75 - 28.0}{1.26} = -1.79$$

Figure 11-2 shows us that $t = -1.79$ falls in the area between $t = -2.797$ and $t = 2.797$, which is our do-not-reject region. Therefore, he must conclude that the difference between the two sample means is not large enough for him to reject the null hypothesis that they came from the same population. In this study, the educator must conclude that the obtained difference in mean scores between the students taught by Method 1 and those taught by Method 2 could have occurred by chance.

Of course, to perform this statistical test, it is not necessary to display the sampling distribution graphically, as we did in Figure 11-2. We drew the curve merely to illustrate the process by which we make decisions using the underlying sampling distribution. In practice, we determine the degrees of freedom associated with the data in our study and use Table 2 to determine the value of t that is needed at a given significance level. We then compute the t ratio, using the appropriate formulas, and compare it with the tabled value. If the obtained t ratio is larger than the tabled t value, we reject the null hypothesis. If it is less than the tabled t value, we do not reject the null hypothesis.

Testing the Difference between Nonindependent Means

The means of samples are nonindependent in studies in which the same individuals are tested at two different times or in which the individuals selected for the two samples have been paired in some way, such as matching them in terms of a variable that could affect their scores. In these studies, we can compute the difference between each pair of scores and use these differences to estimate the population standard error of the mean difference scores, which is represented by $s_{\bar{D}}$.

To compute this estimate, we must first obtain an estimate of the population variance of the difference scores, using Formula 17.

Formula 17 requires that we compute the sum of the difference scores for the N pairs of scores and also compute the sum of the squares of the difference scores. Note that ΣD^2 is not the same as $(\Sigma D)^2$. For ΣD^2, we square each difference score before we sum them; for $(\Sigma D)^2$, we sum the difference scores and then square this sum. In Formula 17, N indicates the number of difference scores.

Formula 17. Estimation of the population variance of difference scores.

$$s_D{}^2 = \frac{N\Sigma D^2 - (\Sigma D)^2}{N(N-1)}$$

where $D = X_1 - X_2$ for each pair of scores.

Formula 18 is then used to estimate the population standard error of the mean difference scores.

Formula 18. Estimation of the population standard error of the mean difference scores. (Formulas 18a and 18b are equivalent.)

$$s_{\bar{D}} = \sqrt{\frac{s_D{}^2}{N}} \qquad \text{(Formula 18a)}$$

$$s_{\bar{D}} = \sqrt{\frac{N\Sigma D^2 - (\Sigma D)^2}{N^2(N-1)}} \qquad \text{(Formula 18b)}$$

in which N = number of pairs of scores

There are two equivalent formulas used to calculate this estimate. Formula 18a uses $s_D{}^2$ in its calculation; Formula 18b uses the difference scores. The t ratio is then computed using Formula 19, in which the degrees of freedom associated with the t distribution is the number of pairs of scores minus one.

Formula 19. Calculation of the t ratio for nonindependent means.

$$t = \frac{\bar{X}_1 - \bar{X}_2}{s_{\bar{D}}}$$

Degrees of freedom: $N - 1$ pairs of scores

We shall illustrate the procedure for testing the difference between nonindependent means using the data given in Example 11-2.

Example 11-2

A high-school typing instructor wished to determine if students taking a typing-proficiency test would score differently depending upon whether the test was administered in the morning or the afternoon. She randomly selected ten students from her typing class and gave each student two typing tests, one in the morning and one in the afternoon. To overcome any bias due to the order of testing, she alternated the sequence of the testing by giving half of the sample the morning test first and the other half the afternoon test first. She obtained the following typing-proficiency scores, and set $P = .05$ as the level of significance.

Student	Morning test scores (X_1)	Afternoon test scores (X_2)	D	D^2
A	18	16	-2	4
B	19	19	0	0
C	17	16	-1	1
D	22	18	-4	16
E	15	17	$+2$	4
F	16	15	-1	1
G	18	14	-4	16
H	19	12	-7	49
I	13	10	-3	9
J	20	17	-3	9
$N = 10$	$\Sigma X_1 = 177$	$\Sigma X_2 = 154$	$\Sigma D = -23$	$\Sigma D^2 = 109$

In Example 11-2, ΣD and ΣD^2 have already been calculated. The estimate of the population variance of morning/afternoon difference scores and the estimate of the population standard error of the mean difference scores are presented below.

$$\bar{X}_1 = \frac{177}{10} = 17.7 \qquad \bar{X}_2 = \frac{154}{10} = 15.4$$

Using Formula 17: $s_D^2 = \dfrac{N \Sigma D^2 - (\Sigma D)^2}{N(N-1)} = \dfrac{10(109) - (-23)^2}{10(10-1)} = 6.23$

Using Formula 18a: $s_{\bar{D}} = \sqrt{\dfrac{s_D^2}{N}} = \sqrt{\dfrac{6.23}{10}} = .79$

or Using Formula 18b: $s_{\bar{D}} = \sqrt{\dfrac{N \Sigma D^2 - (\Sigma D)^2}{N^2 (N-1)}}$

$$= \sqrt{\dfrac{10(109) - (-23)^2}{(10)^2(9)}} = .79$$

The degrees of freedom associated with nonindependent sample means are $N - 1$. Thus, in Example 11-2, the degrees of freedom are $10 - 1$

= 9. Table 2 shows that the values of t that designate $P = .05$ in the tails of the curve ($P = .025$ in each tail) are $t = -2.262$ and $t = 2.262$. The appropriate sampling distribution for this example is the t distribution based on 9 degrees of freedom; it is shown in Figure 11-3.

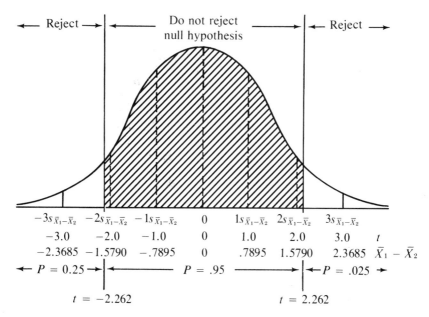

Figure 11-3. The sampling distribution of differences for data in Example 11-2 (t distribution for $df = 9$).

The final step in this procedure is to use Formula 19 to determine the t ratio based on the difference between the two sample means.

Using Formula 19: $t = \dfrac{\bar{X}_1 - \bar{X}_2}{s_{\bar{D}}} = \dfrac{17.7 - 15.4}{.79} = 2.91$

Because the obtained t ratio is larger than the tabled value needed for significance at $P = .05$, it falls in the rejection region, as Figure 11-3 shows. Therefore, the typing instructor should reject the null hypothesis that there is no difference in students' typing-proficiency scores when they are tested in the morning and in the afternoon. The data indicate that students score significantly higher when they are tested in the morning than they do when they are tested in the afternoon. Of course, since the instructor has rejected the null hypothesis at the .05 significance level, she must realize that there is this small a probability that the mean difference she obtained between the two sets of data occurred by chance and was not the result of the different times of testing. However, since she can never prove that there is a real difference, she decides to settle for this quite low probability of her being wrong.

In this chapter, we have discussed two methods for determining whether the observed difference between the means of two samples is a significant one or whether there is a high probability that the difference is merely the result of sampling error. In both methods, the procedures leading to the decision to reject or not reject the null hypothesis are essentially these:

1. A research hypothesis is stated regarding the difference between the means of two populations of scores.
2. The research hypothesis is reworded as a null hypothesis, which states that there is no difference between the population means.
3. The probability level of significance is decided upon. This level represents the risk we are willing to take of being incorrect if we decide to reject the null hypothesis.
4. Two sets of sample data are collected and their means are computed.
5. Assuming that the null hypothesis is true, the appropriate t distribution is specified to serve as the sampling distribution of the differences between pairs of sample means.
6. A t ratio based upon the difference between the obtained sample means and the estimate of the standard error of the difference between the means is computed.
7. The probability of occurrence of the t ratio within the sampling distribution is determined.
8. If the probability of the occurrence of the t ratio is less than the pre-specified significance level, the null hypothesis is rejected; if it is greater, the null hypothesis is not rejected.

Exercises: Group A

1. A swimming instructor wished to determine if there was a difference in the effectiveness of two methods of instruction in swimming. He randomly selected two groups of nonswimmers and gave one group Method A instruction and the other group Method B instruction. He then tested each group and obtained the following data. He set $P = .05$ as the level of significance. Should he reject the null hypothesis?

Method A	Method B
$N_1 = 16$	$N_2 = 11$
$\bar{X}_1 = 40$	$\bar{X}_2 = 44$
$\Sigma x_1^2 = 203$	$\Sigma x_2^2 = 251$

2. A test developer wished to determine if the two forms of his intelligence test were comparable. He randomly selected a group of 10 students and adminis-

tered both Form A and Form B to each student. He obtained the following test data and set $P = .01$ as the level of significance. Should he reject the null hypothesis?

Student	Form A	Form B
A	104	102
B	96	96
C	106	105
D	101	102
E	98	94
F	99	98
G	111	108
H	102	103
I	100	94
J	97	96

3. An experimental psychologist was interested in determining the relative effects of two drugs on guinea pigs. She randomly selected two samples and injected one sample with Drug XX-7 and the other sample with Drug XX-8. After the injections, she gave the members of each group a pain-sensitivity test and obtained the following results. She set $P = .05$ as the level of significance. Should the null hypothesis be rejected?

Drug XX-7	Drug XX-8
$N_1 = 8$	$N_2 = 7$
$\bar{X}_1 = 78$	$\bar{X}_2 = 69$
$s_1^2 = 81$	$s_2^2 = 74$

Exercises: Group B

4. A developmental psychologist wished to see if there was any difference between unlike-sex twins in their ability to perceive geometric shapes at the age of 2 years. She selected a sample of 12 pairs of unlike-sex twins and gave each child a geometric-forms test. She set $P = .05$ as the level of significance and obtained the following data. Should the null hypothesis be rejected?

Boys	Girls
14	17
16	17
15	19
14	14
12	13
17	16
18	22
12	14
10	11
18	17
17	19
17	20

5. An educational researcher made the hypothesis that there is a difference between the discriminatory power of college students in the morning and in the afternoon. He randomly selected samples of students from morning and afternoon classes and administered a cognitive-discrimination test to both samples. He obtained the following data. With $P = .01$ set as the level of significance, should he reject the null hypothesis?

Morning students	Afternoon students
$N_1 = 13$	$N_2 = 14$
$\bar{X}_1 = 36.4$	$\bar{X}_2 = 30.7$
$\Sigma x_1^2 = 197$	$\Sigma x_2^2 = 184$

6. A social worker wondered whether the social adjustment of foster children placed in large families was different from that of foster children placed in small families. He randomly assigned foster children to large and small families, and at the end of two years, he measured their social adjustment. He obtained the following adjustment data. Using $P = .05$ as the level of significance, should he reject the null hypothesis?

Small families	Large families
$N_1 = 29$	$N_2 = 33$
$\bar{X}_1 = 4.17$	$\bar{X}_2 = 4.94$
$s_1^2 = 2.65$	$s_2^2 = 2.49$

CHAPTER 12
MAKING DECISIONS ABOUT
THE NULL HYPOTHESIS

A researcher embarking on a particular research project does not work in a vacuum. Much thought and effort must be expended before we can formulate the research hypothesis, select the appropriate research design, and specify the procedures and techniques for data gathering, analysis, and interpretation.

Our first task is the formulation of the research hypothesis. This hypothesis is usually the outgrowth of considerable study and it reflects our desire to answer a question about the relationship between variables. We conduct our experiment for the express purpose of obtaining objective evidence to corroborate or refute certain aspects of existing theory or to verify relationships between variables that will lead to the development of new theoretical positions.

Of course, theory development depends upon the continued confirmation of hypotheses, rather than on the results of a single isolated experiment. No scientist would be foolhardy enough to develop a theoretical position based on the statistical analysis of one research project!

As we have seen earlier, we are not in a position to test a research hypothesis directly. We must first convert it to a null hypothesis and then, using the sample statistics, we must decide whether or not to reject it. Because we must depend upon sample data to substantiate or refute the hypothesis, we know that we cannot make either decision with certainty. In this process, there is always a chance that the sample data will lead us to an incorrect decision. In fact, the results of a single experiment must be viewed with a degree of skepticism, and they should not form the basis of any definitive judgments about the truth of the hypothesis.

This point is made to emphasize the fact that, although we say that we "reject" or "do not reject" the null hypothesis on the basis of sample data, this does not mean that we have irrevocably decided that the hypothesis is or is not true. The phrase "reject the null hypothesis" should be taken to mean "The statistical analysis of the data obtained from the samples in this experiment indicates that there is such a low probability that they came from the same population that not to reject such a notion would be flying in the face of obtained evidence." The phrase "not reject the null hypothesis" should be taken to mean "The statistical analysis of the data obtained from the samples in this experiment indicates that there is such a low probability that they came from the same population that not to reject such a notion would be flying in the face of obtained evidence." Another way of stating the phrase "not reject the null hypothesis" is "The statistical analysis of the data obtained from this experiment indicates that there is a high probability that the observed difference between the samples could have occurred through sampling error, and that without further evidence, it would be foolish to conclude that the difference was due to some factor other than chance." Although the terms "reject" and "not reject" are used for convenience throughout this book, they should always be interpreted in this manner.

In this chapter we will examine the manner in which a research hypothesis is stated and the effect it has on our decision regarding the null hypothesis. We will also discuss how significance levels are set and the types of errors that are likely to occur when we make decisions about the null hypothesis.

One- and Two-Tail Tests

Sometimes we make a hypothesis stating that one experimental treatment is more effective than another treatment. At other times we do not state which treatment we think is more effective than the other but merely hypothesize that there is a difference in effectiveness between the two treatments. The type of research hypothesis that is made determines how the significance of the difference between the treatments is evaluated.

In either case, the statistical hypothesis used in testing is the null hypothesis. A null hypothesis indicating that there is no difference between the means of two populations is symbolized by:

$$H_0: \mu_1 - \mu_2 = 0$$

In the statistical analysis of data, the research hypothesis is considered an alternate to the null hypothesis. We shall designate the alternate hypothesis H_1. If the alternate hypothesis is "There is a difference in effectiveness between Method 1 and Method 2 in teaching reading to third-grade pupils," it can be expressed as:

$$H_1: \mu_1 \neq \mu_2$$

This expression tells us that the population means of third-grade pupils given Method 1 is not equal to the population mean of comparable pupils given Method 2. In this case, the alternate hypothesis does not state the direction of the difference—that is, which method is superior. It only states that there is a difference. Therefore, the rejection region for the null hypothesis is located in both tails of the sampling distribution, with one tail indicating that Method 1 is superior to Method 2 and with the other tail indicating the opposite possibility. We will reject the null hypothesis if we obtain a difference between the sample means that is located in either rejection region of the sampling distribution.

The examples of hypothesis-testing procedures presented in Chapters 10 and 11 were all concerned with testing nondirectional alternative hypotheses, although we didn't explicitly say so at that time. In all of those examples, the area under the curve representing the significance level, such as $P = .05$, was equally divided between the two tails of the sampling distribution, with half of it ($P = .025$) located in each tail. When the rejection regions are separated in this manner, we are making a *two-tail test*.

The way in which the research hypothesis is stated dictates the nature of H_1. If the research hypothesis is nondirectional, then H_1 is symbolized by H_1: $\mu_1 \neq \mu_2$ and a two-tail test is made. If the research hypothesis indicates which population mean is thought to be superior to the other, the alternate hypothesis is a directional one. For example, if the alternate hypothesis states that Method 1 is superior to Method 2, the direction of the difference is indicated, and the hypothesis is expressed as:

$$H_1: \mu_1 > \mu_2$$

(The symbol $>$ means "greater than," and the symbol $<$ means "less than.") When the hypothesis is a directional one, the rejection region is located entirely in one tail of the sampling distribution, and we make a *one-tail test*. In such cases, we will reject the null hypothesis only if we obtain a difference between sample means that lies in the tail of the sampling distribution that represents the rejection region. The problem of determining whether a research hypothesis should be directional or nondirectional involves a number of considerations that we will take up later in this chapter.

Example 12-1

An educational-products developer has produced a videotape that he claims is superior for teaching basic geometric patterns to first-grade pupils to the conventional flash-card method. Before deciding to purchase this videotape, a school principal decided to test its effectiveness. He hypothesized "Children will score higher on a test of basic geometric patterns when they are taught by the videotape method (Method 1) than when they are taught by the conventional flash-card method (Method 2)." He set $P = .05$ as his level of significance. He randomly selected two groups of first-grade pupils, assigned each group one of the methods, and obtained the following test data:

Method 1	Method 2
$N_1 = 12$	$N_2 = 14$
$\bar{X}_1 = 40$	$\bar{X}_2 = 37.5$
$\Sigma x_1^2 = 125$	$\Sigma x_2^2 = 110$

In Example 12-1, the principal will reject the null hypothesis only if the videotape presentation (Method 1) is superior. His alternate hypothesis is a directional one, so he will make a one-tail statistical test. The hypotheses for this example are:

$$H_0: \mu_1 = \mu_2$$

$$H_1: \mu_1 > \mu_2$$

He will reject H_0 and accept H_1 only if $\bar{X}_1$ is sufficiently larger than $\bar{X}_2$. If $\bar{X}_2$ is larger than $\bar{X}_1$, then, of course, H_1 cannot be substantiated, and he need not proceed with the test of significance. If $\bar{X}_1$ is larger than $\bar{X}_2$, then the difference lies in the hypothesized direction, and he needs to specify the sampling distribution and to ascertain whether the difference between $\bar{X}_1$ and $\bar{X}_2$ is large enough to permit him to reject the null hypothesis at his preset significance level. If he assumes that the data came from normally distributed populations, a one-tail t test for independent means is appropriate for testing the null hypothesis. For the data in Example 12-1, the t ratio is calculated as follows:

Using Formula 14a: $\quad s^2 = \dfrac{\Sigma x_1^2 + \Sigma x_2^2}{N_1 + N_2 - 2} = \dfrac{125 + 110}{12 + 14 - 2} = 9.79$

Using Formula 15: $\quad s_{\bar{X}_1 - \bar{X}_2} = \sqrt{\dfrac{s^2}{N_1} + \dfrac{s^2}{N_2}} = \sqrt{\dfrac{9.79}{12} + \dfrac{9.79}{14}} = 1.23$

Using Formula 11: $\quad t = \dfrac{\bar{X}_1 - \bar{X}_2}{s_{\bar{X}_1 - \bar{X}_2}} = \dfrac{40 - 37.5}{1.23} = 2.03$

$df: N_1 + N_2 - 2 = 12 + 14 - 2 = 24$

The next task is to determine the appropriate sampling distribution and to specify the rejection region for the null hypothesis. Because this is a one-tail test, he must designate $P = .05$ in *one* tail of the sampling distribution, rather than splitting it between the two tails as we did when we were making a two-tail test. He can use Table 2 to determine the critical t value which cuts off .05 in one tail, but he must remember that the column headings in Table 2 indicate the P value divided between the two tails of the sampling distribution. For Example 12-1, where $df = 24$, the column headed $P = .05$ gives the critical value $t = 2.064$, with $P = .025$ in each tail. But for a one-tail test at $P = .05$, the critical t value that designates $P = .05$

in one *tail* must be determined. This value is given in the column headed P = .10, since the values in this column represent P = .10 divided between the two tails (with P = .05 in each tail).

In summary, the column headings in Table 2 give the probabilities associated with different t values for two-tail tests. In order to determine the critical t values for one-tail tests, the P values given in the column headings must be halved. Thus, for one-tail tests, the column headings in Table 2 should read P = .05, P = .025, P = .01, and P = .005. For Example 12-1, where df = 24, the t value designating P = .05 in one tail of the sampling distribution is t = 1.711. The sampling distribution appropriate to this example is shown in Figure 12-1.

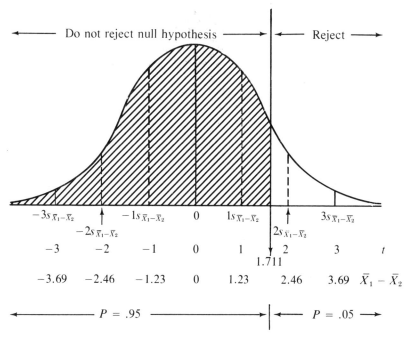

Figure 12-1. The sampling distribution of differences between means for the data in Example 12-1 (t distribution for df = 24).

Notice that in the figure the entire rejection region (P = .05) is placed in the right tail of the sampling distribution. Therefore, only positive t ratios (those favoring Method 1 over Method 2) at or exceeding t = 1.711 will lead to the rejection of the null hypothesis. The data in Example 12-1 yielded a t ratio of 2.03. This value exceeds the critical value t = 1.711 and thus lies in the rejection region for the null hypothesis. The principal should reject the null hypothesis and should conclude that, based upon this study, the videotape presentation is more effective for teaching basic geometric patterns to first-grade pupils than is the conventional flash-card method.

We have seen that the process of determining the t radio from the data in the samples is exactly the same for one- and two-tail tests. The difference between the two types of tests lies in the determination of the critical value for rejection of the null hypothesis.

Let's assume that the principal in Example 12-1 had made a non-directional hypothesis requiring a two-tail test. The hypotheses would be:

$$H_0: \mu_1 = \mu_2$$
$$H_1: \mu_1 \neq \mu_2$$

The rejection region for the null hypothesis would then be divided between both tails of the sampling distribution. For $df = 24$, at $P = .05$, Table 2 gives this critical t value as 2.064. Therefore, the rejection region lies to the left of $t = -2.064$ and to the right of $t = 2.064$. The obtained $t = 2.03$ in Example 12-1, then, would not have led to rejection of the null hypothesis had a two-tail test been made.

We notice that, in the same sampling distribution, we need a t ratio as large as 2.064 (either positive or negative) for a two-tail test, but for a one-tail test we need a t ratio of only 1.711. This leads us to the obvious conclusion that to be significant, an observed t ratio does not have to be as large in a one-tail test as it does in a two-tail test.

Directional versus Nondirectional Hypotheses

Since most research projects are undertaken for the express purpose of demonstrating that the null hypothesis is false and should be rejected, why not always make a directional hypothesis and capitalize on the smaller critical value required to designate the rejection region? The decision to make a one- or a two-tail test should not be a capricious choice of the researcher or a matter of statistical convenience. On the contrary, the choice between the two types of tests is made not on the basis of statistical considerations but on the basis of the decisions that will be made as a result of the findings.

A nondirectional hypothesis should be made in any situation in which a finding in either direction is meaningful for decision making. For example, when the selection of one of two instructional methods will be based on the outcome of a research project, findings in favor of either method will dictate the adoption of that method. Here a nondirectional hypothesis must be made and a two-tail test conducted.

On the other hand, if a decision will be made to adopt a new method only if it is shown to be superior to the old method, a directional hypothesis is appropriate and a one-tail test will provide the basis for rejecting the null hypothesis. Here the researcher is not concerned with the degree to which the new method might be superior to the old one; he is only concerned with whether it is sufficiently superior to warrant its adoption.

Directional hypotheses are sometimes made in research studies conducted to aid in development of a theory; in these cases, only one conclusion can be considered consistent with or supportive of the theory. The rationale for such directional hypotheses is that findings in the opposite direction are contraindicated by all that is known about the variables under study. This reasoning may be faulty, however, and a finding opposite in direction to the predicted outcome may be of immense value in causing modification of heretofore accepted theories. In fact, some practitioners insist that tests in the behavioral sciences should always be two-tail. They assert that so little is known about relationships among socio-psychological variables that it is unwarranted to make hypothetical presumptions of the meaningfulness of findings in only one direction.

A safe position may be that directional hypotheses should be made only in studies where there is no useful difference, in terms of decision making, between a finding that the null hypothesis cannot be rejected and a finding that a difference exists in the direction opposite to the one predicted in the alternative hypothesis, regardless of the magnitude of that difference.

The Level of Significance

Throughout this book we have discussed examples in which either .05 or .01 was designated as the level for significance. Although these are the two conventionally adopted levels, they are by no means universal. We must realize that the researcher's choice of a level of significance prior to the experiment is somewhat arbitrary. It is merely an assertion of the risk the experimenter is willing to run of being wrong if, on the basis of sample data, a decision is made to reject the null hypothesis. In deciding on the extent of this risk, the researcher must gauge the consequences which might follow if he makes an incorrect decision.

In general, a research study is conducted with the intent that a conventional method will be replaced by a new one if the new method is shown to be superior to the conventional one—that is, if the null hypothesis if rejected. Making such a change from the status quo invariably entails changing a number of commonly held assumptions and practices. Consequently, the researcher wants to be relatively certain that the decision to change is the correct one. The level of significance that is chosen depends on the seriousness of the consequences if the null hypothesis is falsely rejected.

In cases where the decision to change will have far reaching effects, such as in medical research, where a new medical treatment may possibly replace a conventional one, the researcher may not be satisfied with a significance level of .01. Studies of this sort may warrant a more stringent level of significance, such as .005 or .001, before the decision to change treatments is made. The researcher wants to be sure that the probability that he will make an incorrect decision is very low before he rejects the null hypothesis.

On the other hand, if a false rejection of the null hypothesis does not carry with it extremely adverse effects, then a higher probability of an incorrect decision may be tolerated—for example, .10. This may be the case when he or she is choosing between two new approaches or instructional methods.

It is considered good research procedure to set the level of significance before conducting the study. If the researcher were to set the significance level after the data were collected, he could be accused of choosing a level that "fits" the outcome of the experiment to his personal desires. This, of course, would be an unprofessional approach to research.

In practice, a researcher usually reports the actual significance level of the research findings if it is smaller than the preset level. For example, suppose we set .05 as the level of significance, conduct a nondirectional t test between independent sample means, and obtain $t = 3.55$. If there are 20 degrees of freedom, this finding will be considered significant and the null hypothesis will be rejected. We will therefore report this finding as "significant beyond the .05 level" or "significant at $P < .05$." If we have an extensive table of the probability values for this particular t distribution, we can specify the actual probability level of this finding. In this example, the actual significance level is $P = .002$. Complete statistical tables are available for determining the actual probabilities associated with the various t values.

It should be evident that although we set .05 as the level of significance, we would be quite elated to report a finding that was significant at .002! At this level, the probability of our making an error in rejecting the null hypothesis is indeed remote.

Type I and Type II Errors

The purpose of conducting an experiment or research project is to provide us with a statistical basis upon which we can make one of two possible decisions regarding the null hypothesis: to reject it or not to reject it. We have seen that neither decision can be made with certainty, because when we work with sample data a degree of sampling error is always present. To make provision for this, we set a probability level representing the amount of risk we are willing to run of being wrong if our decision is to reject the null hypothesis. Incorrect rejection of the null hypothesis is termed a Type I error. Another type of error can also be made. If the statistical test leads us to not reject the null hypothesis when it is in fact false, we have made a Type II error. These two types of errors are defined as follows:

Type I error:
Rejecting the null hypothesis on the basis of sample data when, in fact, no difference exists.

Type II error:
Not rejecting the null hypothesis on the basis of sample data when, in fact, a true difference exists.

The choice between the two alternatives available to us and the types of possible errors can be summarized as follows:

| | | Null hypothesis is, in fact, | |
		TRUE	FALSE
Our decision based upon sample data	REJECT	Type I Error Probability: α	Correct Decision Probability: $1 - \beta$ (Power)
	NOT REJECT	Correct Decision Probability: $1 - \alpha$	Type II Error Probability: β

This chart indicates that there are four possible situations in connection with our decision: two involve correct decisions and two involve incorrect ones.

We have seen that the risk of a Type I error is set by the researcher prior to the experiment and is called the significance level. This probability is sometimes called the *alpha level* and is symbolized by α. Thus, α represents the probability of rejecting the null hypothesis when it is true.

Let's examine more closely the Type II error. The probability of this type of error is usually called the *beta level,* and is symbolized by β. Whereas the level of a Type I error is always specified by the level of significance, the Type II error, unfortunately, is sometimes neglected. Beta is the probability of not rejecting the null hypothesis when it is false. Its complement is the probability of rejecting a false null hypothesis. The probability of correctly rejecting a false null hypothesis is called the *power of the test* and is represented by $1 - \beta$.

Our concerns with regard to Type I and Type II errors may be summed up by the following questions:

1. What probability of being wrong are we permitting ourselves if we decide to reject the null hypothesis? This is determined by the significance level we set before conducting the research study. This is the probability at

which we are willing to risk making a Type I error; it is called the alpha (α) level.

2. What is the probability of our being wrong if we decide not to reject the null hypothesis? In other words, what is the probability that by not rejecting the null hypothesis we have made an error, since some alternative to it is in fact true? This is the probability of making a Type II error and is called the beta (β) level. This probability varies depending on which alternative hypothesis is involved.

3. If the null hypothesis is actually false, what is the probability that our data will lead us to the correct decision—that is, the rejection of the null hypothesis? This probability is the power of the test, and is given by $1 - \beta$.

Let us examine the concept of the power of a statistical test in the context of Example 12-2.

Example 12-2

A nondirectional hypothesis has been made that there is a difference in the effectiveness of Method A and Method B, which is revealed in achievement-test scores. We set .05 as the level of significance, randomly select two groups of students, conduct the experiment, and obtain the following results.

Method A	Method B	
$N_1 = 50$	$N_2 = 60$	
$\bar{X}_1 = 70$	$\bar{X}_2 = 68.5$	$t = 1.50$
		$df = 108$
$\Sigma x_1^2 = 1{,}675.6$	$\Sigma x_2^2 = 1{,}262$	nonsignificant

In Example 12-2, the estimate of the standard error of the difference works out to be 1.00. Because there are many degrees of freedom, the sampling distribution for this test follows the normal curve very closely. For a two-tail test with $\alpha = .05$, a t ratio at or below -1.96 or at or above $+1.96$ is required for significance. The obtained t ratio of 1.50 does not permit us to reject the null hypothesis. Since we have not rejected the null hypothesis, we have not made a Type I error.

But what if there is a true difference between μ_1 and μ_2? If this is the case, then we have made a Type II error. The difficulty in determining the probability of making a Type II error (β), and thereby specifying the power of the test ($1 - \beta$), is that in order to determine it, we must state an alternative hypothesis assigning the population parameter a specific value. Suppose two points is the smallest difference between the μ_1 and μ_2 that we are interested in detecting, if a difference exists at all. That is, if we incorrectly fail to reject the null hypothesis, a difference between μ_1 and μ_2 of less than two points is of no concern to us. To determine the power of our statistical test to lead to the rejection of the null hypothesis if $\mu_1 - \mu_2$ is at least two points, we may state the alternative hypothesis as $\mu_1 - \mu_2 = 2$. If this alternative hypothesis is true, what is the probability that we will make a Type II error? Stated more precisely, our question is, "What is the probability that the null hypothesis will not be rejected when, in fact, $\mu_1 - \mu_2 = 2$?" This probability will be β.

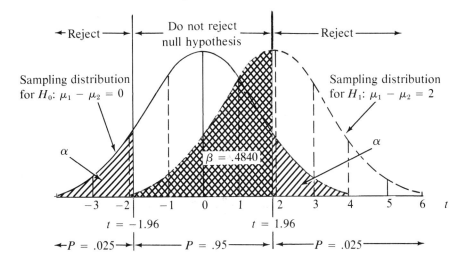

Figure 12-2. Sampling distribution of differences between means based upon H_0: $\mu_1 - \mu_2 = 0$ and H_1: $\mu_1 - \mu_2 = 2$ from data in Example 12-2.

Figure 12-2 presents two sampling distributions: the solid-line curve represents the sampling distribution if the null hypothesis ($\mu_1 - \mu_2 = 0$) is true; the dotted-line curve represents the sampling distribution if the alternative hypothesis ($\mu_1 - \mu_2 = 2$) is true. Notice that the "do not reject" region for the null hypothesis ranges from $t = -1.96$ to $t = 1.96$. Now inspect the dotted curve, which has its mean centered on 2. A large proportion of this curve lies in the "do not reject" region. This area represents the probability that the null hypothesis will be incorrectly "not rejected." This is the probability of our making a Type II error, which, in this instance, is $\beta = .4840$. The power of the test is given by $1 - \beta$, which is $1 - .4840 = .5160$. This is the probability that we will correctly reject the null hypothesis if, in fact, $\mu_1 - \mu_2 = 2$. Of course, this is a very low degree of power. It is only slightly better than flipping a coin to decide whether or not to reject the null hypothesis!

We could have postulated any value for $\mu_1 - \mu_2$ and determined the power in a similar fashion. For example, if we had postulated that $\mu_1 - \mu_2 = 3$, the dotted curve in Figure 12-2 would shift to the left, so that its mean was at 3 and much less of the area under it would lie to the left of $t = 1.96$. In fact, the probability of a Type II error would be $\beta = .1492$, and the power of the test to lead to a correct rejection of the null hypothesis would be .8508.

As these two calculations demonstrate, the power of the test to lead to a correct rejection of the null hypothesis increases as the postulated difference between μ_1 and μ_2 increases. It is possible to compute the power of the test for a multitude of postulated parameter differences. Figure 12-3 presents the power function of the test of the null hypothesis based upon the data in Example 12-2. The range of postulated $\mu_1 - \mu_2$ values is given along the horizontal axis, and the probability of correctly rejecting the null hypothesis (power) is given along the vertical axis. At $\mu_1 - \mu_2 = 0$, the null hypothesis is true, and the .05 probability indicated there is the probability of making a Type I error; this was the level of significance (α) that we set prior to the experiment.

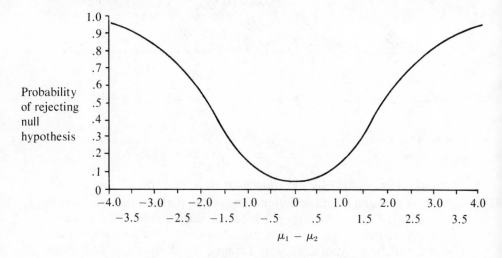

Figure 12-3. Power function for test of H_o: $\mu_1 \sigma \mu_2 = 0$ for data in Example 12-1.

It must be noted that the curve in Figure 12-2 is based upon $s_{\bar{X}_1 - \bar{X}_2} = 1.00$. Other things being equal, the larger the sample, the smaller will be $s_{\bar{X}_1 - \bar{X}_2}$ and the more powerful will be the test that will lead us to reject the null hypothesis. Also, other things being equal, if we reduce the probability of a Type I error, we increase the probability of a Type II error. A power-function curve can be constructed for directional as well as nondirectional hypothesis tests. Again, other things being equal, the probability of making a Type II error is less for a directional than for a nondirectional hypothesis test.

In conducting an experiment, the researcher naturally wants the probability of making either type of error to be small. The researcher is directly responsible for setting the significance level, and he specifies its value in advance of the project. The probability that he selects depends upon his assessment of the consequences of making a Type I error.

The power function of a statistical test can be developed and the probability of making a Type II error can be determined if the researcher specifies the size of the smallest departure from the null hypothesis that he wishes to detect. The β level is the probability of the risk he is willing to take of not detecting a departure of that size.

In Example 12-2, we can decide to reject the null hypothesis if μ_1 and μ_2 differed by as much as 2.5 points. We can then use the power function curve in Figure 12-3 to determine that the power of this test to lead to such a rejection is .71. On the other hand, if we decide that it is important for the test to detect a difference of as much as 1.5 points, the power of the test to do so is only .32. Of course, the power of the test can be increased by increasing the size of the samples in the study.

The setting of the significance level and the evaluation of the beta level are substantive considerations of the researcher; they depend on his assessment of the consequences of either possible wrong decision.

Exercises: Group A

1. A group of social scientists formulated the following research hypothesis: "The grade-point averages of students living at home are higher than the grade-point averages of students living in the university dormitory." They randomly selected two samples and obtained the following data. They set $P = .05$ as the level of significance. Should the null hypothesis be rejected?

Living at home	Living in dormitory
$N_1 = 65$	$N_2 = 70$
$\bar{X}_1 = 3.4$	$\bar{X}_2 = 3.1$
$s_1^2 = 1.7$	$s_2^2 = 1.8$

2. In Exercise 1, if $\mu_1 - \mu_2 = 0.4$, what is the probability that the social scientists will make a Type II error? What is the power of this statistical test to detect that large a difference?

3. In Exercise 1, if $\mu_1 - \mu_2 = 0.2$, what is the probability that the social scientists will make a Type II error? What is the power of this statistical test to detect a difference that large?

4. A physical-education instructor wished to test the hypothesis that athletes who eat Diet A breakfasts will perform differently from those who eat Diet B breakfasts. He randomly assigned athletes to the two breakfast diets and, after

a 6-week period, measured their athletic ability. He set $P = .01$ as his level of significance and obtained the following data. Should he reject the null hypothesis?

Diet A	Diet B
$N_1 = 50$	$N_2 = 70$
$\bar{X}_1 = 84$	$\bar{X}_2 = 80$
$s_1^2 = 107$	$s_2^2 = 104$

5. In Exercise 4, if $\mu_1 - \mu_2 = 9$, what is the probability that the physical-education instructor will make a Type II error? What is the power of this statistical test to detect a difference that large?

6. In Exercise 4, if $\mu_1 - \mu_2 = 1$, what is the probability that the physical-education instructor will make a Type II error? What is the power of this statistical test to detect that large a difference?

Exercises: Group B

7. A biologist randomly assigned white rats to two groups to examine the hypothesis "There will be a difference between the life spans of white rats living in a Type M environment and the life spans of white rats living in a Type N environment." She selected $P = .05$ as the level of significance and obtained the following data. Should the null hypothesis be rejected?

Type M environment	Type N environment
$N_1 = 100$	$N_2 = 112$
$\bar{X}_1 = 16.2$	$\bar{X}_2 = 16.8$
$s_1^2 = 9.5$	$s_2^2 = 9.1$

8. In Exercise 7, if $\mu_1 - \mu_2 = .5$, what is the probability that the biologist will make a Type II error? What is the power of this statistical test to detect a difference that large?

9. In Exercise 7, if $\mu_1 - \mu_2 = -3$, what is the probability that the biologist will make a Type II error? What is the power of this statistical test to detect that great a difference?

10. A signal-corps instructor made the hypothesis that spaced instruction was more effective than concentrated instruction for increasing Morse-code proficiency in recruits. He randomly assigned recruits to the two methods of instruction and administered a Morse-code-proficiency test to them. He set $P = .01$ as the level of significance and obtained the following data. Should he reject the null hypothesis?

Spaced instruction	Concentrated instruction
$N_1 = 70$	$N_2 = 62$
$\bar{X}_1 = 230$	$\bar{X}_2 = 225$
$s_1^2 = 225$	$s_2^2 = 238$

11. In Exercise 10, if $\mu_1 - \mu_2 = 5$, what is the probability that the instructor will make a Type II error? What is the power of this statistical test to detect a difference that large?

12. In Exercise 10, if $\mu_1 - \mu_2 = 10$, what is the probability that the instructor will make a Type II error? What is the power of this statistical test to detect a difference that large?

CHAPTER 13
ANALYSIS OF VARIANCE

Research studies often include more than two samples. Suppose we wish to compare the effects of four different teaching methods on students' arithmetic achievement. If we randomly assign students to the four methods, we can measure their arithmetic achievement at the end of the school year and obtain a mean score for each of the four samples. In this study, the null hypothesis is "There is no difference in the effectiveness of the four teaching methods on students' arithmetic achievement." This hypothesis could be symbolized by H_0: $\mu_A = \mu_B = \mu_C = \mu_D$. The alternate hypothesis is that at least one of the population means is different from the others. Note that the alternate hypothesis does not state that all population means are different; it says only that at least one of them differs from the others. Also, the alternate hypothesis does not state which of the population means will be larger (or smaller). Thus, this is a nondirectional hypothesis.

If we can assume that the samples were randomly selected and came from normally distributed populations, we may use the analysis-of-variance technique (referred to simply as ANOVA) to analyze the variability among the mean scores. If the null hypothesis is true, then the population means are identical. However, we would not expect the means of our four samples to be the same; we expect some variability among them due to sampling error. We wish to ask "If the null hypothesis is true, is the variability among the means of the samples larger than we would expect to occur by chance?" If we can show that the probability is low that the sample means differ as much as they do because of sampling error, then we will reject the null hypothesis and conclude that some factor in addition to sampling error is contributing to their variation.

The ANOVA technique compares two estimates of the population variance to determine the probability that the difference between them is due to sampling error. One of these estimates is obtained by computing a variance estimate for each of the samples separately, and then combining these estimates to obtain one population variance estimate. This is called the *within-groups variance estimate* because it is obtained by estimating variances within the samples.

The other estimate is computed by obtaining the mean score of each of the samples and then calculating a variance estimate using these mean scores and the sizes of the samples in the computation. This is called the *between-groups variance estimate* because it takes into account the variability of the means of the various samples.

Thus, through statistical procedures that will be explained later in this chapter, we obtain two estimates of the population variance. We wish to determine whether the between-groups variance estimate is significantly larger than the within-groups variance estimate. This is the crux of the ANOVA technique, because if we can show that the variance estimate based upon the variability of the sample means is significantly larger than the variance estimate derived from the variability of scores within the samples, we can conclude that the samples did not come from the same population. This conclusion will lead us to reject the null hypothesis. In other words, if the between-groups variance estimate is too large to have occurred as a result of sampling error, we conclude that there is a difference in the effectiveness of the four teaching methods.

If we cannot reject the null hypothesis, we conclude that the samples may have come from the same population and that the variation in the sample means may be due solely to sampling error. In this case, we decide that there is probably no difference in the effectiveness of the four methods of teaching arithmetic.

To apply the ANOVA technique, a ratio is computed between the two variance estimates, using the between-groups variance estimate as the numerator and the within-groups variance estimate as the denominator. This ratio is termed the *F*-ratio and is named after R. A. Fisher, who devised this statistic.

In ANOVA terms, the estimate of the population variance is called a *mean square*, symbolized by *MS*, because it is the average of the sum of squares. (Recall that a variance estimate is calculated by dividing the sum of squares by the *df*, as Formula 12a shows.) We shall use the term mean square rather than variance estimate in connection with the ANOVA technique. Formula 20 gives the procedure for computing the *F* ratio in the ANOVA technique.

Formula 20. *F* test. Formula for computing the *F* ratio in the analysis of variance.

$$F = \frac{\text{Mean Square between groups}}{\text{Mean Square within groups}} = \frac{MS_b}{MS_w}$$

To illustrate the application of the ANOVA technique, we shall examine Example 13-1, in which there are three experimental groups.

Example 13-1

We wish to determine whether levels of illumination affect work production in an electronics firm. We randomly select 41 employees and randomly assign them to three experimental groups, with each group working under a different level of illumination. We select .05 as the level of significance for this study. After a three-month period, we measure the work production of each group and obtain the following data:

Group A		Group B		Group C	
20	16	23	19	25	22
19	15	23	18	24	21
18	15	21	18	24	21
17	14	20	18	23	21
17	13	20	17	23	21
16	12	19	16	22	20
		19	15	22	19
		19			
$N_A = 12$		$N_B = 15$		$N_C = 14$	
$\bar{X}_A = 16$		$\bar{X}_B = 19$		$\bar{X}_C = 22$	

Under the null hypothesis, we assume that all of the data in the three samples in Example 13-1 come from the same population. Therefore, we form one frequency distribution of the data on the 41 employees and compute a total mean. In Example 13-1, the total mean for all 41 employees is $\bar{X}_T = 19.146$.

Figure 13-1 presents a graphic display of the frequency distributions for Groups A, B, and C, and for all three groups combined. The locations of the means of the three groups and of the mean of the total group are indicated by the arrows. Here we can see that the sample means vary around the total mean. Our question is "Is the probability .05 or less that we would get three samples means that vary this much, if they all came from the same population?"

We will illustrate two methods for performing the ANOVA technique with these data. The first method consists of a step-by-step explanatory procedure so that we can grasp the meaning underlying the technique. The second method is an easier procedure for doing the actual computations. Both methods are algebraically equivalent and they lead to identical results.

One important concept in ANOVA can be illustrated by considering the deviation of one individual's score from the mean of the total group and from his own group's mean. In Figure 13-1, subject K belongs to Group C and has a score of 25. Therefore, his score deviates from the total mean of 19.146 by 5.854 points, which is shown as (*t*) in Figure 13-1. It is important to note that this deviation can be divided into two portions. One portion is

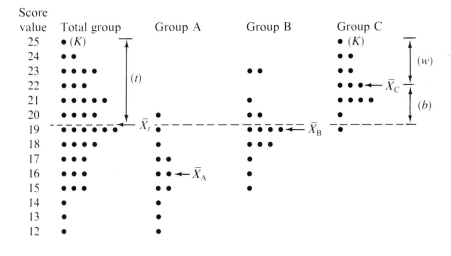

$$N_t = 41 \qquad N_A = 12 \qquad N_B = 15 \qquad N_C = 14$$
$$\overline{X}_t = 19.146 \qquad \overline{X}_A = 16 \qquad \overline{X}_B = 19 \qquad \overline{X}_C = 22$$
$$\Sigma X_t = 785 \qquad \Sigma X_A = 192 \qquad \Sigma X_B = 285 \qquad \Sigma X_C = 308$$
$$\Sigma X_t^2 = 15{,}431 \qquad \Sigma X_A^2 = 3{,}134 \qquad \Sigma X_B^2 = 5{,}485 \qquad \Sigma X_C^2 = 6{,}812$$

Figure 13-1. Frequency distributions of scores for groups A, B, and C and for all three groups combined.

the amount of deviation from his own group's mean, $25 - 22 = 3$ points, which is termed a deviation within a group (w). The other portion is the amount by which his group's mean deviates from the total mean (b), which is $22 - 19.146 = 2.854$. Thus, the deviation of subject K's score from the total mean is exactly equal to its deviation from its group mean plus the deviation of the group mean from the total mean. This is true for each of the scores in all three groups. We shall use these deviation scores to compute variance estimates.

Recall that the variance, as it is given in Formula 12a, is determined by dividing the sum of squares by the df. In ANOVA, the Mean Square (MS) is determined in the same way. Our first concern, then, is with the sum of squares. In ANOVA, the total sum of squares (SS_t) can be divided into two components: the sum of squares between groups (SS_b) and the sum of squares within groups (SS_w), as Formula 21 shows.

These sums of squares can be calculated by applying Formulas 22 through 24 to the data in Figure 13-1.

Formula 21. Composition of the total sum of squares.

Total sum of squares = sum of squares between groups + sum of squares within groups.

$$SS_t = SS_b + SS_w$$

Formulas 22 through 24. Calculation of sum of squares.

Total Sum of Squares $SS_t = \Sigma X^2 - \dfrac{(\Sigma X)^2}{N_t}$ (Formula 22)

Sum of Squares within Groups $SS_w = SS_A + SS_B + SS_C$

(within group) (Formula 23)

Sum of Squares between Groups $SS_b = SS_t - SS_w$ (Formula 24a)

$SS_b = N_A(\bar{X}_A - \bar{X}_t)^2 + N_B(\bar{X}_B - \bar{X}_t)^2 + N_C(\bar{X}_C - \bar{X}_t)^2$ (Formula 24b)

For Example 13-1, the total sum of squares and the sum of squares within each group are calculated as follows:

Using Formula 22: $\quad SS_t = 15{,}431 - \dfrac{(785)^2}{41} = 401.12$

For each group:

$$SS_A = 3{,}134 - \dfrac{(192)^2}{12} = 62$$

$$SS_B = 5{,}485 - \dfrac{(285)^2}{15} = 70$$

$$SS_C = 6{,}812 - \dfrac{(308)^2}{14} = 36$$

Using Formula 23: $\quad SS_w = 62 + 70 + 36 = 168$

To determine the sum of squares between groups, we can use either Formula 24a or Formula 24b.

Using Formula 24a: $\quad SS_b = 401.12 - 168 = 233.12$

Using Formula 24b: $\quad SS_b = 12(16 - 19.146)^2 + 15(19 - 19.146)^2$
$\qquad\qquad\qquad\quad + 14(22 - 19.146)^2 = 233.12$

Of primary interest to us are the SS_w and SS_b. Examination of Formula 23 indicates that SS_w is computed by adding the sum of squares for each sample. Since the sum of squares for a particular group is dependent not on the magnitude of the mean score, but on the variability of scores around it, the differences in the group means do not affect SS_w; that is, the value of SS_w will be the same whether the groups all have identical means or whether their means differ greatly. (In our example, SS_w will be 168 regardless of the values of the group means.)

Formula 24b indicates that the SS_b is affected by how much each group mean differs from the total mean. Thus, $SS_b = 233.12$, due to the specific differences between the group means. If the groups had identical means, then SS_b would be zero. If their means differed greatly, then there would be a large SS_b.

Having calculated two sums of squares, we can determine the mean squares by dividing each SS by its appropriate degrees of freedom; this procedure is shown in Formulas 25 through 27.

Formulas 25 through 27. Calculation of degrees of freedom for analysis of variance.

Degrees of freedom

Total	$df_t = N - 1$	(Formula 25)
Between groups	$df_b = \text{No. of groups} - 1$	(Formula 26)
Within groups	$df_w = df_t - df_b$	(Formula 27)

In Example 13-1, $df_t = 40$, $df_b = 2$, and $df_w = 38$. Formulas 28 and 29 demonstrate how to obtain the mean squares between groups and the mean squares within groups.

Formulas 28 and 29. Calculation of mean squares (variance estimates).

$$MS_b = \frac{SS_b}{df_b} \qquad \text{(Formula 28)}$$

$$MS_w = \frac{SS_w}{df_w} \qquad \text{(Formula 29)}$$

Applying these formulas to the data in our example we obtain:

$$MS_b = \frac{233.12}{2} = 116.56$$

$$MS_w = \frac{168}{38} = 4.42$$

These mean squares represent estimates of the population variance that are calculated from the same data but computed from two independent sources of variability, the variability within each group and the variability between the group means. Under the null hypothesis, we would expect these two estimates to be approximately the same. Obviously, the MS_b in Example 13-1 is quite a bit larger than the MS_w. We now need to determine if the difference is great enough to permit us to reject the null hypothesis. Since we set our significance level at .05, we wish to determine whether the probability is .05 or less that we would obtain variance estimates differing as much as these do if the null hypothesis is true. To make this decision, we must compute an F ratio using Formula 20. Using the data in our example, $F = 116.56/4.42 = 26.37$. To evaluate the significance of this F ratio, we must specify the appropriate sampling distribution of F.

The F Distribution

As was the case with the t distributions, there is a family of F distributions. The shape of each F distribution is determined by the degrees of freedom associated with two variance estimates. To see how an F distribution is formed, suppose that we select from a normally distributed population a multitude of samples of size $N_1 = 4$, and also select a multitude of samples of size $N_2 = 31$. For each sample, we estimate the population variance, s^2, using Formula 12. The df associated with the estimate derived from each sample of $N_1 = 4$ is $df_1 = 3$; the df associated with the estimate from each sample of $N_2 = 31$ is $df_2 = 30$.

If we randomly pair estimates of differing dfs and compute the ratios between the variance estimates, always placing the s_1^2 based upon $df_1 = 3$ in the numerator, we obtain an array of ratios called F ratios. The ratio of each pair of estimates is determined by

$$F = \frac{s_1^2 \quad \leftarrow \text{variance estimate with } df_1 = 3}{s_2^2 \quad \leftarrow \text{variance estimate with } df_2 = 30}$$

The distribution of the array of F ratios calculated from all possible pairs of samples forms a sampling distribution of F. The shape of a particular F distribution depends on the df associated with the numerator and the df associated with the denominator. The particular F distribution that applies to our example, in which $df_1 = 3$ and $df_2 = 30$, is shown in Figure 13-2. As this figure shows, the lowest possible value of F is zero, and this value can occur only when s_1^2 is zero. The distribution of F ratios is skewed to the right and theoretically extends to infinity. Virtually all tests of significance using an F distribution are used to determine whether s_1^2 is significantly larger than s_2^2. Therefore, when we use them, we are generally concerned with probabilities associated with areas in the right tail of the F distribution.

Figure 13-2 indicates that for this particular F distribution the probability is .05 that an F ratio will be obtained that is 2.92 or larger. The

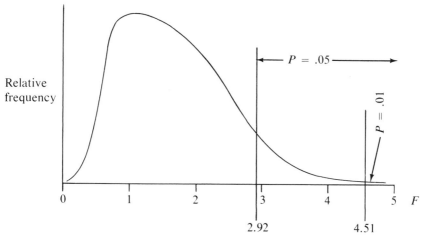

Figure 13-2. Sampling distribution of F with $df_1 = 3$ and $df_2 = 30$.

probability is .01 of obtaining an F ratio of 4.51 or larger. This represents the sampling distribution of F for 3 and 30 degrees of freedom and specifies the critical values of F commonly used in deciding to reject the null hypothesis.

To illustrate the use of this distribution, suppose we wish to test the hypothesis that Population 1 has a larger variance than Population 2—that is, that $H_1: \sigma_1^2 > \sigma_2^2$. The null hypothesis is $H_0: \sigma_1^2 = \sigma_2^2$. Suppose we set .05 as our level of significance. A sample of size $N_1 = 31$ is selected from the first population and a sample of $N_2 = 4$ from the second. Variance estimates from these samples are computed to be $s_1^2 = 290.4$ and $s_2^2 = 75.2$, respectively. The F ratio, therefore, is $290.4/75.2 = 3.86$. Figure 13-2 indicates that this F ratio exceeds the critical value of F at the .05 significance level. Thus, we reject the null hypothesis that the two variance estimates come from populations having the same variance, and conclude that σ_1^2 is larger than σ_2^2. (Had we set .01 as the level of significance, we could not reject the null hypothesis, since an F ratio of 4.51 is needed to reject it at that level.)

Since the shape of the sampling distribution of F differs for each combination of dfs, the values of F needed at .05 and .01 differ for each combination of dfs. Table 3 at the back of the book lists the values of F that represent the .05 and .01 areas in the right tail of each F distribution. This table is structured so that the dfs associated with the greater mean square (variance estimate) are located across the top of the table and the dfs associated with the smaller mean square are located along the side. Figures in roman type in the body of Table 3 indicate the F ratios needed for significance at the .05 level; figures in boldface type give the ratios needed at the .01 level.

Returning now to Example 13-1, if we wish to evaluate the significance of the F ratio 26.37, we consult the columns in Table 3 showing $df_b = 2$ (for our greater mean square) and $df_w = 38$ (for our smaller mean square) and find that we need an F ratio of approximately 3.23 (tabled value for the intersection of 2 and 40 dfs) to be significant at .05. Our obtained F ratio of 26.37 is far in excess of the critical value; therefore, we reject the null hypothesis that the three groups came from the same population.

The format for reporting the results of the ANOVA technique for Example 13-1 is as follows:

	Sum of squares	Degrees of freedom	Mean square	F
Between groups	$SS_b = 233.12$	$df_b = 2$	$MS_b = 116.56$	26.37 $P < .05$
Within groups	$SS_w = 168$	$df_w = 38$	$MS_w = 4.42$	
Total	$SS_t = 401.12$	$df_t = 40$		

The variance estimate based on the variability of the sample means (MS_b) has been shown to be significantly greater than the variance estimate based on within-group variability (MS_b). Therefore, we conclude that some factor other than chance has affected the level of the group means, and has thereby caused the large MS_b. If our research study has been well designed, with extraneous factors controlled, we may conclude that this difference is due to the different treatments given to the three groups.

As we mentioned at the beginning of this chapter, there is an easier way to compute the sums of squares for the ANOVA technique. This method and its format are presented in Formula 30.

Formula 30. Computational formulas for sums of squares.

	Group A	Group B	Group C	Total
	ΣX_A	ΣX_B	ΣX_C	ΣX_t
	$\Sigma X_A{}^2$	$\Sigma X_B{}^2$	$\Sigma X_C{}^2$	$\Sigma X_t{}^2$
	N_A	N_B	N_C	N_t

Step 1 Correction term

$$C = \frac{(\Sigma X_t)^2}{N_t}$$

Step 2 Total sum of squares

$$SS_t = \Sigma X_t{}^2 - C$$

Step 3 Sum of squares between groups

$$SS_b = \frac{(\Sigma X_A)^2}{N_A} + \frac{(\Sigma X_B)^2}{N_B} + \frac{(\Sigma X_C)^2}{N_C} - C$$

Step 4 Sum of squares within groups

$$SS_w = SS_t - SS_b$$

Formula 30 shows that first we compute a correction term that is then used in Steps 2 and 3 to compute SS_t and SS_b. Then we find SS_w, which is the difference between SS_t and SS_b. The use of these formulas is illustrated below, using the data given in Example 13-1. Notice that this simplified method yields values that are identical with those we computed using the first method.

Group A	Group B	Group C	Total
$\Sigma X_A = 192$	$\Sigma X_B = 285$	$\Sigma X_C = 308$	$\Sigma X_t = 785$
$\Sigma X_A^2 = 3{,}134$	$\Sigma X_B^2 = 5{,}485$	$\Sigma X_C^2 = 6{,}812$	$\Sigma X_t^2 = 15{,}431$
$\bar{X}_A = 16$	$\bar{X}_B = 19$	$\bar{X}_C = 22$	$\bar{X}_t = 19.146$
$N_A = 12$	$N_B = 15$	$N_C = 14$	$N_t = 41$

Step 1 $\quad C = \dfrac{(785)^2}{41} = 15{,}029.88$

Step 2 $\quad SS_t = 15{,}431 - 15{,}029.88 = 401.12$

Step 3 $\quad SS_b = \dfrac{(192)^2}{12} + \dfrac{(285)^2}{15} + \dfrac{(308)^2}{14} - 15{,}029.88 = 233.12$

Step 4 $\quad SS_w = 401.12 - 233.12 = 168$

Notice that in the ANOVA technique, we always place the MS_b in the numerator and the MS_w in the denominator. The MS_b is almost always larger than the MS_w. Although it is possible for the MS_w to be larger than the MS_b, it is highly unlikely. This would mean that the variability of the sample means was less than would be expected by chance! (Such a finding might lead us to question whether the samples were truly randomly selected.) When an F ratio is less than 1.00, then, of course, we cannot reject the null hypothesis. It is only when an F ratio exceeds 1.00 that we must determine whether the difference is significantly larger than we would expect as a result of sampling error. The result is that we invariably deal with only the right tail of the F distribution, even though we are testing a nondirectional hypothesis.

In studies in which the application of the ANOVA technique does not yield a significant F ratio, we must conclude that the null hypothesis of no difference among the population means is tenable. But what are we to conclude if the F ratio is large enough to permit us to reject the null hypothesis? In Example 13-1, where the null hypothesis was rejected, we can only conclude that at least one of the population means differs from the other two: the statistical test does not indicate which one differs from the others, nor does it indicate whether all three population means differ.

There are various advanced statistical techniques that we can use to make multiple comparisons among our samples.[1]

We have presented only the simplest form of the analysis-of-variance technique. It can be applied to any number of groups by extending the formulas to include the additional groups. This technique can also be applied to experiments involving groups within groups, including both independent and nonindependent samples. However, these advanced techniques are beyond the scope of this text.

On page 130, where we were illustrating the use of the sampling distribution of F, we tested the hypothesis that $\sigma_1^2 > \sigma_2^2$. A more common situation is one in which we have two variance estimates, s_1^2 and s_2^2, and wish to test the nondirectional hypothesis that the variances of the two populations differ. In this case we are concerned with H_1: $\sigma_1^2 \neq \sigma_2^2$. The null hypothesis, H_0: $\sigma_1^2 = \sigma_2^2$, will be rejected if s_1^2 is significantly larger than s_2^2, or if s_2^2 is significantly larger than s_1^2. Table 3, however, only gives F values larger than 1.00. Therefore, to test a nondirectional hypothesis, we must always put the larger s^2 in the numerator and compute an F ratio as shown in Formula 31.

Formula 31. Calculation of the F-ratio for comparison of two variance estimates.

$$F = \frac{\text{larger } s^2}{\text{smaller } s^2}$$

Since we put either s_1^2 or s_2^2 in the numerator, depending upon which is larger, the level of significance given in Table 3 must be doubled. This means that in testing nondirectional hypotheses about differences between variance estimates, the tabled values represent the critical values at $P = .10$ and $P = .02$ rather than at $P = .05$ and $P = .01$.

To illustrate the use of Formula 31, suppose we wish to test the hypothesis H_1: $\sigma_1^2 \neq \sigma_2^2$, using .02 as the level of significance. We obtain two samples and compute the following variance estimates:

$$N_1 = 19 \qquad N_2 = 6$$
$$s_1^2 = 230 \qquad s_2^2 = 490$$

---

[1]Two of the commonly used multiple-comparison techniques are those developed by Tukey and Scheffé, called the HSD method and the S method, respectively. Both methods are clearly described in Roger E. Kirk, *Experimental Design: Procedures for the Behavioral Sciences* (Monterey, Calif.: Brooks/Cole, 1968), pp. 88–91, and in Gene V. Glass and Julian C. Stanley, *Statistical Methods in Education and Psychology* (Englewood Cliffs, N.J.: Prentice-Hall, 1970), pp. 383–397.

Applying Formula 31, we obtain:

$$F = \frac{490}{230} = 2.13$$

Table 3 indicates that for $df = 18$ for the greater s^2 and $df = 5$ for the smaller s^2, an F ratio of 4.25 is needed at the .02 level of significance. In this example, therefore, we cannot reject the null hypothesis that the samples came from populations with equal variances. Extensive tables of F are available for the conventional significance levels of .05 and .01; these give the critical F-ratios at these levels for nondirectional hypothesis tests.

Exercises: Group A

1. An educational researcher wished to determine if there was a difference in the effectiveness of three methods of reading instruction. She randomly assigned students to Methods A, B, and C and tested them at the conclusion of the instructional period. She set $P = .05$ as the level of significance and obtained the following data. Prepare a summary table for these data. Should the null hypothesis be rejected?

Method A	Method B	Method C
30	32	40
29	31	38
28	31	37
27	30	37
27	30	36
27	30	36
24	27	
21		

2. A high-school teacher wished to test the hypothesis that one sex is more variable than the other in terms of public-speaking ability. She selected a random sample of boys and a random sample of girls from the local high-school enrollment and tested them on their public-speaking ability. She set $P = .01$ as the level of significance and obtained the following frequency distribution of scores. Should the null hypothesis be rejected?

Public speaking scores	Boys f	Girls f
30		2
29		2
28	1	2
27	2	3
26	4	5
25	5	4
24	4	3
23	2	2
22	1	1
21		1

3. Four samples of white rats were randomly selected and given different types of liquid diets for a two-week period. At the end of the period they were weighed; their weights are given below. Using $P = .01$ as the level of significance, should the null hypothesis that the liquids have no differential effects on the weights of the white rats be rejected?

Group 1	Group 2	Group 3	Group 4
10	11	9	10
11	12	13	11
13	13	13	12
13	13	15	13
13	15		14
15			16
16			

Exercises: Group B

4. A camp director randomly selected three samples of Girl Scouts and gave each sample a different style of leadership during a summer encampment. At the conclusion of the camping period, each Girl Scout answered a questionnaire designed to measure her attitude toward the camp. The camp director obtained the following attitude measurements. She set $P = .05$ as the level of significance. Should the null hypothesis be rejected?

Democratic	Authoritarian	Laissez-faire
17	18	17
16	15	14
16	15	13
15	11	12
11		10
		8

5. Four samples of college freshmen were given a writing-proficiency test after receiving different methods of writing instruction. The level of significance was set at $P = .01$. Should the null hypothesis that there is no difference in the effectiveness of the four methods of writing instruction be rejected?

Method A	Method B	Method C	Method D
14	15	9	7
15	16	11	10
17	16	12	11
17	16	14	12
19	17	12	14
	14	12	15
	12		

6. A sociologist wished to test the hypothesis that the flexibility in child-rearing practices of parents in a low socioeconomic level is just as variable as that of parents in a high socioeconomic level. He administered a child-rearing questionnaire to a random sample of parents of both socioeconomic classes and obtained the following data. Setting $P = .05$ as the level of significance, should the null hypothesis be rejected?

Low socioeconomic-level parents	High socioeconomic-level parents
$N_1 = 41$	$N_2 = 25$
$\bar{X}_1 = 17.6$	$\bar{X}_2 = 17.5$
$s_1 = 9.4$	$s_2 = 16.6$

CHAPTER 14
CORRELATION

As researchers, we are concerned with detecting relationships between and among phenomena. Many research studies are designed to find out whether there is an association between two variables. For example, we may wish to determine if people's ages are related to their blood pressures, or whether students' anxiety levels are related to their achievement scores. By discovering a relationship between variables, we can often predict a person's status on a given variable if we know how he or she performs on the other variable. Since prediction is one of the major goals of any science, the discovery of relationships is of paramount importance. In this chapter, we will present a way to show the relationship between two sets of data and one commonly used technique for measuring this relationship. In Chapter 15, we will demonstrate a method for making predictions about associated variables.

We should note that the statistical techniques presented so far describe frequency distributions or measure differences between sets of data where scores were obtained for only one variable. In these cases, each datum represented a measurement based on only one characteristic, and we made statistical inferences using the sampling distribution that was appropriate for that statistic.

Now we shall consider another very useful statistical technique that allows us to measure the relationship between two sets of data obtained from the same sample, or between data from two samples where individuals in the samples have been matched on some basis. For example, this technique will permit us to specify the relationship between the pretest and posttest achievement-test scores for fourth-grade students, or the motivation ratings and aptitude scores for a group of college freshmen, or the high-school grade-point averages and the college senior grade-point averages for a group of students. In such studies, we are not looking for differences between two groups of individuals; instead, we want to discover to what extent two sets of data are related. This statistical technique is called *correlation*. To illustrate its use, suppose we have the following arithmetic- and spelling-achievement scores for eight students:

Student	Arithmetic-achievement scores	Spelling-achievement scores
A	6	6
B	4	4
C	3	3
D	2	2
E	8	8
F	5	5
G	1	1
H	7	7

To depict graphically the correlation between the variables on arithmetic achievement and spelling achievement, we shall draw what is called a *scatter diagram*. To draw this diagram, which is shown in Figure 14-1, we choose one of the variables, for instance arithmetic achievement, to be represented on the vertical axis, and the other variable, spelling achievement, to be represented on the horizontal axis. Notice that in this diagram the arithmetic scores are ranged along the vertical axis with the lowest score placed at the bottom, and the spelling scores are ranged along the horizontal axis with the lowest score placed at the left. This is the conventional method for arranging the scores in a scatter diagram, and it is consistent with the traditional Cartesian coordinate system.

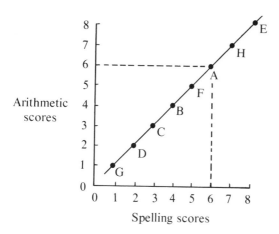

Figure 14-1. Scatter diagram of arithmetic scores and spelling scores.

Our data indicate that Student A received an arithmetic score of 6 and a spelling score of 6. To plot these two scores for Student A, we must locate both scores in the diagram and make one dot that will represent both scores. To do this, we locate value 6 on the arithmetic axis and extend a horizontal line from this position across the diagram. Next we locate value

6 on the spelling axis and extend a line vertically from this position. At the point where these two lines intersect we place a dot. This one dot now represents both scores for Student A, as Figure 14-1 shows.

Following the same procedure for each student in the group, we form a scatter diagram of the scores for all the students. We then find that we can draw a straight line connecting all of these dots in the scatter diagram in Figure 14-1.

This diagram shows that for every increase in score value on one variable, there is a corresponding increase on the other variable. Since this is true for every pair of scores in our data, we conclude that the relationship between arithmetic scores and spelling scores is *perfect*. In statistical terms, we would call this particular relationship a *perfect positive correlation*. It is called *perfect* because the amount of increase in a score on one variable is exactly proportional to the amount of increase in the score on the corresponding variable, with no exceptions. It is called *positive* because an *increase* in a score on one variable is associated with an increase in the score on the corresponding variable.

Now let's look at a scatter diagram that depicts a *perfect negative correlation*. Figure 14-2 is a scatter diagram that represents the relationship between the speeds of runners and the amounts of weight they are carrying. It is evident from this diagram that the speed of each runner is inversely related to the amount of weight he or she is carrying. Again in statistical terms, we would say that there is a perfect negative correlation between these two variables, because we can draw a straight line that runs through all of the dots in Figure 14-2. It is a *negative* correlation because the two variables are inversely related; that is, an increase in a score on one variable is associated with a decrease in the score on the corresponding variable.

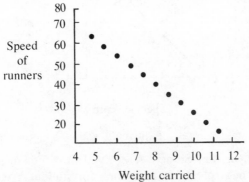

Speed of runners

Weight carried

Figure 14-2. A perfect negative correlation.

To express the relationship between two variables statistically, we must have some numerical index showing the degree of correlation. This index is termed the *correlation coefficient,* and its magnitude indicates the degree to which two frequency distributions of data are related.

There are many different correlation techniques available to the statistician. Which one is appropriate for use in a particular situation depends upon the nature of the data being analyzed. This chapter presents a method for computing one type of correlation coefficient—the *Pearson product-moment correlation coefficient.* It is named after its originator, Karl Pearson, and is derived by examining functions of deviations of values from the "best-fit" line. The term *moment* is taken from the science of mechanics and refers to certain functions of deviations. The symbol for this correlation coefficient is *r.* It is one of the more commonly used correlational techniques. To use it properly, however, we must assume that the variables are linearly related, and that the scores on each variable come from normally distributed populations. If these assumptions cannot be made, this type of correlation analysis is inappropriate and other techniques must be used. (In Chapter 15 we will examine a correlation technique that can be used for data that do not meet these requirements.)

The coefficient of correlation for the perfect positive correlation shown in Figure 14-3(a) is $r = 1.00$. The coefficient for the perfect negative

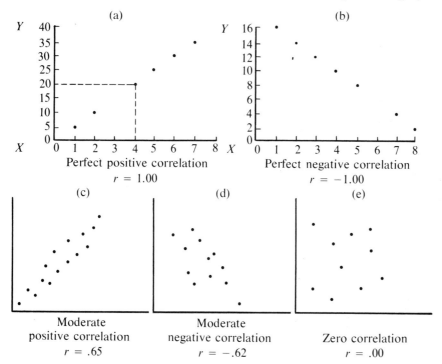

Figure 14-3. Scatter diagrams depicting various levels of correlation.

correlation shown in Figure 14-3(b) is $r = -1.00$. These are the maximum values for r. Notice that the sign of the correlation coefficient indicates whether the correlation is positive or negative and that the size of the perfect correlation is the same (1.00) regardless of whether it is positive or negative. This is an important point to keep in mind because people sometimes mistakenly think that a coefficient of $r = -1.00$ represents no correlation. The coefficient that indicates no degree of correlation is $r = .00$. This condition occurs when scores on one variable are not related in any way to scores on the other variable. Figure 14-3(e) is a scatter diagram of uncorrelated data, representing the relationships between the IQs of soldiers and their rifle-marksmanship scores.

As you may imagine, a perfect correlation between two variables rarely occurs. Almost every time a relationship exists between two variables, it is less than perfect. In such cases, the coefficient is less than 1.00. For example, $r = .85$ indicates that there is a fairly strong positive correlation between two variables, $r = .54$ indicates that the positive correlation is not as strong, and $r = .03$ indicates that there is practically no positive correlation; likewise, $r = -.75$ indicates a fairly strong negative correlation, and $r = -.12$ indicates a weak negative correlation. Thus, we see that all positive coefficients indicate direct relationships and all negative coefficients indicate inverse relationships, and that the size of the coefficient indicates the strength of the relationship. Figures 14-3(c) and 14-3(d) depict scatter diagrams showing moderate positive and negative correlations.

Suppose we obtain IQs and reading scores for a group of students and prepare the scatter diagram shown in Figure 14-4. We can see that the dots on the diagram tend to lie in a positive direction, although they certainly do not lie in a straight line. This indicates that the correlation is positive, but less than perfect. We can compute the correlation coefficient for these data; in this case, $r = .75$.

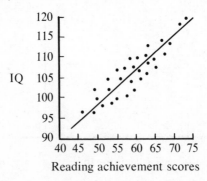

Figure 14-4. Scatter diagram of IQs and reading scores.

Let's see how we determine the size of a correlation coefficient from the scatter of the dots in the diagram. First we draw a straight line through the dots that best represents the linear trend shown in the diagram. This line is positioned in the scatter diagram so that the average distance of the dots from it is as small as possible, as Figure 14-4 shows. If we measure the perpendicular distance of each dot from this line, square each distance, and sum these squared distances, the sum will be smaller than the sum we could obtain by placing the line in any other position in the diagram. A line placed in this fashion is called a *best-fitting* line.

The total of the distances that the dots lie from this best-fitting line is inversely related to the size of the correlation coefficient. For example, if the dots are widely scattered, then the distances of the dots from the best-fitting line are great and the size of the coefficient is small. On the other hand, if the dots deviate very little from the best-fitting line, then the coefficient is large. If there is no deviation from the best-fitting line, as in Figures 14-3(a) and 14-3(b), the coefficient will be either 1.00 or -1.00.

Computation of the Correlation Coefficient

We do not need to prepare a scatter diagram to determine the degree of correlation between two variables; we have a statistical procedure that allows us to compute the correlation coefficient directly from the data. However, a scatter diagram is helpful because it gives us a visual indication of the linearity of the relationship and the variability of the data on each variable.

Formula 32 presents the formula for calculating the Pearson product-moment correlation coefficient.

Formula 32. Calculation of the Pearson product-moment correlation coefficient.

$$r = \frac{N\Sigma XY - (\Sigma X)(\Sigma Y)}{\sqrt{[N\Sigma X^2 - (\Sigma X)^2][N\Sigma Y^2 - (\Sigma Y)^2]}}$$

N = number of pairs of scores

Degrees of freedom: $N - 2$

Since we are dealing with two sets of data, we generally assign the symbol X to the scores on one variable and the symbol Y to the scores on the other variable. The expression $N\Sigma XY$ in the numerator of Formula 32 indicates that we obtain the product of each pair of scores, sum these products, and then multiply this sum by the number of pairs of scores (N).

To illustrate the application of Formula 32 with a very simple example, suppose a teacher wishes to determine if the scores fourth-grade students obtain on a spelling test are directly related to their reading scores. This is a directional hypothesis stating that there will be a positive relationship between these two variables. Suppose the significance level is set at .05. The teacher obtains spelling scores (X) and reading scores (Y) for 12 fourth-grade students; these scores are shown in Table 14-1. The computation of the correlation coefficient, using Formula 32, is given below the table.

Table 14-1. Computation of the Pearson product-moment correlation coefficient

Spelling scores X	Reading scores Y	X^2	Y^2	XY
1	1	1	1	1
2	4	4	16	8
3	2	9	4	6
4	4	16	16	16
4	6	16	36	24
5	2	25	4	10
6	3	36	9	18
6	7	36	49	42
7	5	49	25	35
8	4	64	16	32
8	9	64	81	72
9	8	81	64	72
$\Sigma X = 63$	$\Sigma Y = 55$	$\Sigma X^2 = 401$	$\Sigma Y^2 = 321$	$\Sigma XY = 336$

Using Formula 32: $r = \dfrac{12(336) - (63)(55)}{\sqrt{[12(401) - (63)^2][12(321) - (55)^2]}} = .679$

The Sampling Distribution of r

As is true of all statistical procedures described in this book, we do not want merely to describe the correlation between the two sets of sample data, but to make inferences from these data about the extent of correlation between the variables in the population from which the samples are drawn. We know that sample statistics are always subject to sampling error; this is also true of correlation coefficients.

One of the major purposes of correlational analysis of sample data is to test the null hypothesis that there is zero correlation between the variables in the population. In these cases, we must determine the probability that our obtained r is a result of sampling error and not a reflection of a true relationship between the variables. If our test leads us to reject the null hypothesis, then we will conclude that the two variables are correlated in the population.

As in all statistical tests, we need to develop a sampling distribution of *r*. It will reflect the distribution of sample *r*'s that result solely from sampling error when the population correlation is in fact zero. If the null hypothesis is true, correlation coefficients based upon small samples will fluctuate more around a mean of zero than will coefficients based upon large samples.

If the null hypothesis is true, the sampling distribution of correlation coefficients will be symmetrical around zero and will be similar in form to the *t* distributions (but not quite identical with them). The specific shape of the sampling distribution of *r* depends upon the degrees of freedom associated with the coefficient. For *r*, the degrees of freedom are $N - 2$, where *N* is the number of pairs of scores used in the calculation.

Of course, hypotheses regarding correlations between variables can be directional or nondirectional. A hypothesis which states that there is a relationship between *X* and *Y* is considered nondirectional, since a sufficiently large correlation coefficient that is either positive or negative can lead to the rejection of the null hypothesis.

On the other hand, a hypothesis that states that there will be a positive relationship between two variables is a directional one, and the null hypothesis will be rejected only if a sufficiently large positive coefficient is obtained.

Table 4 at the back of the book lists the critical values of *r* at varying significance levels for use in testing nondirectional hypotheses. Therefore, the tabled values of *r* indicate both the critical positive and the critical negative values, with the probability level equally divided between the two tails of the sampling distribution. For example, if the .05 level of significance is adopted for a test of a nondirectional hypothesis when $df = 21$, the critical value for rejecting the null hypothesis is .413. This means that an obtained *r* of this magnitude or greater, whether positive or negative, will lead to the rejection of the null hypothesis.

When directional hypotheses are being tested, the probability levels listed in Table 4 must be doubled, thereby placing the entire rejection region in one tail of the sampling distribution. For directional tests, the probability headings in Table 4 become $P = .05$, $P = .025$, $P = .01$, and $P = .005$.

From Table 4 we can see that *r*'s derived from small samples (small *df*) must be larger than those derived from large samples (large *df*) to be statistically significant. In the example given in Table 14-1, the teacher is concerned with a directional hypothesis about the positive relationship between spelling and reading scores. A correlation of $r = .679$ was computed from the scores of the 12 students. Therefore, the *df* associated with this correlation coefficient is $N - 2 = 10$. Table 4 indicates that for $df = 10$, the critical *r* at $P = .05$ for this directional hypothesis is .497 (in the column headed $P = .10$). Since the obtained r of .679 exceeds the critical value, the teacher should reject the null hypothesis that there is no correlation between the spelling and reading scores in the population of fourth-grade students.

The magnitude of a correlation coefficient can be affected by several factors. First, if the relationship between the variables is not linear, the Pearson product-moment correlation coefficient will yield an underestimate of the true relationship between the variables. There are other statistical methods for determining the correlation between variables that have curvilinear relationships. Also, the correlation between heterogeneous variables tends to be greater than the correlation between variables that have a curtailed range of values.

A word of caution is needed on the interpretation of a correlation coefficient. Although the coefficient indicates the degree to which two variables are related, this does not necessarily mean that there is a causal relationship between them. Correlation does not imply that one variable is causing the variation in the other. A simple example will illustrate that correlation cannot be interpreted in this way. Suppose we find a correlation between childrens' neatness of appearance and their punctuality in arriving at school. By no stretch of the imagination can we say that being neat causes the children to be on time or that being punctual causes them to be neat. This relationship may actually be caused by a third variable, such as the kind of parental attention the children receive.

Another caution should also be observed in interpreting correlation coefficients. Because they are indexes of relationship, they cannot be interpreted as percentages of agreement. A coefficient of $r = .30$ does not indicate that there is a 30% agreement between the two sets of scores. Also, it is not proper to say that a correlation of $r = .40$ is twice as strong as a correlation of $r = .20$ just because it is twice as large.

If we wish to make statements regarding the meaning of a correlation, we can compute the *coefficient of determination,* which is obtained by squaring the correlation coefficient. This value, r^2, can be properly interpreted as the proportion (or percentage) of the variance of the X scores that is associated with the variance of the Y scores. To illustrate, in the example in Table 14-1, where $r = .679$, the coefficient of determination, $r^2 = (.679)^2 = .461$, indicates that 46% of the variance of the X scores is accounted for by the variance of the Y scores.

Lastly, we must be aware of the distinction between statistical significance and the practical utility of a correlation coefficient. As we have observed in Table 4, a small coefficient can be statistically significant in cases where the coefficient is computed by using data obtained from a very large sample. For example, in the case of a directional hypothesis, for

$df = 100$, a coefficient as small as $r = .164$ is significant at the .05 level. But the coefficient of determination, $r^2 = .027$, indicates that, for all practical purposes, the relationship between them is too small to be useful, since only about 3% of the variance in one variable is associated with the variance in the other variable.

Exercises: Group A

1. An industrial-arts teacher wished to determine if there was any relationship between students' mechanical comprehension and their divergent-thinking ability. He randomly selected a group of students and measured them on these two variables. He selected $P = .05$ as the level of significance and obtained the following data. Compute the Pearson product-moment correlation coefficient. Should the null hypothesis be rejected?

Mechanical comprehension	Divergent thinking
10	30
11	32
15	27
17	29
19	34
21	34
26	39
29	37

2. Compute the coefficient of determination for the data in Exercise 1. What does it indicate about the relationship between the variables of mechanical comprehension and divergent thinking?

3. An elementary-school teacher wished to test the hypothesis that the longer it took her pupils to complete a spelling quiz, the less accurate would be their answers. She randomly selected a sample of pupils and obtained the following data. She set $P = .05$ as the level of significance. Compute the Pearson product-moment correlation coefficient. Should the null hypothesis be rejected?

Spelling scores	Time (in minutes)	Spelling scores	Time (in minutes)
25	5.5	31	4.2
26	5.4	33	3.6
28	5.7	35	5.0
28	4.6	37	4.7
29	4.9	42	4.0
30	4.8	43	4.9
30	4.9		

4. Compute the coefficient of determination for the data in Exercise 3. What does it indicate about the relationship between the variables of spelling ability and completion times?

Exercises: Group B

5. A developmental psychologist had the hypothesis that there would be a positive relationship between children's self-concept ratings provided by their teachers and those provided by the children's parents. Using a self-concept scale, the psychologist obtained the following data. She set $P = .05$ as the level of significance. Calculate the Pearson product-moment correlation coefficient for these data. Should the null hypothesis be rejected?

Teacher ratings	Parent ratings	Teacher ratings	Parent ratings
20	23	27	24
21	21	29	25
23	20	30	29
25	26	35	36
25	28	38	38

6. Compute the coefficient of determination for the data in Exercise 5. What does it indicate about the relationship between the variables of teacher ratings and parent ratings of children's self concepts?

7. A probation officer wished to determine if there was any relationship between the ages at which juveniles are arrested and their adjustment scores at the end of their probationary period. He set $P = .01$ as the level of significance and obtained the following data. Should the null hypothesis be rejected?

Age at arrest	Adjustment score	Age at arrest	Adjustment score
12	30	15	36
13	35	16	37
14	34	16	32
14	33	17	37
15	34	18	34
15	30		

8. Compute the coefficient of determination for the data in Exercise 7. What does it indicate about the relationship between ages of arrest of juveniles and their adjustment scores after probation?

CHAPTER 15
REGRESSION

We have seen that the correlation coefficient is a useful statistical index for describing the degree of relationship between two variables. It follows that if two variables are correlated, it should be possible to estimate the score an individual would obtain on one variable if we know his score on the related variable. For example, if we know that social competence is positively correlated with chronological age, we can predict that 8-year-old children will receive higher social competence scores than 5-year-old children. However, this estimate usually is not precise enough for our purposes. We need a method for predicting the values of social-competence scores for children at various age levels. For the data given in Figure 14-1 (page 139), we could "predict" that an individual with a spelling score of 5 would obtain an arithmetic score of 5. This prediction could be made with complete accuracy, because the correlation between these two variables was perfect. Variables in the behavioral sciences seldom correlate perfectly, but even with less than perfect correlations, we can make a fairly good prediction of an individual's score on one variable, if we are given his score on another related variable, by a statistical method known as *regression analysis*.

Through the formulas used in regression analysis, we can make theoretical predictions based on examination of the relationship between the data on the predictor variable and the data on the predicted variable from a sample of individuals. In this context, the term *prediction* is not limited solely to making future projections; it also means estimating a person's present status on one variable, given his present status on the related variable.

As we did in the case of correlations, we shall consider only the situation in which two variables are linearly related. The method we will use is called *linear regression;* it is based upon our ability to place a best-fitting straight line, called a *regression line*, through two sets of correlated data. We shall develop a method, known as the *regression equation*, for mathematically describing the regression line.

In regression analysis, we assign the symbol X to the *predictor* variable, and Y to the *predicted* variable. The regression equation permits us to predict an individual's Y score if we know his X score. To illustrate this procedure, we will use the data presented in Example 15-1.

Example 15-1
A school librarian noticed that students who spend a good deal of time in the library tend to receive higher achievement scores than those who use the library infrequently. He wished to establish a method for predicting a student's achievement score once he knew the number of hours the student spent in the library. The librarian collected the following data on 24 students:

Average number of hours per week in library (X)	Achievement-test scores (Y)	Average number of hours per week in library (X)	Achievement-test scores (Y)
1	1	6	3
2	1	6	5
2	3	6	7
2	4	7	5
3	2	7	5
3	2	7	7
4	4	8	4
4	4	8	8
4	6	8	9
5	2	9	7
5	3	9	8
5	6	9	9

In Example 15-1, the predictor variable (X) is the average number of hours per week students spend in the library and the predicted variable (Y) is their achievement scores. Figure 15-1 shows the scatter diagram for these data.

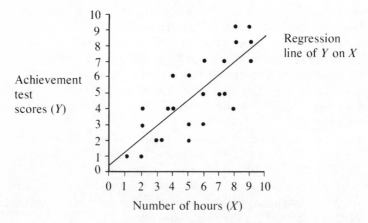

Figure 15-1. Scatter diagram of achievement-test scores and number of hours in library, with the regression line of Y on X.

Suppose we know that a student spends an average of two hours per week in the library, and we wish to predict his achievement score. The data in this study indicate that three students in the sample averaged two hours per week in the library, and they received achievement scores of 1, 3, and 4. Therefore, one way to predict this student's score is to take the average of these three scores, which is 2.67, and use it as the predicted score. By this process, we predict that a student averaging two hours per week in the library will receive an achievement score of 2.67. But this estimate is based on a sample of only three students! Logic tells us that a prediction based on such a small sample is of limited value because of the amount of sampling error that is likely to be involved. We will feel more confident if we can use all of the data obtained in our sample to determine the predicted value. We need to establish the trend of the Y scores as they relate to the X scores, and this trend should be derived from all of the available data.

Our first task, then, is to determine the best-fitting line in this scatter diagram that can be used to predict Y scores on the basis of X scores. Such a line is called the *regression line of Y on X*. This line should be positioned in the diagram so that the sum of squares of the vertical distances of the data from the regression line is as small as possible. To position this line precisely in the scatter diagram, we must locate at least two points on it. The regression line can then be drawn through these two points. To locate points on the regression line, we use the regression equation, which is given in Formula 33.

Formula 33. Calculation of the regression equation.

$$\tilde{Y} = a + b_{yx}X$$

in which $\tilde{Y}$ is the predicted value of Y

In Formula 33, the symbol $\tilde{Y}$ indicates a predicted value of Y that corresponds to a given X. The symbol b_{yx} is called the *regression coefficient of Y on X*, and the symbol a is called the *Y intercept*. First, we shall illustrate how this formula is used to position the regression line in the scatter diagram, and then we will present the formulas used to compute b_{yx} and a.

The regression coefficient, b_{yx}, describes the *slope of the best-fitting line,* by specifying the amount of increase on the Y variable that accompanies one unit of increase on the X variable. The regression coefficient can be described as b_{yx} = vertical change/horizontal change.

Figure 15-2 shows a regression line of Y on X developed from data on two related variables. The actual scatter of the data around this regression line has been omitted in the figure. The regression of Y on X in Figure 15-2 indicates that for every 10 units of horizontal change (on the X variable), there are 5 units of vertical change (on the Y variable). Therefore,

$$b_{yx} = 5 \text{ units}/10 \text{ units} = .5,$$

which is the ratio of vertical change to horizontal change.

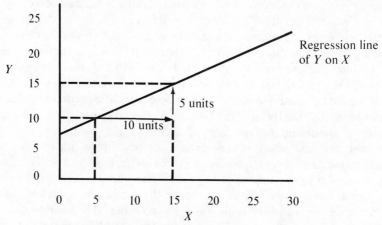

Figure 15-2. Regression line of Y on X (data omitted).

The b_{yx} indicates the amount of increase in Y that is accompanied by an increase in X. A negative b_{yx} value indicates that an increase in Y is accompanied by a *decrease* in X.

In Formula 33, a is called the Y *intercept*, and it represents the value of Y that corresponds to $X = 0$; that is, it is the value of Y at the point where the regression line crosses the Y axis. In Figure 15-2, the regression line of Y on X intersects the Y axis at $Y = 7$; that is, when $X = 0$, $Y = 7$. Therefore, in this example, $a = 7$.

From the regression line in Figure 15-2 we have determined the values of b_{yx} and a. By substituting these values in Formula 33, we can state the regression equation for this figure as $\tilde{Y} = 7 + .5X$. This equation can be used to obtain the predicted value of Y (symbolized by $\tilde{Y}$) for a given X value by substituting the X value in the equation and solving for $\tilde{Y}$. For example, for $X = 25$, $\tilde{Y} = 7 + .5(25) = 19.5$. Here, we have used the regression equation to predict that a person receiving an X of 25 will have a Y of 19.5.

We have used Figure 15-2 to illustrate how we determine b_{yx} and a by examining the placement and slope of the regression line in a scatter diagram. In actual practice, however, if we wish to draw the regression line for Y on X, we proceed in reverse fashion, using the obtained data on two variables to determine the values of b_{yx} and a, which we then use to form the regression equation. Thus, to develop the regression equation from the data given in Example 15-1, and to draw the regression line in the scatter diagram in Figure 15-1, we need to compute the values represented by b_{yx} and a.

Formula 34 shows the calculation of the regression coefficient of Y on X from sample data.

Formula 34. Calculation of the regression coefficient of Y on X.

$$b_{yx} = \frac{\Sigma XY - \dfrac{(\Sigma X)(\Sigma Y)}{N}}{\Sigma X^2 - \dfrac{(\Sigma X)^2}{N}}$$

Applying this formula to the data in Example 15-1, where $\Sigma X = 130$, $\Sigma Y = 115$, $\Sigma X^2 = 844$, $\Sigma Y^2 = 689$, and $\Sigma XY = 733$, we obtain:

$$\text{Using Formula 34: } b_{yx} = \frac{733 - \dfrac{(130)(115)}{24}}{844 - \dfrac{(130)^2}{24}} = .79$$

Formula 35 is the formula for calculating the value of the Y intercept.

Formula 35. Calculation of the Y intercept.

$$a = \bar{Y} - b_{yx}\,\bar{X}$$

In Example 15-1, $\bar{Y} = 4.79$ and $\bar{X} = 5.42$. We determine the value of the Y intercept by using Formula 35: $a = 4.79 - .79(5.42) = .51$.

Having calculated both b_{yx} and a, we can use Formula 33 to state the regression equation of Y and X for Example 15-1.

Using Formula 33: $\tilde{Y} = .51 + .79X$

We may now use this regression equation to predict the value of Y for any selected value of X. Using the data in Example 15-1, suppose we wish to predict a student's achievement score when we know that he has used the library for two hours per week, or for eight hours per week. Using the regression equation:

For $X = 2$: $\tilde{Y} = .51 + .79(2) = 2.09$

For $X = 8$: $\tilde{Y} = .51 + .79(8) = 6.83$

If we wish to draw the regression line of Y on X in Figure 15-1, we simply place a dot at $X = 2$, $Y = 2.09$ and a dot at $X = 8$, $Y = 6.83$, and draw the regression line through these two dots.

Another way of locating the regression line is based on the fact that the line always passes through the point in the scatter diagram where the means of the two variables coincide. Therefore, we know that the regression line passes through the point at which $\bar{X} = 5.42$ and $\bar{Y} = 4.79$. We learned earlier that a gives the value of Y corresponding to $X = 0$. In our example, $a = .51$, so we know that the regression line also passes through the point at which $X = 0$ and $Y = .51$. Therefore, using the mean values and a, we can determine two points in the scatter diagram through which we can draw the regression line. The regression line can be used directly to obtain a predicted Y value for any given X value merely by locating the point on the line directly above the X value and reading the corresponding Y value on the vertical axis.

It should be obvious that we do not have to actually prepare a scatter diagram and draw the regression line to be able to predict Y scores. All we have to do is to use Formulas 33, 34, and 35 to develop the regression equation, and then use this equation to calculate Y for any X value.

The Regression of X on Y

Up to this point we have been concerned with defining one regression line, that of Y on X. It is possible to develop a second regression equation that will permit us to predict X values for given values of Y. This second regression line and its regression equation describe the regression of X on Y. The line depicting the regression of X on Y will differ from the regression line of Y on X whenever the correlation between the two variables is less than perfect. Only when $r = 1.00$ or -1.00 will the two regression lines be identical.

The formulas for predicting X values corresponding to given Y variables are Formulas 36, 37, and 38.

Formulas 36 through 38. Formulas for calculation of the regression of X on Y.

Formula 36 $\qquad \tilde{X} = a + b_{xy}Y$ (regression equation)

Formula 37 $\qquad b_{xy} = \dfrac{\Sigma XY - \dfrac{(\Sigma X)(\Sigma Y)}{N}}{\Sigma Y^2 - \dfrac{(\Sigma Y)^2}{N}}$ (regression coefficient)

Formula 38 $\qquad a = \bar{X} - b_{xy}\bar{Y}$

in which $\tilde{X}$ is the predicted value of X

Formula 36 gives the regression equation for X on Y, with the predicted value of X symbolized by $\tilde{X}$. Formula 37 is the formula for determining the regression coefficient of X on Y, which is symbolized by b_{xy} (rather than b_{yx}, as in Formula 34). The numerator of this formula is identical to the numerator of Formula 34, but the denominator represents the sum of squares for the Y variable. Formula 38 shows how to calculate the X intercept, and it yields the value of X corresponding to $Y = 0$. Thus, it gives the value of X at the point where the regression line crosses the Y axis. The regression lines cross each other at the point in the scatter diagram where $\bar{X}$ and $\bar{Y}$ coincide.

To illustrate the computation of the regression equation for X on Y and the location of the regression line, suppose the librarian in Example 15-1 wished to predict the average number of hours a student used the library corresponding to a given achievement score. (This seems somewhat unlikely, but such a prediction can be made using regression techniques.) Applying Formulas 36, 37 and 38 to the data in Example 15-1, we obtain:

$$\text{Using Formula 37: } b_{xy} = \frac{733 - \dfrac{(130)(115)}{24}}{689 - \dfrac{(115)^2}{24}} = .80$$

Using Formula 38: $a = 5.42 - .80(4.79) = 1.59$

Using Formula 36: $\tilde{X} = 1.59 + .80Y$

We can use the regression equation given in Formula 36 to predict X values corresponding to given Y values. For example, if a student received an achievement score of $Y = 4$, we can predict that the average time he has spent in the library has been $\tilde{X} = 1.59 + .80(4) = 4.79$ hours per week. For a student with $Y = 9$, we can predict that his average weekly library time has been $\tilde{X} = 1.59 + .80(9) = 8.79$ hours per week.

Figure 15-3 depicts the same scatter diagram as Figure 15-1, but it shows both regression lines. Notice that the regression line of X on Y crosses the X axis at $X = 1.59$ (the value of a, which is computed by using Formula 38), and also that the two regression lines intersect at the point where the means of the X and Y scores coincide.

Although we have shown that regression equations can be used to predict values on both the X and Y variables, we must stress that it would be foolish to conclude that a student with a particular X value would, in fact, have the precise value of Y that the equation predicted. A more correct interpretation is that the average Y score of students who have a given X score will tend to be close to the predicted Y value. Thus, the regression line can be thought to represent a kind of continuous mean that gives us the expected value, or mean, of Y for a particular X value. In fact, there are statistical techniques that permit us to develop confidence intervals for the population mean of Y for any given value of X (and for the population mean of X for any given value of Y).

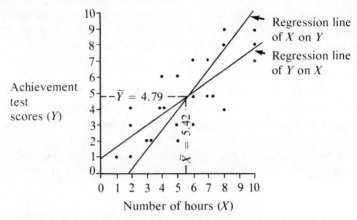

Figure 15-3. Scatter diagram of achievement-test scores and number of hours in library, with regression lines of Y on X and X on Y.

Exercises: Group A

1. A random sample of 14-year-old educable mentally retarded children was selected, and each child's mother and father were asked to rate the child's problem-solving ability. The following ratings were obtained. Using X for the mother ratings and Y for the father ratings, determine the regression equation for father ratings on mother ratings.

Mother Rating	Father Rating	Mother Rating	Father Rating
5	10	25	35
10	15	30	25
10	20	35	35
15	5	40	25
15	15	40	35
20	15	40	45
20	25	45	35
25	20	50	25

2. Using the regression equation developed in Exercise 1, predict the father rating for an educable mentally retarded child who receives a mother rating of 15. For one who receives a mother rating of 40.

3. Construct a scatter diagram of the distribution in Exercise 1 and draw in the regression line of Y on X.

4. For the data in Exercise 1, determine the regression equation of mother ratings on father ratings.

5. Using the regression equation developed in Exercise 4, predict the mother rating for an educable mentally retarded child who receives a father rating of 20. For one who receives a father rating of 45.

6. In the scatter diagram for Exercise 3, draw the regression line of X on Y.

Exercises: Group B

7. A university admissions officer collected the high-school grade-point averages (GPAs) and the university entrance-examination scores of a randomly selected group of applicants. The following data were obtained. Using X for the GPAs and Y for the entrance-examination scores, determine the regression equation for entrance-examination scores on GPAs.

GPA	Entrance-examination scores
2.8	22
2.8	23
2.9	23
2.9	25
3.0	24
3.0	26
3.1	23
3.1	26
3.2	24
3.2	27
3.3	23
3.3	26
3.4	25
3.4	27
3.5	25
3.5	28
3.6	27
3.6	29

8. Using the regression equation developed in Exercise 7, predict the entrance-examination score for a student who received a high-school GPA of 2.9. For one who received a GPA of 3.5.

9. Draw a scatter diagram of the data in Exercise 7 and draw in the regression line of Y on X.

10. For the data in Exercise 7, determine the regression equation for GPAs on entrance-examination scores.

11. Using the regression equation developed in Exercise 10, predict the GPA for a student who receives an entrance-examination score of 23. For one who receives an entrance-examination score of 28.

12. In the scatter diagram for Exercise 9, draw in the regression line of X on Y.

CHAPTER 16
THE SPEARMAN
RANK-ORDER
CORRELATION

In the preceding chapters, we have explored a variety of statistical techniques for testing research hypotheses. In all of the tests presented, we have made several assumptions regarding the population distribution from which the sample or samples were selected. One of these assumptions is that the variable or variables in the population under study are normally distributed. Other assumptions were made for specific tests. For example, an assumption underlying the use of the Pearson product-moment correlation is that the variables are linearly related. To use these tests properly, we had to make some assumptions about the parameters of the population or populations from which the sample data were obtained. Therefore, such tests are called *parametric* tests.

Statistical methods that do not require assumptions about population parameters are termed *distribution-free,* or *nonparametric* statistical techniques.

In this chapter and in Chapter 17, we will examine two of the most commonly used distribution-free statistical methods. First, we will consider a correlational technique called the Spearman rank-order correlation, in which no assumptions about the population distribution are required. This correlation gives us a measure of the relationship between two variables where the data are in the form of relative rankings of individuals on each variable. In such cases, the data represent measurements on the ordinal scale. The Spearman rank-order correlation is represented by the Greek letter *rho* (ρ).

Example 16-1 gives a typical correlational study in which rho is the appropriate technique for data analysis.

Example 16-1
A high-school counselor wished to determine if there is a relationship (either positive or negative) between students' athletic ability and their level of anxiety. He ranked 12 students according to their level of anxiety as he perceived them during counseling sessions. He asked the physical-education instructor to rank these students according to their athletic ability. He set .05 as the level of significance. The following data were obtained:

Student	Athletic-ability rank	Anxiety-level rank	Student	Athletic-ability rank	Anxiety-level rank
A	1	4	G	7	10
B	2	3	H	8	8
C	3	1	I	10	7
D	4.5	6	J	10	9
E	4.5	5	K	10	12
F	6	2	L	12	11

The data given in Example 16-1 on the two variables, athletic ability and anxiety, represent the rank order of the students. It is customary, though not necessary, to assign the rank of 1 to the individual with the highest score on a variable. Where more than one individual occupies the same position in the order—that is, where two or more are "tied"—each is assigned the average of the rank that he would otherwise have received.

In Example 16-1, Student A is rated highest in athletic ability and is assigned the rank of 1. Students D and E are rated as having the same degree of athletic ability. Since they occupy the fourth and fifth positions in the rank order, each of them is assigned the average of these two ranks, which is 4.5.

The rankings in Example 16-1 indicate that there is a tendency for students who are ranked high on one variable to be ranked high on the other variable also. To make a statistical test of this relationship, we proceed in a manner similar to that used in calculating the Pearson product-moment correlation coefficient. The null hypothesis to be tested can be stated as "There is no relationship between the variables of athletic ability and anxiety in high-school students." Our task is to answer the statistical question "What is the probability that the obtained relationship between the rankings of a sample of individuals on these two variables is a result of sampling error?" In Example 16-1, the counselor set .05 as the level of significance. In this study the counselor is interested in detecting a relationship, either positive or negative, between the two variables. Therefore, a nondirectional hypothesis test is appropriate.

The statistical technique appropriate for testing the null hypothesis in this example is the Spearman rank-order correlation. Formula 39 shows the method of computation for this correlation coefficient.

Formula 39. Calculation of Spearman's rank-order correlation coefficient (rho).

$$\rho = 1 - \frac{6\Sigma D^2}{N(N^2 - 1)}$$

in which D = difference between a pair of ranks
N = number of pairs of ranks

Formula 39 indicates that we must determine ΣD^2, which is obtained by taking the difference between each student's two rankings, squaring each difference, and then summing the squares. In Formula 39, the value 6 is a constant, and N is the number of pairs of rankings, or the number of individuals in the study. The computation of rho for the data in Example 16-1 is shown in Table 16.1

Table 16-1. Computation for rho for data in Example 16-1

Student	Athletic-ability ranking	Anxiety-level ranking	D	D₂
A	1	4	3	9
B	2	3	1	1
C	3	1	-2	4
D	4.5	6	1.5	2.25
E	4.5	5	0.5	0.25
F	6	2	-4	16
G	7	10	3	9
H	8	8	0	0
I	10	7	-3	9
J	10	9	-1	1
K	10	12	2	4
L	12	11	-1	1
$N = 12$				$\Sigma D^2 = 56.5$

Using Formula 39: $\rho = 1 - \dfrac{6(56.5)}{12(12^2 - 1)} = .802$

Table 5 in the back of the book is used to evaluate the significance of ρ. The column headings in this table are the same as those used in Table 4. Notice that the first column on the left-hand side is designated N, the number of pairs of ranks in the correlation. The concept of degrees of freedom does not apply when we use this statistical technique.

The values of ρ given in the body of Table 5 represent the critical values at varying significance levels for nondirectional hypothesis tests. Therefore, these values indicate both the positive and negative critical values of ρ, with the probability level divided equally between the two tails of the various sampling distributions of ρ.

In Example 16-1, where the counselor designated .05 as the significance level for making a nondirectional hypothesis test, and where $N = 12$, Table 5 indicates that a ρ of .591 or larger is needed to reject the null hypothesis. The obtained $\rho = .802$ is therefore large enough to permit the rejection of the null hypothesis. Thus, the data indicate that students with exceptional athletic ability tend to be more anxious than students with low athletic ability. The counselor may then conclude that there is a positive relationship between athletic ability and anxiety levels of high-school students.

The Spearman rank-order correlation is also commonly used in situations in which the assumption that the variables are normally distributed in the population is unwarranted. Such an instance is described in Example 16-2.

Example 16-2

A special-education teacher gave each of the eight educable mentally retarded students in the class a manual-dexterity test. The teacher hypothesized that there is a positive relationship between the students' manual dexterity and their IQ scores. The level of significance was set at .01. The teacher obtained the following data:

Student	Manual-dexterity scores	IQ scores
A	21	84
B	6	70
C	18	84
D	22	85
E	9	84
F	4	73
G	21	79
H	20	75

The data in Example 16-2 reveal that manual dexterity scores cannot be assumed to be normally distributed in the population of educable mentally retarded students. Also, we cannot assume that IQ scores are normally distributed in this particular population. If either or both variables cannot meet the assumption of normality, then the parametric Pearson product-moment correlation is not warranted, and we must turn to the nonparametric rank-order correlation.

To apply this technique, we must first convert the scores on each variable to rankings. For the variable of manual dexterity, we assign a rank of 1 to student D, who has the highest score. Two students, A and G, had scores of 21, so each is assigned the average of ranks 2 and 3, which is 2.5. The other manual-dexterity scores are ranked in order of magnitude. The same procedure is followed for the IQ scores. Students A, C, and E all have the same IQ and occupy ranks 2, 3, and 4. Accordingly, each is assigned the average rank of 3. The rankings of the scores on each variable and the computation of ρ appear in Table 16-2 on page 162.

Using Formula 39: $\rho = 1 - \dfrac{6(25.5)}{8(8^2 - 1)} = .696$

Because the teacher hypothesized that there would be a positive correlation between these two variables in the population, a directional test is made. When we test directional hypotheses, we must double the probability levels listed in Table 5, just as we did for Table 4, thereby placing the entire rejection region in one tail of the sampling distribution of ρ. Thus, for directional tests, the column headings in Table 5 become $P = .05, P = .025,$ $P = .01,$ and $P = .005.$

In Example 16-2, where $N = 8$, a ρ of at least .833 is required to reject the null hypothesis for a directional test at the .01 significance level. Our obtained correlation, $\rho = .696$, is not large enough to permit us to reject the null hypothesis, and we must conclude that this correlation may be due solely to sampling error.

Table 16-2. Computation of rho for data in Example 16-2.

Student	Manual-dexterity Score	Rank	IQ Score	Rank	D	D_2
A	21	2.5	84	3	0.5	0.25
B	6	7	70	8	1	1
C	18	5	84	3	−2	4
D	22	1	85	1	0	0
E	9	6	84	3	−3	9
F	4	8	73	7	−1	1
G	21	2.5	79	5	2.5	6.25
H	20	4	75	6	2	4
$N = 8$					$\Sigma D^2 = 25.5$	

Of course, the validity of our decision regarding the null hypothesis rests on the assumption that the individuals in the sample have been randomly selected and are representative (within sampling error) of the population to which we wish to generalize. This is true of all statistical tests. In Examples 16-1 and 16-2, both samples were deliberately kept small for computational convenience. In reality, much larger samples would be needed to provide definitive findings. (It is highly unlikely that the eight students in the educable mentally retarded class are representative of all such students!)

In summary, the nonparametric technique of Spearman's rank-order correlation provides us with a way to calculate the degree of relationship between two variables where the data are in the form of ordinal measurements, or where the assumption that the variables are normally distributed in the population is untenable and the data are in interval or ratio form.

Various nonparametric techniques that are not presented in this text may be used instead of the parametric techniques we have discussed, such as the *t* test and the analysis of variance, where the shape of the population distribution is either unknown or known to be nonnormal. The question arises "If nonparametric techniques do not require us to assume anything about the shape of the population distribution, why don't we always use them rather than the parametric techniques?"

Parametric techniques are preferred when they are appropriate because they are more powerful than their nonparametric counterparts. If a correlation (or difference between means) exists in the population, a parametric technique is more likely to produce a significant finding; thus, the probability of making a Type II error (not rejecting a true null hypothesis) is less with a parametric technique.

Also, studies have shown that parametric tests are quite robust in cases where the underlying assumptions are violated. This means that even if a population distribution is quite nonnormal in shape, the parametric tests still tend to give us valid findings. This is especially true when sample sizes are large.

For these reasons, we find parametric tests used even when the assumption of normality in the population is questionable. On the other hand, the use of nonparametric techniques is becoming increasingly widespread, especially when small samples are involved.

Exercises: Group A

1. A college professor wished to determine if there was any relationship between the length of time students took to complete an English final exam and the grades they received on the exam. She rank-ordered the finishing times, assigning the rank of 1 to the fastest student. She set $P = .05$ as the level of significance and obtained the following data. Should the null hypothesis be rejected?

Rank of completion times	Scores on English exam	Rank of completion times	Scores on English exam
1	39	7	33
2.5	42	7	37
2.5	36	7	41
4	38	9	40
5	42	10	41

2. A developmental psychologist wished to test the hypothesis that there is a direct relationship between the scores that pairs of twins receive on a spacial-relations test. She selected 14 pairs of twins and obtained the following test data. She could not assume that the scores were normally distributed in the population. Setting $P = .01$ as the level of significance, should the null hypothesis be rejected?

Score of first twin	Score of second twin	Score of first twin	Score of second twin
25	26	23	19
18	17	27	32
20	24	24	23
17	19	24	21
25	31	32	27
21	19	24	29
33	34	29	29

3. A school psychologist wished to determine if there was any relationship between the IQs of high-school students and the degree to which they were accepted by their peers. He randomly selected a sample of students and ranked them according to peer ratings, assigning a rank of 1 to the most accepted student. Below are the IQs and the peer-acceptance rankings. He set $P = .05$ as the level of significance. Should the null hypothesis be rejected?

IQ	Rank of peer Acceptance	IQ	Rank of peer Acceptance
91	9	102	3
95	11	104	8
96	10	104	5
99	1	104	13
99	5	110	7
100	2	115	14
101	12	119	15
101	5	122	16

Exercises: Group B

4. Two samples of seventh-grade students were matched on the basis of their IQs; one group was given Form A of a social-studies test and the other group was given Form B of the same test. The test developers wished to test the hypothesis that there was a positive relationship between the two sets of data. They could not assume that the scores were normally distributed in the population. They set $P = .01$ as the level of significance. Should the null hypothesis be rejected?

Form A	Form B	Form A	Form B
141	139	145	143
154	146	149	150
149	157	145	139
160	157	132	130
145	145	129	134
156	159		

5. A high-school athletic coach wished to test the hypothesis that there was no relationship between the swimming ability and height in students. She ranked the students on their swimming ability, assigning a rank of 1 to the best swimmer, and also measured their heights. She set $P = .05$ as the level of significance. From the following data, should the null hypothesis be rejected?

Swimming ranks	Heights in inches	Swimming ranks	Heights in inches
1	68	4	70
3	66	5.5	70
5.5	63	8	65
2	70	9	69
7	64		

6. A director of a preschool program wished to determine if there was a positive relationship between teacher and parent evaluations of the level of social competence of preschool children. She asked a random sample of parents to rate their children on social competence, and also obtained the teacher's rankings for the same children, with the rank of 1 assigned to the most socially competent child. She obtained the following data. Setting $P = .01$ as the level of significance, should the null hypothesis be rejected?

Parent ratings	Teacher rankings	Parent ratings	Teacher rankings
69	8	60	9.5
61	13	80	4
57	12	64	14
84	2	69	6
59	11	75	9.5
72	6	89	3
79	1	85	6

CHAPTER 17
CHI SQUARE

Statistical problems are frequently encountered in which the data are in the form of frequencies rather than score values; in these cases, our job is to determine whether the distribution of the frequencies across a set of categories differs from a set of expected frequencies. The statistical procedure that is appropriate for such problems is a commonly used nonparametric technique called *chi square*. It is symbolized by χ^2, using the capital Greek letter, chi (rhymes with eye). Whenever data can be classified into a set of mutually exclusive categories, we can use a chi-square sampling distribution to determine the probability that the distribution of observed frequencies differs from the distribution of expected frequencies, based upon a given hypothesis.

The chi-square technique is appropriate to use when we are solving three basic types of problems involving the comparison of observed and expected frequencies. These three types, which will be examined in this chapter, are the test for goodness of fit, the test for the independence of two variables, and the test for equality of proportions. The three types differ in the hypothesis that is to be tested and in the method by which the expected frequencies are determined. Each of these tests involves the use of a chi-square sampling distribution.

The Test for Goodness of Fit

Problems in which we wish to determine whether the distribution of frequencies across a set of categories observed in a sample can reasonably be regarded as fitting a hypothetical set of frequencies in a population require a goodness-of-fit test. Example 17-1 illustrates the simplest form of a study involving the goodness-of-fit test.

Example 17-1
A marketer wished to determine whether there was a difference in the preference of U.S. business executives for Brand A and Brand B cigarettes. He randomly selected 50 business executives, had each of them try both

brands, and noted that 17 preferred Brand A and 33 preferred Brand B. He chose .05 as his significance level for making a statistical test.

Notice that the type of data collected in Example 17-1 is not in the form of scores or ranks, but in terms of frequencies of responses to the two brands of cigarettes. These data represent the nominal level of measurement since they are merely frequencies that fall into alternative categories. In addition, the data represent frequencies of occurrence of discrete events; thus, they represent discrete measurements rather than continuous variables. This means that an individual event, such as the choice between brands in our example, falls either into one category or into the other; a person's choice cannot be split between categories. The result is that the data are in the form of integers, such as 40-10, 38-12, or 29-21, indicating that one brand is favored over the other.

Using the chi-square technique, we can determine the probability that the frequencies we observe in our sample differ from a set of hypothesized frequencies. In Example 17-1, the null hypothesis being tested is that there is no difference between the number of business executives in the population who prefer Brand A and the number who prefer Brand B. If the null hypothesis is correct, we would expect 25 of the 50 executives to choose Brand A and 25 to choose Brand B. In the chi-square test, these are called the expected frequencies; that is, they are the frequencies we would expect to occur by chance.

Since we found that 17 business executives preferred Brand A and 33 preferred Brand B, these are called the observed frequencies. The data indicate that more executives preferred Brand B than Brand A, but, as is true of all situations in which we obtain data from samples, there is a possibility that the difference between the preferences is due to sampling error and not to a true difference in the population. Our question, then, is "Are the observed frequencies sufficiently different from the expected frequencies to justify rejection of the null hypothesis?"

The chi-square test provides us with a statistic based on the differences between observed and expected frequencies. The test tells us at what level of probability (for instance, the $P = .01$ or the $P = .05$ level) the difference between observed and expected frequencies is significant. Thus, by this test we determine whether the observed frequencies in our sample differ significantly from the expected frequencies based on the null hypothesis. If they do, we reject the null hypothesis and conclude that the population of business executives prefers Brand B over Brand A. If they do not differ significantly, we conclude that the difference in frequencies obtained from our sample may be due to sampling error.

In preparation for chi-square analysis, the observed and expected frequencies in Example 17-1 are presented in a summary table below:

	Observed (O)	Expected (E)
Brand A	17	25
Brand B	33	25
Total	50	50

We are now ready to test the null hypothesis using the chi-square technique. Formula 40 is the formula for the simplest type of chi-square analysis, the type used in Example 17-1, where observed frequencies fall into only two categories, which are called *cells* in chi-square tests.

Formula 40. Calculation of the chi square when $df = 1$.

$$\chi^2 = \sum \frac{(|O - E| - .5)^2}{E}$$

in which O = observed frequency
E = expected frequency

The subtraction of .5 from each $|O - E|$ represents Yates's correction for continuity.

In using Formula 40 to compute χ^2, we are concerned with the difference between O and E in each cell. In the formula the two vertical bars encompassing $O - E$ indicate that we are only interested in the absolute difference between O and E. This means that we only consider the magnitude of the difference, regardless of whether it is positive or negative.

Formula 40 indicates that for the first cell (Brand A), we subtract .5 from the absolute difference, square the remainder, and divide by its expected frequency (E). We then follow the same process for the second cell (Brand B), and sum the values for both cells (indicated by Σ) to arrive at the chi-square statistic. The calculation of χ^2, using Formula 40 for the data in Example 17-1, is given below:

	O	E	O − E	|O − E| − .5
Brand A	17	25	−8	7.5
Brand B	33	25	8	7.5

Using Formula 40: $\chi^2 = \dfrac{(7.5)^2}{25} + \dfrac{(7.5)^2}{25} = 4.50$

We now need to evaluate this χ^2 using the appropriate chi-square sampling distribution. As was the case with the t distributions and F distributions, there is a family of chi-square distributions, with each distribution based upon a specific number of degrees of freedom. However, the degrees of freedom associated with a particular χ^2 test do not depend upon the size of the sample, as they did in the t and F distributions, but represent the number of cells in which observed frequencies are "free to vary." For the simplest use of the χ^2 technique, the df are determined by the number of cells minus one. This is because if there are 50 frequencies in the study, any number of them may be assigned to one cell, for example, Brand A; that is, the frequencies in this cell are "free to vary." However, once the frequency in that cell is ascertained, the frequency in the other cell is fixed— that is, not free to vary. In the example involving the 50 business executives, any number could have chosen Brand A. However, once it is determined that 17 executives actually did so, then the number of executives choosing Brand B is fixed at 33. Thus, in this example, the frequency in only one cell was free to vary; therefore, $df = 1$.

Figure 17-1 shows the shapes of the sampling distributions of chi square for 1, 5, and 15 degrees of freedom. Every possible value of the degrees of freedom has its own distinct curve. Examination of these curves reveals some interesting properties of χ^2 distributions. First, χ^2 values depicted on the horizontal axis are all positive, with $\chi^2 = 0$ as the left-hand limit of the distributions. Secondly, as the df increases, the shapes of the χ^2 distributions approach the normal curve. Thirdly, if we assume that the null hypothesis is true, we expect the value of chi square to be equal to the df associated with it. That is, for chi square with $df = 5$, we would expect to obtain $\chi^2 = 5$ if the null hypothesis is true. As we have found in other statistical tests, the sampling distribution of χ^2 around this expected value is due to sampling error. The expected chi-square values for $df = 1$, $df = 5$, and $df = 15$ are shown as dotted lines in Figure 17-1.

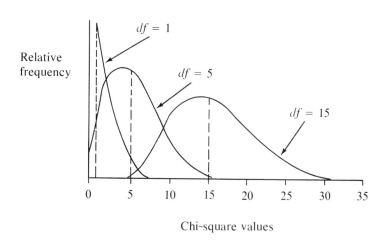

Figure 17-1. Sampling distributions of χ^2 for $df = 1$, $df = 5$, and $df = 15$.

Chi-square tests are always tests of nondirectional hypotheses, in which the right-hand tail of the appropriate χ^2 sampling distribution represents the area for rejection of the null hypothesis. Thus, the chi-square technique determines whether there is a significant difference between the O and E frequencies in the cells, not whether a particular cell has a smaller or a larger frequency than expected.

In performing a χ^2 test, we are deciding whether our obtained χ^2 is so large that it is unlikely to have come from the appropriate χ^2 sampling distribution. Large χ^2 values are located in the right-hand tail of the distribution, and they become more improbable as they grow larger. Critical values of χ^2 designating $P = .05$ and $P = .01$ in the right-hand tail of the various sampling distributions of χ^2 are given in Table 6 at the back of the book. For χ^2 with $df = 1$, a value of 3.84 is needed for significance at $P = .05$. In Example 17-1, we obtained $\chi^2 = 4.50$. Therefore, we reject the null hypothesis that there is no difference in the preferences of business executives for Brand A and Brand B cigarettes, since the data indicate that Brand B is preferred.

Formula 40 shows that the size of the obtained chi square is determined by the size of the discrepancies between O and E in the cells. The evaluation of the significance of a chi square is based on the comparison of the obtained test statistic with the appropriate sampling distribution of χ^2. Since the test statistic is derived from actual sample data, which are discrete measurements, Formula 40 provides for a correction factor that results in a test statistic whose sampling distribution more closely approximates the continuous sampling distribution of chi square. This correction, called *Yates's correction for continuity,* is incorporated in Formula 40 in the form of the subtraction of .5 from the absolute discrepancies between O and E for each cell. Its function is to reduce the discrepancies between O and E and to bring the obtained χ^2, which is based on discrete frequencies, more in line with the continuous function of the sampling distribution. Yates's correction for continuity is appropriate for all chi-square analyses in which $df = 1$.

The chi-square test illustrated above involves categorizing the data on one variable for a single sample. It is called a goodness-of-fit test because it provides an index of how close the fit is between the observed and expected frequencies, and it is appropriate for testing a variety of hypotheses since it can test the goodness of fit between the observed frequencies and any set of expected frequencies. In Example 17-1, instead of testing the null hypothesis that Brand A and Brand B were equally preferred by business executives, we could have tested the hypothesis that 75% of them preferred Brand A. In this case, we would set 37.5 (75% of 50) as the expected frequency for Brand A and 12.5 (25% of 50) as the expected frequency for Brand B. We would then use these expected frequencies in Formula 40 to calculate chi square.

The Test for Independence of Two Variables

In the goodness-of-fit test, we employed the chi-square technique to the one-variable situation. Chi square can also be employed to test the hypothesis that the population frequency distribution among the categories on one variable is independent of the distribution on the other variable.

Example 17-2

A scout executive wished to determine if there was a difference between 11-year-old and 14-year-old scouts in their preference for swimming or hiking activities. He randomly selected 28 11-year-olds and 30 14-year-olds from the membership of the local scout council and did a survey. He set .05 as his level of significance and obtained the following data:

	Age of scouts		
	11 years	14 years	Total
Hiking	19	12	31
Swimming	9	18	27
Total	28	30	58

Example 17-2 presents data involving the two variables of age and activity preference for a group of scouts. The data given in this example are called contingency data, and the table is referred to as a contingency table. In this example, we wish to determine whether the frequency distribution of respondents according to age is independent of the frequency distribution according to activity preference, or whether activity preference is in some way contingent upon the ages of the scouts. The null hypothesis to be tested is that the population distribution of activity preferences is independent of the ages of scouts.

The degrees of freedom in Example 17-2 are $df = 1$ because, given the row and column totals shown, once the frequency in any one of the four cells is ascertained, the frequencies of the other three cells are fixed—that is, they are not free to vary. Thus, if 19 is given as the frequency of 11-year-olds choosing hiking, the frequencies in the other three cells must be as they are shown in the example.

In general, the degrees of freedom for a chi-square analysis are determined by: (number of rows $- 1$) (number of columns $- 1$). In Example 17-2, where there is a 2×2 matrix, $df = (2 - 1)(2 - 1) = 1$. Therefore, Formula 40 is appropriate because it incorporates Yates's correction for continuity.

To apply Formula 40, the first step is to determine the expected frequency for each cell in the matrix. If the null hypothesis that there is no difference in the preferences of 11- and 14-year-old scouts for hiking and swimming activities is true, then, since 31/58 (or 53.4%) of the total group preferred hiking, we would expect that 53.4% of the 11-year-olds (which is

53.4% of 28, or 14.95 of them) would choose hiking. For the 14-year-olds, we would expect that 53.4% of 30, or 16.02 would choose hiking. These, then, become the expected frequencies for the two categories of hiking.

Because 27/58 (or 46.6%) of the total group preferred swimming, we calculate the expected frequency of 11-year-olds preferring this activity to be 46.6% of 28, which is 13.05. The expected frequency of 14-year-olds preferring swimming is 46.6% of 30, which is 13.98. As we have seen, expected frequencies in chi-square analyses can be fractional, even though the observed frequencies cannot.

We can summarize the observed and expected frequencies for Example 17-2 as follows:

| | Ages of scouts | | | | Totals | |
| | 11 years | | 14 years | | | |
	Observed	Expected	Observed	Expected	Observed	Expected
Hiking	19	14.95	12	16.02	31	31
Swimming	9	13.05	18	13.98	27	27
Totals	28	28	30	30	58	58

This matrix illustrates the principle that the sum of the expected frequencies must equal the sum of the observed frequencies for each row and column.

To compute χ^2 using the data in this matrix:

Using Formula 40:
$$\chi^2 = \frac{(|19 - 14.95| - .5)^2}{14.95} + \frac{(|9 - 13.05| - .5)^2}{13.05}$$
$$+ \frac{(|12 - 16.02| - .5)^2}{16.02} + \frac{(|18 - 13.98| - .5)^2}{13.98} = 3.47$$

In this study, in which $df = 1$ and .05 is the level of significance, Table 6 indicates that the critical value of χ^2 is 3.84. Therefore, we cannot reject the null hypothesis that activity preference is independent of the ages of the scouts. Of course, this finding only applies to the preferences for hiking and swimming among 11- and 14-year-old scouts.

The Test for Equality of Proportions

The use of the chi-square technique is not limited to situations involving only a 2 × 2 contingency table of frequencies. Chi square can also be used to test hypotheses where frequency data are collected on a number of categories of a variable for a number of samples. Example 17-3 presents a study involving multiple samples that have yielded frequencies for multiple categories of a variable.

Example 17-3

A researcher wished to determine if preschool children whose parents were of different socioeconomic levels would have different preference patterns for animals as pets. He randomly selected children whose parents were from three socioeconomic levels and asked each child to indicate his or her favorite pet. He set .01 as the level for significance and obtained the following frequency data.

	Socioeconomic level			
Animal selected	High	Middle	Low	Row totals
Dog	17	11	7	35
Cat	16	14	9	39
Rabbit	6	11	14	31
Mouse	10	9	16	35
Column Totals	49	45	46	140

For this test, the null hypothesis is that the proportion of individuals selecting each category (animals) is the same for each of the populations sampled (socioeconomic levels); that is, it states that the proportion of children selecting dogs will be the same for the high, middle, and low socioeconomic levels. The same hypothesis is made about the proportions of children selecting cats, rabbits, and mice.

Although the null hypothesis deals with the equality of proportions, the determination of chi square does not involve the proportions in its calculation but is based instead on the frequencies given in the contingency table.

Example 17-3 presents a 4×3 matrix of frequencies. The degrees of freedom associated with the chi-square test in this example are (rows $- 1$)(columns $- 1$) $= (4 - 1)(3 - 1) = 6$. Since there are more than 1 degrees of freedom, we use Formula 41, the general formula for chi square, which does not employ Yates's correction for continuity. Before using this formula, however, we must compute the expected frequencies for each of the cells. Formula 42 gives a method for calculating the expected frequency for each cell, using row, column, and frequency totals.

To illustrate the use of Formula 42, we shall compute the expected frequency of the selection of dogs as pets by children with parents in a high

---

Formula 41. Calculation of the chi square when *df* is larger than 1.

$$\chi^2 = \sum \frac{(O - E)^2}{E}$$

Formula 42. Calculation of the expected frequency (E) of a cell.

$$E = \frac{(N_{row})(N_{col})}{N_{total}}$$

Degrees of Freedom: (number of rows $-$ 1)(number of columns $-$ 1)

---

socioeconomic level. For this cell, $N_{row} = 35$, the total frequency of children in the sample who are high socioeconomic level; $N_{col} = 49$, the total frequency of children selecting dogs as pets; and $N_{total} = 140$.

Using Formula 42: $E = \dfrac{(35)(49)}{140} = 12.25$

Therefore, we would expect that 12.25 children whose parents belong to a high socioeconomic level would select dogs as pets. The expected frequency for each of the other 11 cells in the matrix is computed in the same manner, using Formula 42 and the appropriate row and column totals. These frequencies follow.

Expected frequencies for Example 17-3

Socioeconomic level

Animal selected	High	Middle	Low	Row totals
Dog	12.25	11.25	11.50	35
Cat	13.65	12.54	12.81	39
Rabbit	10.85	9.96	10.19	31
Mouse	12.25	11.25	11.50	35
Column totals	49	45	46	140

We can now employ Formula 41 to compute the chi square, using the observed frequencies in Example 17-3 and the expected frequencies already computed.

Using Formula 41: $\chi^2 = \dfrac{(17 - 12.25)^2}{12.25} + \dfrac{(11 - 11.25)^2}{11.25} + \dfrac{(7 - 11.50)^2}{11.50}$

$$+ \frac{(16 - 13.65)^2}{13.65} + \frac{(14 - 12.54)^2}{12.54} + \frac{(9 - 12.81)^2}{12.81}$$

$$+ \frac{(6 - 10.85)^2}{10.85} + \frac{(11 - 9.96)^2}{9.96} + \frac{(14 - 10.19)^2}{10.19}$$

$$+ \frac{(10 - 12.25)^2}{12.25} + \frac{(9 - 11.25)^2}{11.25} + \frac{(16 - 11.50)^2}{11.50}$$

$$= 11.65$$

Table 6 indicates that for $df = 6$, a chi square of 16.81 is needed to be significant at the .01 level. Therefore, the obtained $\chi^2 = 11.65$ is not large enough to permit the researcher to reject the null hypothesis in Example 17-3.

The chi-square technique is a very useful statistical tool, because it can be used with any number of samples divided into any number of categories of responses. Chi-square tests are not limited solely to nominal data. In Example 17-3, the variable of socioeconomic class was divided into three categories: low, middle, and high. This variable is essentially ordinal in nature (although it can even be measured on the interval scale, if the measurement instrument is calibrated into equal intervals), but for chi-square purposes, it was considered to consist of three categories. The chi-square technique requires only that the frequency of responses be assigned to specific categories of a variable, regardless of whether the nominal, the ordinal, the interval, or the ratio level of measurement is used.

Even though chi square is a highly versatile nonparametric technique that makes no assumptions about population values, certain requirements must be met in using it properly to analyze data. These requirements are:

1. The sample or samples must have been randomly selected. This requirement applies to all statistical techniques.

2. Each response must be independent of the other responses in the study; that is, the way in which one response is categorized must in no way influence the way in which the other responses are categorized. In Example 17-3, we assumed that the choice of a pet by one child had no effect on the choice of a pet by any other child. Implicit in this requirement of independence is the assumption that each frequency must represent a different individual.

3. If the observed frequencies are obtained from a multitude of samples, they must be normally distributed around the expected frequency. This requirement is not met when the expected frequency is very small. For chi square to be properly used, each cell must have an expected frequency of at least 5 when the $df = 1$. When the df is greater than 1, this requirement may be relaxed somewhat without invalidating the chi-square procedure. Some authorities suggest that when the df is 2 or more, at least 80% of the cells should have expected frequencies of 5 or more. Note that the above discussion relates to expected frequencies, not to observed frequencies.

Exercises: Group A

1. A statistics instructor wished to determine if students differed in their preference for two types of instructional techniques. He asked a random sample of 96 students whether they preferred programmed instruction or a conventional

text. He obtained the following responses. Setting $P = .01$ as the level of significance, should the null hypothesis be rejected?

Type of Instruction	f
Programmed Instruction	57
Conventional Text	39

2. A toy manufacturer wished to know if there was a difference between boys and girls in their preference for two types of swimming-pool floats. He selected a random sample of children and asked them to choose between Type A and Type B floats. The following data were obtained. Setting $P = .05$ as the level of significance, should the null hypothesis be rejected?

	Type A	Type B
Boys	30	12
Girls	15	19

3. A social psychologist asked random samples of adults in three socioeconomic levels to specify their preferences among four types of television programs. She obtained the following responses. If $P = .01$ is set as the level of significance, should the null hypothesis be rejected?

Socioeconomic Level	Drama	Documentary	Comedy	Musical
High	14	17	9	8
Middle	8	18	10	12
Low	10	9	17	9

Exercises: Group B

4. A researcher wished to determine if students in urban high schools differed from students in rural high schools in their preference for night football games. He selected two random samples and obtained the following responses. Setting $P = .05$ as the level of significance, should the null hypothesis be rejected?

	Prefer night football	
High school	Yes	No
Urban	6	13
Rural	21	12

5. An experimental psychologist wished to determine if rats had a preference for eating out of red or yellow bowls. He randomly selected a sample of rats and

observed the following choices. Setting $P = .05$ as the level of significance, should the null hypothesis be rejected?

Bowl color	f
Red	13
Yellow	47

6. A preschool director wished to determine if working and nonworking mothers differed in their preference for the scheduling of preschool classes for their children. She obtained the following responses. Setting $P = .01$ as the level of significance, should the null hypothesis be rejected?

		Time of classes	
Parents	Morning	Early afternoon	Late afternoon
Working	10	36	14
Nonworking	23	17	7

ANSWERS TO GROUP - A EXERCISES

Chapter 2

1.

Flavor	f
Vanilla	9
Chocolate	7
Strawberry	5
Rocky Road	4

2.

Flavor	Rank
Vanilla	1
Chocolate	2
Strawberry	3
Rocky Road	4

3.

Score	f	Score	f	Score	f
28	1	21	2	14	2
27	1	20	2	13	1
26	1	19	3	12	0
25	0	18	1	11	0
24	1	17	1	10	0
23	1	16	1	9	1
22	2	15	2		

4.

Interval	f
27–29	2
24–26	2
21–23	5
18–20	6
15–17	4
12–14	3
9–11	1

5. 11.5, 19.5, 16.5, 99.5

Chapter 3

1. Mode $= 28$; $Mdn = 25.67$; $\bar{X} = 27$
2. $\bar{X} = 27$
3. Tom: $X = 26.97$; Sam: $X = 28.14$

4. Charlie: 90.9th percentile; Danny: 13.6th percentile
5. Modal interval, 84–87; $Mdn = 83.50$; $\bar{X} = 82.17$
6. $\bar{X} = 82.17$
7. Susan: $X = 87.34$; Janice: $X = 80.80$
8. Sally: 54.17th percentile; Judy: 17.36th percentile

Chapter 4

1.

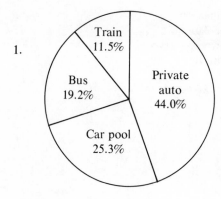

Segment of circle:

Private auto	158.4°
Car pool	91.1°
Bus	69.1°
Train	41.4°

2.

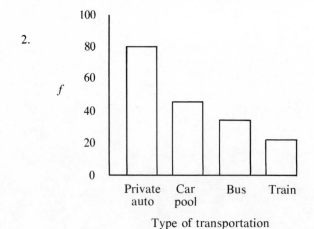

3.

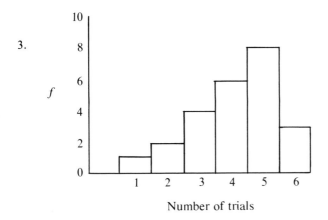

Number of trials

4.

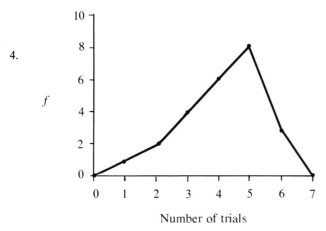

Number of trials

5.

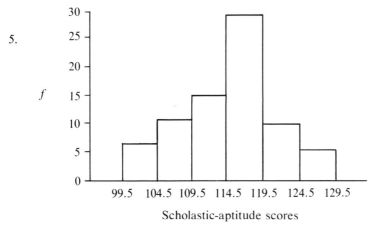

Scholastic-aptitude scores

6.

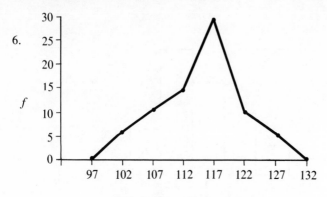

Scholastic-aptitude scores

Chapter 5

1. Range $= 6$
2. $Q = 1.31$
3. $A.D. = 1.38$
4. $s'^2 = 2.85$
5. $s'^2 = 2.85$
6. $s' = 1.69$
7. for $X = 53$: $z = 1.18$
8. for $X = 50$: $z = -0.59$

Chapter 6

1. .0668
2. .0401
3. .5859
4. .1747
5. .1498

Chapter 7

1. $P = .3300$
2. $P = .3707$
3. $P = .0949$

4. $P = .3535$
5. $P = .7553$

Chapter 8

1. $\Sigma x^2 = 40$
2. $df = 13$
3. $s^2 = 3.08$
4. $s = 1.75$
5. $s_{\bar{x}} = .47$
6. $\Sigma x^2 = 486$
7. $df = 19$
8. $s^2 = 25.58$
9. $s = 5.06$
10. $s_{\bar{x}} = 1.13$

Chapter 9

1. $57.77 - 62.23$
2. $57 - 63$
3. $17.27 - 18.73$
4. $16.99 - 19.01$
5. $73.75 - 76.25$
6. $73.35 - 76.65$

Chapter 10

1. There is a difference in effectiveness between the variable method and the constant method for teaching chickens to peck at a red circle.
2. There is no difference in effectiveness between the variable method and the constant method for teaching chickens to peck at a red circle.
3. $\bar{X}_1 - \bar{X}_2 = -10$; cutoff point: $-1.96 \times 4 = -7.84$; reject the null hypothesis.
4. $\bar{X}_1 - \bar{X}_2 = 6$; cutoff point: $1.96 \times 4 = 7.84$; do not reject the null hypothesis.
5. There is a difference in the levels of scores students obtain on Group-A exercises and Group-B exercises.
6. There is no difference in the levels of scores students obtain on Group-A exercises and Group-B exercises.

7. $\bar{X}_1 - \bar{X}_2 = 4$; cutoff point: $1.96 \times 2.5 = 4.9$; do not reject the null hypothesis.

8. $\bar{X}_1 - \bar{X}_2 = -7$; cutoff point: $-1.96 \times 2.5 = -4.9$; reject the null hypothesis.

Chapter 11

1. $s^2 = 18.16$; $s_{\bar{X}_1-\bar{X}_2} = 1.67$; $t = -2.40$; $df = 25$; reject the null hypothesis.

2. $s_{\bar{D}}^2 = 4.93$; $s_{\bar{D}} = 0.702$; $t = 2.28$; $df = 9$; do not reject the null hypothesis.

3. $s^2 = 77.77$; $s_{\bar{X}_1-\bar{X}_2} = 4.56$; $t = 1.97$,$df = 13$; do not reject the null hypothesis.

Chapter 12

1. $s^2 = 1.75$; $s_{\bar{X}_1-\bar{X}_2} = .23$; $t = 1.30$; do not reject the null hypothesis.

2. Probability of a Type II error: $\beta = .4602$; power: $1 - \beta = .5398$.

3. Probability of a Type II error: $\beta = .7794$; power: $1 - \beta = .2206$.

4. $s^2 = 105.25$; $s_{\bar{X}_1-\bar{X}_2} = 1.90$; $t = 2.11$; do not reject the null hypothesis.

5. Probability ot a Type II error: $\beta = .0154$; power: $1 - \beta = .9846$.

6. Probability of a Type II error: $\beta = .9789$; power: $1 - \beta = .0211$.

Chapter 13

1.

	Sum of squares	Degrees of freedom	Mean square	F
Between groups	398.50	2	199.25	42.67 P < .05
Within groups	84.07	18	4.67	
Total	482.57	20		

Reject the null hypothesis.

2. Boys: $s^2 = 2.33$; girls: $s^2 = 5.64$; $F = 2.42$; do not reject the null hypothesis.

3.

	Sum of squares	Degrees of freedom	Mean square	F
Between groups	0.73	3	0.24	0.06 N.S.
Within groups	77.13	18	4.28	
Total	77.86	21		

Do not reject the null hypothesis.

Chapter 14

1. $r = .785$; nondirectional hypothesis; $df = 6$; reject the null hypothesis.

2. $r^2 = .616$. Approximately 61.6% of the variance in mechanical-comprehension scores is associated with the variance in divergent-thinking scores.

3. $r = -.473$; directional hypothesis; $df = 11$; do not reject the null hypothesis.

4. $r^2 = .224$. Approximately 22.4% of the variance in spelling scores is associated with the variance in completion times.

Chapter 15

1. $\tilde{Y} = 8.92 + .57X$

2. For $X = 15$: $\tilde{Y} = 17.47$
   For $X = 40$: $\tilde{Y} = 31.72$

3.

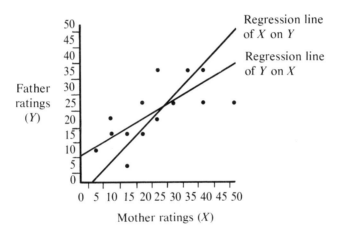

4. $\tilde{X} = 3.94 + .94Y$

5. For $Y = 20$: $\tilde{X} = 22.74$
   For $Y = 45$: $\tilde{X} = 46.24$

6. Regression line of X on Y shown in answer to Exercise 3.

Chapter 16

1. $\rho = -.030$; nondirectional hypothesis; do not reject the null hypothesis.

2. $\rho = .837$; directional hypothesis; reject the null hypothesis.

3. $\rho = .456$; nondirectional hypothesis; do not reject the null hypothesis.

Chapter 17

1. $\chi^2 = 3.01$; $df = 1$; do not reject the null hypothesis.
2. $\chi^2 = 4.73$; $df = 1$; reject the null hypothesis.
3. $\chi^2 = 9.10$; $df = 6$; do not reject the null hypothesis.

TABLES

TABLE 1. AREAS OF THE STANDARD NORMAL CURVE

z	μ to z	z	μ to z	z	μ to z	z	μ to z	z	μ to z	z	μ to z	z	μ to z	z	μ to z
0.00	.0000	0.25	.0987	0.50	.1915	0.75	.2734	1.00	.3413	1.25	.3944	1.50	.4332	1.75	.4599
0.01	.0040	0.26	.1026	0.51	.1950	0.76	.2764	1.01	.3438	1.26	.3962	1.51	.4345	1.76	.4608
0.02	.0080	0.27	.1064	0.52	.1985	0.77	.2794	1.02	.3461	1.27	.3980	1.52	.4357	1.77	.4616
0.03	.0120	0.28	.1103	0.53	.2019	0.78	.2823	1.03	.3485	1.28	.3997	1.53	.4370	1.78	.4625
0.04	.0160	0.29	.1141	0.54	.2054	0.79	.2852	1.04	.3508	1.29	.4015	1.54	.4382	1.79	.4633
0.05	.0199	0.30	.1179	0.55	.2088	0.80	.2881	1.05	.3531	1.30	.4032	1.55	.4394	1.80	.4641
0.06	.0239	0.31	.1217	0.56	.2123	0.81	.2910	1.06	.3554	1.31	.4049	1.56	.4406		
0.07	.0279	0.32	.1255	0.57	.2157	0.82	.2939	1.07	.3577	1.32	.4066	1.57	.4418		
0.08	.0319	0.33	.1293	0.58	.2190	0.83	.2967	1.08	.3599	1.33	.4082	1.58	.4429		
0.09	.0359	0.34	.1331	0.59	.2221	0.84	.2995	1.09	.3621	1.34	.4099	1.59	.4441		
0.10	.0398	0.35	.1368	0.60	.2257	0.85	.3023	1.10	.3643	1.35	.4115	1.60	.4452		
0.11	.0438	0.36	.1406	0.61	.2291	0.86	.3051	1.11	.3665	1.36	.4131	1.61	.4463		
0.12	.0478	0.37	.1443	0.62	.2324	0.87	.3078	1.12	.3686	1.37	.4147	1.62	.4474		
0.13	.0517	0.38	.1480	0.63	.2357	0.88	.3106	1.13	.3708	1.38	.4162	1.63	.4484		
0.14	.0557	0.39	.1517	0.64	.2389	0.89	.3133	1.14	.3729	1.39	.4177	1.64	.4495		
0.15	.0596	0.40	.1554	0.65	.2422	0.90	.3159	1.15	.3749	1.40	.4192	1.65	.4505		
0.16	.0636	0.41	.1591	0.66	.2454	0.91	.3186	1.16	.3770	1.41	.4207	1.66	.4515		
0.17	.0675	0.42	.1628	0.67	.2486	0.92	.3212	1.17	.3790	1.42	.4222	1.67	.4525		
0.18	.0714	0.43	.1664	0.68	.2517	0.93	.3238	1.18	.3810	1.43	.4236	1.68	.4535		
0.19	.0753	0.44	.1700	0.69	.2549	0.94	.3264	1.19	.3830	1.44	.4251	1.69	.4545		
0.20	.0793	0.45	.1736	0.70	.2580	0.95	.3289	1.20	.3849	1.45	.4265	1.70	.4554		
0.21	.0832	0.46	.1772	0.71	.2611	0.96	.3315	1.21	.3869	1.46	.4279	1.71	.4564		
0.22	.0871	0.47	.1808	0.72	.2642	0.97	.3340	1.22	.3888	1.47	.4292	1.72	.4573		
0.23	.0910	0.48	.1844	0.73	.2673	0.98	.3365	1.23	.3907	1.48	.4306	1.73	.4582		
0.24	.0948	0.49	.1879	0.74	.2704	0.99	.3389	1.24	.3925	1.49	.4319	1.74	.4591		
0.25	.0987	0.50	.1915	0.75	.2734	1.00	.3413	1.25	.3944	1.50	.4332	1.75	.4599		

188

z	μ to z	z	μ to z	z	μ to z	z	μ to z	z	μ to z	z	μ to z
1.80	.4641	2.05	.4798	2.30	.4893	2.55	.4946	2.80	.4974	3.05	.4989
1.81	.4649	2.06	.4803	2.31	.4896	2.56	.4948	2.81	.4975	3.06	.4989
1.82	.4656	2.07	.4808	2.32	.4898	2.57	.4949	2.82	.4976	3.07	.4989
1.83	.4664	2.08	.4812	2.33	.4901	2.58	.4951	2.83	.4977	3.08	.4990
1.84	.4671	2.09	.4817	2.34	.4904	2.59	.4952	2.84	.4977	3.09	.4990
1.85	.4678	2.10	.4821	2.35	.4906	2.60	.4953	2.85	.4978	3.10	.4990
1.86	.4686	2.11	.4826	2.36	.4909	2.61	.4955	2.86	.4979	3.11	.4991
1.87	.4693	2.12	.4830	2.37	.4911	2.62	.4956	2.87	.4979	3.12	.4991
1.88	.4699	2.13	.4834	2.38	.4913	2.63	.4957	2.88	.4980	3.13	.4991
1.89	.4706	2.14	.4838	2.39	.4916	2.64	.4959	2.89	.4981	3.14	.4992
1.90	.4713	2.15	.4842	2.40	.4918	2.65	.4960	2.90	.4981	3.15	.4992
1.91	.4719	2.16	.4846	2.41	.4920	2.66	.4961	2.91	.4982	3.16	.4992
1.92	.4726	2.17	.4850	2.42	.4922	2.67	.4962	2.92	.4982	3.17	.4992
1.93	.4732	2.18	.4854	2.43	.4925	2.68	.4963	2.93	.4983	3.18	.4993
1.94	.4738	2.19	.4857	2.44	.4927	2.69	.4964	2.94	.4984	3.19	.4993
1.95	.4744	2.20	.4861	2.45	.4929	2.70	.4965	2.95	.4984	3.20	.4993
1.96	.4750	2.21	.4864	2.46	.4931	2.71	.4966	2.96	.4985	3.21	.4993
1.97	.4756	2.22	.4868	2.47	.4932	2.72	.4967	2.97	.4985	3.22	.4994
1.98	.4761	2.23	.4871	2.48	.4934	2.73	.4968	2.98	.4986	3.23	.4994
1.99	.4767	2.24	.4875	2.49	.4936	2.74	.4969	2.99	.4986	3.24	.4994
2.00	.4772	2.25	.4878	2.50	.4938	2.75	.4970	3.00	.4987	3.30	.4995
2.01	.4778	2.26	.4881	2.51	.4940	2.76	.4971	3.01	.4987	3.40	.4997
2.02	.4783	2.27	.4884	2.52	.4941	2.77	.4972	3.02	.4987	3.50	.4998
2.03	.4788	2.28	.4887	2.53	.4943	2.78	.4973	3.03	.4988	3.60	.4998
2.04	.4793	2.29	.4890	2.54	.4945	2.79	.4974	3.04	.4988	3.70	.4999
2.05	.4798	2.30	.4893	2.55	.4946	2.80	.4974	3.05	.4989		

Adapted from Table 1, E. S. Pearson and H. O. Hartley (Eds.), *Biometrika Tables for Statisticians* (3rd Ed.). Copyright 1966. Reprinted by permission of the Biometrika Trustees.

189

TABLE 2. DISTRIBUTION OF *t*

df	P = .10	P = .05	P = .02	P = .01
1	6.314	12.706	31.821	63.657
2	2.920	4.303	6.965	9.925
3	2.353	3.182	4.541	5.841
4	2.132	2.776	3.747	4.604
5	2.015	2.571	3.365	4.032
6	1.943	2.447	3.143	3.707
7	1.895	2.365	2.998	3.499
8	1.860	2.306	2.896	3.355
9	1.833	2.262	2.821	3.250
10	1.812	2.228	2.764	3.169
11	1.796	2.201	2.718	3.106
12	1.782	2.179	2.681	3.055
13	1.771	2.160	2.650	3.012
14	1.761	2.145	2.624	2.977
15	1.753	2.131	2.602	2.947
16	1.746	2.120	2.583	2.921
17	1.740	2.110	2.567	2.898
18	1.734	2.101	2.552	2.878
19	1.729	2.093	2.539	2.861
20	1.725	2.086	2.528	2.845
21	1.721	2.080	2.518	2.831
22	1.717	2.074	2.508	2.819
23	1.714	2.069	2.500	2.807
24	1.711	2.064	2.492	2.797
25	1.708	2.060	2.485	2.787
26	1.706	2.056	2.479	2.779
27	1.703	2.052	2.473	2.771
28	1.701	2.048	2.467	2.763
29	1.699	2.045	2.462	2.756
30	1.697	2.042	2.457	2.750
60	1.671	2.000	2.390	2.660
∞	1.645	1.960	2.326	2.576

Abridged from Table III of Fisher and Yates: *Statistical Tables for Biological, Agricultural and Medical Research*, published by Longman Group Ltd., London (previously published by Oliver & Boyd, Edinburgh), by permission of the authors and publishers.

TABLE 3. TABLE OF F FOR .05 (ROMAN) and .01 (BOLDFACE) LEVELS OF SIGNIFICANCE

Degrees of Freedom for Greater Mean Square

	1	2	3	4	5	6	8	12	24	∞
1	161.45 **4052.10**	199.50 **4999.03**	215.72 **5403.49**	224.57 **5625.14**	230.17 **5764.08**	233.97 **5859.39**	238.89 **5981.34**	243.91 **6105.83**	249.04 **6234.16**	254.32 **6366.48**
2	18.51 **98.49**	19.00 **99.01**	19.16 **99.17**	19.25 **99.25**	19.30 **99.30**	19.33 **99.33**	19.37 **99.36**	19.41 **99.42**	19.45 **99.46**	19.50 **99.50**
3	10.13 **34.12**	9.55 **30.81**	9.28 **29.46**	9.12 **28.71**	9.01 **28.24**	8.94 **27.91**	8.84 **27.49**	8.74 **27.05**	8.64 **26.60**	8.53 **26.12**
4	7.71 **21.20**	6.94 **18.00**	6.59 **16.69**	6.39 **15.98**	6.26 **15.52**	6.16 **15.21**	6.04 **14.80**	5.91 **14.37**	5.77 **13.93**	5.63 **13.46**
5	6.61 **16.26**	5.79 **13.27**	5.41 **12.06**	5.19 **11.39**	5.05 **10.97**	4.95 **10.67**	4.82 **10.27**	4.68 **9.89**	4.53 **9.47**	4.36 **9.02**
6	5.99 **13.74**	5.14 **10.92**	4.76 **9.78**	4.53 **9.15**	4.39 **8.75**	4.28 **8.47**	4.15 **8.10**	4.00 **7.72**	3.84 **7.31**	3.67 **6.88**
7	5.59 **12.25**	4.74 **9.55**	4.35 **8.45**	4.12 **7.85**	3.97 **7.46**	3.87 **7.19**	3.73 **6.84**	3.57 **6.47**	3.41 **6.07**	3.23 **5.65**
8	5.32 **11.26**	4.46 **8.65**	4.07 **7.59**	3.84 **7.01**	3.69 **6.63**	3.58 **6.37**	3.44 **6.03**	3.28 **5.67**	3.12 **5.28**	2.93 **4.86**
9	5.12 **10.56**	4.26 **8.02**	3.86 **6.99**	3.63 **6.42**	3.48 **6.06**	3.37 **5.80**	3.23 **5.47**	3.07 **5.11**	2.90 **4.73**	2.71 **4.31**
10	4.96 **10.04**	4.10 **7.56**	3.71 **6.55**	3.48 **5.99**	3.33 **5.64**	3.22 **5.39**	3.07 **5.06**	2.91 **4.71**	2.74 **4.33**	2.54 **3.91**
11	4.84 **9.65**	3.98 **7.20**	3.59 **6.22**	3.36 **5.67**	3.20 **5.32**	3.09 **5.07**	2.95 **4.74**	2.79 **4.40**	2.61 **4.02**	2.40 **3.60**
12	4.75 **9.33**	3.88 **6.93**	3.49 **5.95**	3.26 **5.41**	3.11 **5.06**	3.00 **4.82**	2.85 **4.50**	2.69 **4.16**	2.50 **3.78**	2.30 **3.36**
14	4.60 **8.86**	3.74 **6.51**	3.34 **5.56**	3.11 **5.03**	2.96 **4.69**	2.85 **4.46**	2.70 **4.14**	2.53 **3.80**	2.35 **3.43**	2.13 **3.00**
16	4.49 **8.53**	3.63 **6.23**	3.24 **5.29**	3.01 **4.77**	2.85 **4.44**	2.74 **4.20**	2.59 **3.89**	2.42 **3.55**	2.24 **3.18**	2.01 **2.75**

Degrees of Freedom for Smaller Mean Square

Degrees of Freedom for Smaller Mean Square	1	2	3	4	5	6	8	12	24	∞
18	4.41 **8.28**	3.55 **6.01**	3.16 **5.09**	2.93 **4.58**	2.77 **4.25**	2.66 **4.01**	2.51 **3.71**	2.34 **3.37**	2.15 **3.01**	1.92 **2.57**
20	4.35 **8.10**	3.49 **5.85**	3.10 **4.94**	2.87 **4.43**	2.71 **4.10**	2.60 **3.87**	2.45 **3.56**	2.28 **3.23**	2.08 **2.86**	1.84 **2.42**
25	4.24 **7.77**	3.38 **5.57**	2.99 **4.68**	2.76 **4.18**	2.60 **3.86**	2.49 **3.63**	2.34 **3.32**	2.16 **2.99**	1.96 **2.62**	1.71 **2.17**
30	4.17 **7.56**	3.32 **5.39**	2.92 **4.51**	2.69 **4.02**	2.53 **3.70**	2.42 **3.47**	2.27 **3.17**	2.09 **2.84**	1.89 **2.47**	1.62 **2.01**
40	4.08 **7.31**	3.23 **5.18**	2.84 **4.31**	2.61 **3.83**	2.45 **3.51**	2.34 **3.29**	2.18 **2.99**	2.00 **2.66**	1.79 **2.29**	1.52 **1.82**
50	4.03 **7.17**	3.18 **5.06**	2.79 **4.20**	2.56 **3.72**	2.40 **3.41**	2.29 **3.19**	2.13 **2.89**	1.95 **2.56**	1.74 **2.18**	1.44 **1.68**
60	4.00 **7.08**	3.15 **4.98**	2.76 **4.13**	2.52 **3.65**	2.37 **3.34**	2.25 **3.12**	2.10 **2.82**	1.92 **2.50**	1.70 **2.12**	1.39 **1.60**
70	3.98 **7.01**	3.13 **4.92**	2.74 **4.07**	2.50 **3.60**	2.35 **3.29**	2.23 **3.07**	2.07 **2.78**	1.89 **2.45**	1.67 **2.07**	1.35 **1.53**
80	3.96 **6.96**	3.11 **4.88**	2.72 **4.04**	2.49 **3.56**	2.33 **3.26**	2.21 **3.04**	2.06 **2.74**	1.88 **2.42**	1.65 **2.03**	1.31 **1.47**
90	3.95 **6.92**	3.10 **4.85**	2.71 **4.01**	2.47 **3.53**	2.32 **3.23**	2.20 **3.01**	2.04 **2.72**	1.86 **2.39**	1.64 **2.00**	1.28 **1.43**
100	3.94 **6.90**	3.09 **4.82**	2.70 **3.98**	2.46 **3.51**	2.30 **3.21**	2.19 **2.99**	2.03 **2.69**	1.85 **2.37**	1.63 **1.98**	1.26 **1.39**
200	3.89 **6.97**	3.04 **4.71**	2.65 **3.88**	2.42 **3.41**	2.26 **3.11**	2.14 **2.89**	1.98 **2.60**	1.80 **2.28**	1.57 **1.88**	1.14 **1.21**
∞	3.84 **6.64**	2.99 **4.60**	2.60 **3.78**	2.37 **3.32**	2.21 **3.02**	2.09 **2.80**	1.94 **2.51**	1.75 **2.18**	1.52 **1.79**	

Abridged from Table V of Fisher and Yates: *Statistical Tables for Biological, Agricultural and Medical Research*, published by Longman Group Ltd., London (previously published by Oliver & Boyd, Edinburgh), by permission of the authors and publishers.

TABLE 4. CRITICAL VALUES OF *r*

df	$P = .10$	$P = .05$	$P = .02$	$P = .01$
1	.988	.997	.9995	.9999
2	.900	.950	.980	.990
3	.805	.878	.934	.959
4	.729	.811	.882	.917
5	.669	.754	.833	.874
6	.622	.707	.789	.834
7	.582	.666	.750	.798
8	.549	.632	.716	.765
9	.521	.602	.685	.735
10	.497	.576	.658	.708
11	.476	.553	.634	.684
12	.458	.532	.612	.661
13	.441	.514	.592	.641
14	.426	.497	.574	.623
15	.412	.482	.558	.606
16	.400	.468	.542	.590
17	.389	.456	.528	.575
18	.378	.444	.516	.561
19	.369	.433	.503	.549
20	.360	.423	.492	.537
21	.352	.413	.482	.526
22	.344	.404	.472	.515
23	.337	.396	.462	.505
24	.330	.388	.453	.496
25	.323	.381	.445	.487
26	.317	.374	.437	.479
27	.311	.367	.430	.471
28	.306	.361	.423	.463
29	.301	.355	.416	.456
30	.296	.349	.409	.449
35	.275	.325	.381	.418
40	.257	.304	.358	.393
45	.243	.288	.338	.372
50	.231	.273	.322	.354
60	.211	.250	.295	.325
70	.195	.232	.274	.302
80	.183	.217	.256	.283
90	.173	.205	.242	.267
100	.164	.195	.230	.254

Abridged from Table VI of Fisher and Yates: *Statistical Tables for Biological, Agricultural and Medical Research*, published by Longman Group Ltd., London (previously published by Oliver & Boyd, Edinburgh), by permission of the authors and publishers.

TABLE 5. CRITICAL VALUES OF SPEARMAN'S RANK CORRELATION COEFFICIENT (rho)

N	$P = 0.10$	$P = 0.05$	$P = 0.02$	$P = 0.01$
5	0.900	–	–	–
6	0.829	0.886	0.943	–
7	0.714	0.786	0.893	0.929
8	0.643	0.738	0.833	0.881
9	0.600	0.683	0.783	0.833
10	0.564	0.648	0.745	0.794
11	0.523	0.623	0.736	0.818
12	0.497	0.591	0.703	0.780
13	0.475	0.566	0.673	0.745
14	0.457	0.545	0.646	0.716
15	0.441	0.525	0.623	0.689
16	0.425	0.507	0.601	0.666
17	0.412	0.490	0.582	0.645
18	0.399	0.476	0.564	0.625
19	0.388	0.462	0.549	0.608
20	0.377	0.450	0.534	0.591
21	0.368	0.438	0.521	0.576
22	0.359	0.428	0.508	0.562
23	0.351	0.418	0.496	0.549
24	0.343	0.409	0.485	0.537
25	0.336	0.400	0.475	0.526
26	0.329	0.392	0.465	0.515
27	0.323	0.385	0.456	0.505
28	0.317	0.377	0.448	0.496
29	0.311	0.370	0.440	0.487
30	0.305	0.364	0.432	0.478

Adapted from "Distribution of the Sum of Squares of Rank Differences for Small Numbers of Individuals," by E. G. Olds, *Annals of Mathematical Statistics*, 1938, *9*, 133–148, and "The 5 Percent Significance Levels for Sums of Squares of Rank Differences and a Correction," by E. G. Olds, *Annals of Mathematical Statistics*, 1949, *20*, 117–118. Reprinted by permission.

TABLE 6. CRITICAL VALUES OF CHI SQUARE (χ^2)

df	$P = .05$	$P = .01$
1	3.84	6.64
2	5.99	9.21
3	7.82	11.34
4	9.49	13.28
5	11.07	15.09
6	12.59	16.81
7	14.07	18.48
8	15.51	20.09
9	16.92	21.67
10	18.31	23.21
11	19.68	24.72
12	21.03	26.22
13	22.36	27.69
14	23.68	29.14
15	25.00	30.58
16	26.30	32.00
17	27.59	33.41
18	28.87	34.80
19	30.14	36.19
20	31.41	37.57
21	32.67	38.93
22	33.92	40.29
23	35.17	41.64
24	36.42	42.98
25	37.65	44.31
26	38.88	45.64
27	40.11	46.96
28	41.34	48.28
29	42.56	49.59
30	43.77	50.89

Reprinted from Table IV of Fisher and Yates: *Statistical Tables for Biological, Agricultural and Medical Research*, published by Longman Group Ltd., London (previously published by Oliver & Boyd, Edinburgh), by permission of the authors and publishers.

TABLE 7. SQUARES AND SQUARE ROOTS

There are a few points to watch in using the table on the following pages. We shall discuss these briefly. First of all, observe that the first column lists all numbers, n, from 1.00 through 10.00. Each number in the second column is the square, n^2 of the corresponding number, n, in the first column. For example, $(1.78)^2 = 3.1684$ and $(7.17)^2 = 51.4089$.

The second column can also be used to obtain the squares of other numbers having the same succession of digits as the numbers given in the first column. For example, the square of 17.8 will also have the same succession of digits, 31684, as the square of 1.78. However, the position of the decimal point is not the same and $(17.8)^2 = 316.84$. This can be explained by the fact that we must multiply 1.78 by 10 to get 17.8. When the number is squared, the 10 is also squared $[(17.8)^2 = (10)^2 \cdot (1.78)^2]$. Thus the answer is 100 times 3.1684 or 316.84. Similarly, $(717)^2 = 514,089$ because 7.17 must be multiplied by 100 to give 717 and the square of 7.17 is then multiplied by the square of 100, which is 10,000. Note that in each case *the decimal point is moved twice as many places in the square as in the number that is squared.* Consider now the effect of moving the decimal point in the opposite direction. $(.178)^2$ will again contain the digits 31684 but this time the correct answer is .031684. The explanation is that 1.78 must be multiplied by .1 to give .178. The answer is then multiplied by $(.1)^2$ or .01 thus giving .031684. As another example, $(.0717)^2 = .00514089$. Note that the italicized statement holds regardless of the direction that the decimal point is moved.

The operation of taking the square root is the inverse of the operation of squaring, just as division is the inverse operation of multiplication. The discussion in the preceding paragraph is, therefore, also helpful in understanding the use of the third column of the table. This column gives the square root, $\sqrt{n}$, of the corresponding number, n, in the first column of the table. To further simplify the use of the table for finding square roots, the fourth column, $\sqrt{10n}$, has been added.

Since the first column contains all numbers from 1.00 to 10.00, we know that the third column contains the square roots of all these numbers. For example, $\sqrt{1.78} = 1.33417$ and $\sqrt{7.17} = 2.67769$. The fourth column enables us also to find directly the square roots, $\sqrt{10n}$, of all numbers from 10 (1.00) to 10(10.00), that is, from 10.0 to 100.0, where now each number is given only to the nearest tenth. For example, we find from the fourth column opposite 1.78 that $\sqrt{17.8} = 4.21900$ and opposite 7.17 that $\sqrt{71.7} = 8.46759$. Hence from the third and fourth columns we can read directly the square roots of all numbers from 1.00

through 100.0. However, just as we extended the use of the table for squares, so we can extend its use for square roots.

Suppose we want $\sqrt{717}$. From the table we can read both $\sqrt{7.17}$ and $\sqrt{71.7}$. Which should we use? This question is answered when we consider the placement of the decimal point. Remembering that taking the square root is the inverse of squaring, and looking back at the italicized statement earlier in the discussion, we see that *the decimal point is moved half as many places in the square root as in the number.* Now, half of an odd number isn't a whole number and a decimal point can't be moved a fraction of a place. So we must move the decimal point an *even number* of places to begin with when converting a number in order to apply the table and find its square root. Therefore, in our example we want the digits in $\sqrt{7.17}$ that are 267769 and by application of the last italicized statement we have $\sqrt{717} = 26.7769$, since the decimal point is moved two places from 7.17 to 717 and half of two is one. Had the problem been to find $\sqrt{7170}$, we would again have moved the decimal point an *even* number of places in order to obtain a number whose square root we could read directly from the table. In this case we would have the digits in $\sqrt{71.7}$ or 846759. Observing the rule for placement of the decimal point would give us the answer, 84.6759. The problem of finding $\sqrt{.00717}$ leads to the same sequence of digits (moving the decimal point four places), but the answer this time is .0846759. Again, the last italicized statement holds regardless of the direction that the decimal point is moved.

n	n^2	$\sqrt{n}$	$\sqrt{10n}$	n	n^2	$\sqrt{n}$	$\sqrt{10n}$
1.00	1.0000	1.00000	3.16228	1.50	2.2500	1.22474	3.87298
1.01	1.0201	1.00499	3.17805	1.51	2.2801	1.22882	3.88587
1.02	1.0404	1.00995	3.19374	1.52	2.3104	1.23288	3.89872
1.03	1.0609	1.01489	3.20936	1.53	2.3409	1.23693	3.91152
1.04	1.0816	1.01980	3.22490	1.54	2.3716	1.24097	3.92428
1.05	1.1025	1.02470	3.24037	1.55	2.4025	1.24499	3.93700
1.06	1.1236	1.02956	3.25576	1.56	2.4336	1.24900	3.94968
1.07	1.1449	1.03441	3.27109	1.57	2.4649	1.25300	3.96232
1.08	1.1664	1.03923	3.28634	1.58	2.4964	1.25698	3.97492
1.09	1.1881	1.04403	3.30151	1.59	2.5281	1.26095	3.98748
1.10	1.2100	1.04881	3.31662	1.60	2.5600	1.26491	4.00000
1.11	1.2321	1.05357	3.33167	1.61	2.5921	1.26886	4.01248
1.12	1.2544	1.05830	3.34664	1.62	2.6244	1.27279	4.02492
1.13	1.2769	1.06301	3.36155	1.63	2.6569	1.27671	4.03733
1.14	1.2996	1.06771	3.37639	1.64	2.6896	1.28062	4.04969
1.15	1.3225	1.07238	3.39116	1.65	2.7225	1.28452	4.06202
1.16	1.3456	1.07703	3.40588	1.66	2.7556	1.28841	4.07431
1.17	1.3689	1.08167	3.42053	1.67	2.7889	1.29228	4.08656
1.18	1.3924	1.08628	3.43511	1.68	2.8224	1.29615	4.09878
1.19	1.4161	1.09087	3.44964	1.69	2.8561	1.30000	4.11096
1.20	1.4400	1.09545	3.46410	1.70	2.8900	1.30384	4.12311
1.21	1.4641	1.10000	3.47851	1.71	2.9241	1.30767	4.13521
1.22	1.4884	1.10454	3.49285	1.72	2.9584	1.31149	4.14729
1.23	1.5129	1.10905	3.50714	1.73	2.9929	1.31529	4.15933
1.24	1.5376	1.11355	3.52136	1.74	3.0276	1.31909	4.17133
1.25	1.5625	1.11803	3.53553	1.75	3.0625	1.32288	4.18330
1.26	1.5876	1.12250	3.54965	1.76	3.0976	1.32665	4.19524
1.27	1.6129	1.12694	3.56371	1.77	3.1329	1.33041	4.20714
1.28	1.6384	1.13137	3.57771	1.78	3.1684	1.33417	4.21900
1.29	1.6641	1.13578	3.59166	1.79	3.2041	1.33791	4.23084
1.30	1.6900	1.14018	3.60555	1.80	3.2400	1.34164	4.24264
1.31	1.7161	1.14455	3.61939	1.81	3.2761	1.34536	4.25441
1.32	1.7424	1.14891	3.63318	1.82	3.3124	1.34907	4.26615
1.33	1.7689	1.15326	3.64692	1.83	3.3489	1.35277	4.27785
1.34	1.7956	1.15758	3.66060	1.84	3.3856	1.35647	4.28952
1.35	1.8225	1.16190	3.67423	1.85	3.4225	1.36015	4.30116
1.36	1.8496	1.16619	3.68782	1.86	3.4596	1.36382	4.31277
1.37	1.8769	1.17047	3.70135	1.87	3.4969	1.36748	4.32435
1.38	1.9044	1.17473	3.71484	1.88	3.5344	1.37113	4.33590
1.39	1.9321	1.17898	3.72827	1.89	3.5721	1.37477	4.34741
1.40	1.9600	1.18322	3.74166	1.90	3.6100	1.37840	4.35890
1.41	1.9881	1.18743	3.75500	1.91	3.6481	1.38203	4.37035
1.42	2.0164	1.19164	3.76829	1.92	3.6864	1.38564	4.38178
1.43	2.0449	1.19583	3.78153	1.93	3.7249	1.38924	4.39318
1.44	2.0736	1.20000	3.79473	1.94	3.7636	1.39284	4.40454
1.45	2.1025	1.20416	3.80789	1.95	3.8025	1.39642	4.41588
1.46	2.1316	1.20830	3.82099	1.96	3.8416	1.40000	4.42719
1.47	2.1609	1.21244	3.83406	1.97	3.8809	1.40357	4.43847
1.48	2.1904	1.21655	3.84708	1.98	3.9204	1.40712	4.44972
1.49	2.2201	1.22066	3.86005	1.99	3.9601	1.41067	4.46094

n	n^2	$\sqrt{n}$	$\sqrt{10n}$	n	n^2	$\sqrt{n}$	$\sqrt{10n}$
2.00	4.0000	1.41421	4.47214	2.50	6.2500	1.58114	5.00000
2.01	4.0401	1.41774	4.48330	2.51	6.3001	1.58430	5.00999
2.02	4.0804	1.42127	4.49444	2.52	6.3504	1.58745	5.01996
2.03	4.1209	1.42478	4.50555	2.53	6.4009	1.59060	5.02991
2.04	4.1616	1.42829	4.51664	2.54	6.4516	1.59374	5.03984
2.05	4.2025	1.43178	4.52769	2.55	6.5025	1.59687	5.04975
2.06	4.2436	1.43527	4.53872	2.56	6.5536	1.60000	5.05964
2.07	4.2849	1.43875	4.54973	2.57	6.6049	1.60312	5.06952
2.08	4.3264	1.44222	4.56070	2.58	6.6564	1.60624	5.07937
2.09	4.3681	1.44568	4.57165	2.59	6.7081	1.60935	5.08920
2.10	4.4100	1.44914	4.58258	2.60	6.7600	1.61245	5.09902
2.11	4.4521	1.45258	4.59347	2.61	6.8121	1.61555	5.10882
2.12	4.4944	1.45602	4.60435	2.62	6.8644	1.61864	5.11859
2.13	4.5369	1.45945	4.61519	2.63	6.9169	1.62173	5.12835
2.14	4.5796	1.46287	4.62601	2.64	6.9696	1.62481	5.13809
2.15	4.6225	1.46629	4.63681	2.65	7.0225	1.62788	5.14782
2.16	4.6656	1.46969	4.64758	2.66	7.0756	1.63095	5.15752
2.17	4.7089	1.47309	4.65833	2.67	7.1289	1.63401	5.16720
2.18	4.7524	1.47648	4.66905	2.68	7.1824	1.63707	5.17687
2.19	4.7961	1.47986	4.67974	2.69	7.2361	1.64012	5.18652
2.20	4.8400	1.48324	4.69042	2.70	7.2900	1.64317	5.19615
2.21	4.8841	1.48661	4.70106	2.71	7.3441	1.64621	5.20577
2.22	4.9284	1.48997	4.71169	2.72	7.3984	1.64924	5.21536
2.23	4.9729	1.49332	4.72229	2.73	7.4529	1.65227	5.22494
2.24	5.0176	1.49666	4.73286	2.74	7.5076	1.65529	5.23450
2.25	5.0625	1.50000	4.74342	2.75	7.5625	1.65831	5.24404
2.26	5.1076	1.50333	4.75395	2.76	7.6176	1.66132	5.25357
2.27	5.1529	1.50665	4.76445	2.77	7.6729	1.66433	5.26308
2.28	5.1984	1.50997	4.77493	2.78	7.7284	1.66733	5.27257
2.29	5.2441	1.51327	4.78539	2.79	7.7841	1.67033	5.28205
2.30	5.2900	1.51658	4.79583	2.80	7.8400	1.67332	5.29150
2.31	5.3361	1.51987	4.80625	2.81	7.8961	1.67631	5.30094
2.32	5.3824	1.52315	4.81664	2.82	7.9524	1.67929	5.31037
2.33	5.4289	1.52643	4.82701	2.83	8.0089	1.68226	5.31977
2.34	5.4756	1.52971	4.83735	2.84	8.0656	1.68523	5.32917
2.35	5.5225	1.53297	4.84768	2.85	8.1225	1.68819	5.33854
2.36	5.5696	1.53623	4.85798	2.86	8.1796	1.69115	5.34790
2.37	5.6169	1.53948	4.86826	2.87	8.2369	1.69411	5.35724
2.38	5.6644	1.54272	4.87852	2.88	8.2944	1.69706	5.36656
2.39	5.7121	1.54596	4.88876	2.89	8.3521	1.70000	5.37587
2.40	5.7600	1.54919	4.89898	2.90	8.4100	1.70294	5.38516
2.41	5.8081	1.55242	4.90918	2.91	8.4681	1.70587	5.39444
2.42	5.8564	1.55563	4.91935	2.92	8.5264	1.70880	5.40370
2.43	5.9049	1.55885	4.92950	2.93	8.5849	1.71172	5.41295
2.44	5.9536	1.56205	4.93964	2.94	8.6436	1.71464	5.42218
2.45	6.0025	1.56525	4.94975	2.95	8.7025	1.71756	5.43139
2.46	6.0516	1.56844	4.95984	2.96	8.7616	1.72047	5.44059
2.47	6.1009	1.57162	4.96991	2.97	8.8209	1.72337	5.44977
2.48	6.1504	1.57480	4.97996	2.98	8.8804	1.72627	5.45894
2.49	6.2001	1.57797	4.98999	2.99	8.9401	1.72916	5.46809

n	n^2	$\sqrt{n}$	$\sqrt{10n}$	n	n^2	$\sqrt{n}$	$\sqrt{10n}$
3.00	9.0000	1.73205	5.47723	3.50	12.2500	1.87083	5.91608
3.01	9.0601	1.73494	5.48635	3.51	12.3201	1.87350	5.92453
3.02	9.1204	1.73781	5.49545	3.52	12.3904	1.87617	5.93296
3.03	9.1809	1.74069	5.50454	3.53	12.4609	1.87883	5.94138
3.04	9.2416	1.74356	5.51362	3.54	12.5316	1.88149	5.94979
3.05	9.3025	1.74642	5.52268	3.55	12.6025	1.88414	5.95819
3.06	9.3636	1.74929	5.53173	3.56	12.6736	1.88680	5.96657
3.07	9.4249	1.75214	5.54076	3.57	12.7449	1.88944	5.97495
3.08	9.4864	1.75499	5.54977	3.58	12.8164	1.89209	5.98331
3.09	9.5481	1.75784	5.55878	3.59	12.8881	1.89473	5.99166
3.10	9.6100	1.76068	5.56776	3.60	12.9600	1.89737	6.00000
3.11	9.6721	1.76352	5.57674	3.61	13.0321	1.90000	6.00833
3.12	9.7344	1.76635	5.58570	3.62	13.1044	1.90263	6.01664
3.13	9.7969	1.76918	5.59464	3.63	13.1769	1.90526	6.02495
3.14	9.8596	1.77200	5.60357	3.64	13.2496	1.90788	6.03324
3.15	9.9225	1.77482	5.61249	3.65	13.3225	1.91050	6.04152
3.16	9.9856	1.77764	5.62139	3.66	13.3956	1.91311	6.04979
3.17	10.0489	1.78045	5.63028	3.67	13.4689	1.91572	6.05805
3.18	10.1124	1.78326	5.63915	3.68	13.5424	1.91833	6.06630
3.19	10.1761	1.78606	5.64801	3.69	13.6161	1.92094	6.07454
3.20	10.2400	1.78885	5.65685	3.70	13.6900	1.92354	6.08276
3.21	10.3041	1.79165	5.66569	3.71	13.7641	1.92614	6.09098
3.22	10.3684	1.79444	5.67450	3.72	13.8384	1.92873	6.09918
3.23	10.4329	1.79722	5.68331	3.73	13.9129	1.93132	6.10737
3.24	10.4976	1.80000	5.69210	3.74	13.9876	1.93391	6.11555
3.25	10.5625	1.80278	5.70088	3.75	14.0625	1.93649	6.12372
3.26	10.6276	1.80555	5.70964	3.76	14.1376	1.93907	6.13188
3.27	10.6929	1.80831	5.71839	3.77	14.2129	1.94165	6.14003
3.28	10.7584	1.81108	5.72713	3.78	14.2884	1.94422	6.14817
3.29	10.8241	1.81384	5.73585	3.79	14.3641	1.94679	6.15630
3.30	10.8900	1.81659	5.74456	3.80	14.4400	1.94936	6.16441
3.31	10.9561	1.81934	5.75326	3.81	14.5161	1.95192	6.17252
3.32	11.0224	1.82209	5.76194	3.82	14.5924	1.95448	6.18061
3.33	11.0889	1.82483	5.77062	3.83	14.6689	1.95704	6.18870
3.34	11.1556	1.82757	5.77927	3.84	14.7456	1.95959	6.19677
3.35	11.2225	1.83030	5.78792	3.85	14.8225	1.96214	6.20484
3.36	11.2896	1.83303	5.79655	3.86	14.8996	1.96469	6.21289
3.37	11.3569	1.83576	5.80517	3.87	14.9769	1.96723	6.22093
3.38	11.4244	1.83848	5.81378	3.88	15.0544	1.96977	6.22896
3.39	11.4921	1.84120	5.82237	3.89	15.1321	1.97231	6.23699
3.40	11.5600	1.84391	5.83095	3.90	15.2100	1.97484	6.24500
3.41	11.6281	1.84662	5.83952	3.91	15.2881	1.97737	6.25300
3.42	11.6964	1.84932	5.84808	3.92	15.3664	1.97990	6.26099
3.43	11.7649	1 85203	5 85662	3.93	15.4449	1.98242	6.26897
3.44	11.8336	1.85472	5.86515	3.94	15.5236	1.98494	6.27694
3.45	11.9025	1.85742	5.87367	3.95	15.6025	1.98746	6.28490
3.46	11.9716	1.86011	5.88218	3.96	15.6816	1.98997	6.29285
3.47	12.0409	1.86279	5.89067	3.97	15.7609	1.99249	6.30079
3.48	12.1104	1.86548	5.89915	3.98	15.8408	1.99499	6.30872
3.49	12.1801	1.86815	5.90762	3.99	15.9201	1.99750	6.31664

200

n	n^2	$\sqrt{n}$	$\sqrt{10n}$	n	n^2	$\sqrt{n}$	$\sqrt{10n}$
4.00	16.0000	2.00000	6.32456	4.50	20.2500	2.12132	6.70820
4.01	16.0801	2.00250	6.33246	4.51	20.3401	2.12368	6.71565
4.02	16.1604	2.00499	6.34035	4.52	20.4304	2.12603	6.72309
4.03	16.2409	2.00749	6.34823	4.53	20.5209	2.12838	6.73053
4.04	16.3216	2.00998	6.35610	4.54	20.6116	2.13073	6.73795
4.05	16.4025	2.01246	6.36396	4.55	20.7025	2.13307	6.74537
4.06	16.4836	2.01494	6.37181	4.56	20.7936	2.13542	6.75278
4.07	16.5649	2.01742	6.37966	4.57	20.8849	2.13776	6.76018
4.08	16.6464	2.01990	6.38749	4.58	20.9764	2.14009	6.76757
4.09	16.7281	2.02237	6.39531	4.59	21.0681	2.14243	6.77495
4.10	16.8100	2.02485	6.40312	4.60	21.1600	2.14476	6.78233
4.11	16.8921	2.02731	6.41093	4.61	21.2521	2.14709	6.78970
4.12	16.9744	2.02978	6.41872	4.62	21.3444	2.14942	6.79706
4.13	17.0569	2.03224	6.42651	4.63	21.4369	2.15174	6.80441
4.14	17.1396	2.03470	6.43428	4.64	21.5296	2.15407	6.81175
4.15	17.2225	2.03715	6.44205	4.65	21.6225	2.15639	6.81909
4.16	17.3056	2.03961	6.44981	4.66	21.7156	2.15870	6.82642
4.17	17.3889	2.04206	6.45755	4.67	21.8089	2.16102	6.83374
4.18	17.4724	2.04450	6.46529	4.68	21.9024	2.16333	6.84105
4.19	17.5561	2.04695	6.47302	4.69	21.9961	2.16564	6.84836
4.20	17.6400	2.04939	6.48074	4.70	22.0900	2.16795	6.85565
4.21	17.7241	2.05183	6.48845	4.71	22.1841	2.17025	6.86294
4.22	17.8084	2.05426	6.49615	4.72	22.2784	2.17256	6.87023
4.23	17.8929	2.05670	6.50384	4.73	22.3729	2.17486	6.87750
4.24	17.9776	2.05913	6.51153	4.74	22.4676	2.17715	6.88477
4.25	18.0625	2.06155	6.51920	4.75	22.5625	2.17945	6.89202
4.26	18.1476	2.06398	6.52687	4.76	22.6576	2.18174	6.89928
4.27	18.2329	2.06640	6.53452	4.77	22.7529	2.18403	6.90652
4.28	18.3184	2.06882	6.54217	4.78	22.8484	2.18632	6.91375
4.29	18.4041	2.07123	6.54981	4.79	22.9441	2.18861	6.92098
4.30	18.4900	2.07364	6.55744	4.80	23.0400	2.19089	6.92820
4.31	18.5761	2.07605	6.56506	4.81	23.1361	2.19317	6.93542
4.32	18.6624	2.07846	6.57267	4.82	23.2324	2.19545	6.94262
4.33	18.7489	2.08087	6.58027	4.83	23.3289	2.19773	6.94982
4.34	18.8356	2.08327	6.58787	4.84	23.4256	2.20000	6.95701
4.35	18.9225	2.08567	6.59545	4.85	23.5225	2.20227	6.96419
4.36	19.0096	2.08806	6.60303	4.86	23.6196	2.20454	6.97137
4.37	19.0969	2.09045	6.61060	4.87	23.7169	2.20681	6.97854
4.38	19.1844	2.09284	6.61816	4.88	23.8144	2.20907	6.98570
4.39	19.2721	2.09523	6.62571	4.89	23.9121	2.21133	6.99285
4.40	19.3600	2.09762	6.63325	4.90	24.0100	2.21359	7.00000
4.41	19.4481	2.10000	6.64078	4.91	24.1081	2.21585	7.00714
4.42	19.5364	2.10238	6.64831	4.92	24.2064	2.21811	7.01427
4.43	19.6249	2.10476	6.65582	4.93	24.3049	2.22036	7.02140
4.44	19.7136	2.10713	6.66333	4.94	24.4036	2.22261	7.02851
4.45	19.8025	2.10950	6.67083	4.95	24.5025	2.22486	7.03562
4.46	19.8916	2.11187	6.67832	4.96	24.6016	2.22711	7.04273
4.47	19.9809	2.11424	6.68581	4.97	24.7009	2.22935	7.04982
4.48	20.0704	2.11660	6.69328	4.98	24.8004	2.23159	7.05691
4.49	20.1601	2.11896	6.70075	4.99	24.9001	2.23383	7.06399

n	n^2	$\sqrt{n}$	$\sqrt{10n}$	n	n^2	$\sqrt{n}$	$\sqrt{10n}$
5.00	25.0000	2.23607	7.07107	5.50	30.2500	2.34521	7.41620
5.01	25.1001	2.23830	7.07814	5.51	30.3601	2.34734	7.42294
5.02	25.2004	2.24054	7.08520	5.52	30.4704	2.34947	7.42967
5.03	25.3009	2.24277	7.09225	5.53	30.5809	2.35160	7.43640
5.04	25.4016	2.24499	7.09930	5.54	30.6916	2.35372	7.44312
5.05	25.5025	2.24722	7.10634	5.55	30.8025	2.35584	7.44983
5.06	25.6036	2.24944	7.11337	5.56	30.9136	2.35797	7.45654
5.07	25.7049	2.25167	7.12039	5.57	31.0249	2.36008	7.46324
5.08	25.8064	2.25389	7.12741	5.58	31.1364	2.36220	7.46994
5.09	25.9081	2.25610	7.13442	5.59	31.2481	2.36432	7.47663
5.10	26.0100	2.25832	7.14143	5.60	31.3600	2.36643	7.48331
5.11	26.1121	2.26053	7.14843	5.61	31.4721	2.36854	7.48999
5.12	26.2144	2.26274	7.15542	5.62	31.5844	2.37065	7.49667
5.13	26.3169	2.26495	7.16240	5.63	31.6969	2.37276	7.50333
5.14	26.4196	2.26716	7.16938	5.64	31.8096	2.37487	7.50999
5.15	26.5225	2.26936	7.17635	5.65	31.9225	2.37697	7.51665
5.16	26.6256	2.27156	7.18331	5.66	32.0356	2.37908	7.52330
5.17	26.7289	2.27376	7.19027	5.67	32.1489	2.38118	7.52994
5.18	26.8324	2.27596	7.19722	5.68	32.2624	2.38328	7.53658
5.19	26.9361	2.27816	7.20417	5.69	32.3761	2.38537	7.54321
5.20	27.0400	2.28035	7.21110	5.70	32.4900	2.38747	7.54983
5.21	27.1441	2.28254	7.21803	5.71	32.6041	2.38956	7.55645
5.22	27.2484	2.28473	7.22496	5.72	32.7184	2.39165	7.56307
5.23	27.3529	2.28692	7.23187	5.73	32.8329	2.39374	7.56968
5.24	27.4576	2.28910	7.23878	5.74	32.9476	2.39583	7.57628
5.25	27.5625	2.29129	7.24569	5.75	33.0625	2.39792	7.58288
5.26	27.6676	2.29347	7.25259	5.76	33.1776	2.40000	7.58947
5.27	27.7729	2.29565	7.25948	5.77	33.2929	2.40208	7.59605
5.28	27.8784	2.29783	7.26636	5.78	33.4084	2.40416	7.60263
5.29	27.9841	2.30000	7.27324	5.79	33.5241	2.40624	7.60920
5.30	28.0900	2.30217	7.28011	5.80	33.6400	2.40832	7.61577
5.31	28.1961	2.30434	7.28697	5.81	33.7561	2.41039	7.62234
5.32	28.3024	2.30651	7.29383	5.82	33.8724	2.41247	7.62889
5.33	28.4089	2.30868	7.30068	5.83	33.9889	2.41454	7.63544
5.34	28.5156	2.31084	7.30753	5.84	34.1056	2.41661	7.64199
5.35	28.6225	2.31301	7.31437	5.85	34.2225	2.41868	7.64853
5.36	28.7296	2.31517	7.32120	5.86	34.3396	2.42074	7.65506
5.37	28.8369	2.31733	7.32803	5.87	34.4569	2.42281	7.66159
5.38	28.9444	2.31948	7.33485	5.88	34.5744	2.42487	7.66812
5.39	29.0521	2.32164	7.34166	5.89	34.6921	2.42693	7.67463
5.40	29.1600	2.32379	7.34847	5.90	34.8100	2.42899	7.68115
5.41	29.2681	2.32594	7.35527	5.91	34.9281	2.43105	7.68765
5.42	29.3764	2.32809	7.36205	5.92	35.0464	2.43311	7.69415
5.43	29.4849	2.33024	7.36885	5.93	35.1649	2.43516	7.70065
5.44	29.5936	2.33238	7.37564	5.94	35.2836	2.43721	7.70714
5.45	29.7025	2.33452	7.38241	5.95	35.4025	2.43926	7.71362
5.46	29.8116	2.33666	7.38918	5.96	35.5216	2.44131	7.72010
5.47	29.9209	2.33880	7.39594	5.97	35.6409	2.44336	7.72658
5.48	30.0304	2.34094	7.40270	5.98	35.7604	2.44540	7.73305
5.49	30.1401	2.34307	7.40945	5.99	35.8801	2.44745	7.73951

n	n^2	$\sqrt{n}$	$\sqrt{10n}$	n	n^2	$\sqrt{n}$	$\sqrt{10n}$
6.00	36.0000	2.44949	7.74597	6.50	42.2500	2.54951	8.06226
6.01	36.1201	2.45153	7.75242	6.51	42.3801	2.55147	8.06846
6.02	36.2404	2.45357	7.75887	6.52	42.5104	2.55343	8.07465
6.03	36.3609	2.45561	7.76531	6.53	42.6409	2.55539	8.08084
6.04	36.4816	2.45764	7.77174	6.54	42.7716	2.55734	8.08703
6.05	36.6025	2.45967	7.77817	6.55	42.9025	2.55930	8.09321
6.06	36.7236	2.46171	7.78460	6.56	43.0336	2.56125	8.09938
6.07	36.8449	2.46374	7.79102	6.57	43.1649	2.56320	8.10555
6.08	36.9664	2.46577	7.79744	6.58	43.2964	2.56515	8.11172
6.09	37.0881	2.46779	7.80385	6.59	43.4281	2.56710	8.11788
6.10	37.2100	2.46982	7.81025	6.60	43.5600	2.56905	8.12404
6.11	37.3321	2.47184	7.81665	6.61	43.6921	2.57099	8.13019
6.12	37.4544	2.47386	7.82304	6.62	43.8244	2.57294	8.13634
6.13	37.5769	2.47588	7.82943	6.63	43.9569	2.57488	8.14248
6.14	37.6996	2.47790	7.83582	6.64	44.0896	2.57682	8.14862
6.15	37.8225	2.47992	7.84219	6.65	44.2225	2.57876	8.15475
6.16	37.9456	2.48193	7.84857	6.66	44.3556	2.58070	8.16088
6.17	38.0689	2.48395	7.85493	6.67	44.4889	2.58263	8.16701
6.18	38.1924	2.48596	7.86130	6.68	44.6224	2.58457	8.17313
6.19	38.3161	2.48797	7.86766	6.69	44.7561	2.58650	8.17924
6.20	38.4400	2.48998	7.87401	6.70	44.8900	2.58844	8.18535
6.21	38.5641	2.49199	7.88036	6.71	45.0241	2.59037	8.19146
6.22	38.6884	2.49399	7.88670	6.72	45.1584	2.59230	8.19756
6.23	38.8129	2.49600	7.89303	6.73	45.2929	2.59422	8.20366
6.24	38.9376	2.49800	7.89937	6.74	45.4276	2.59615	8.20975
6.25	39.0625	2.50000	7.90569	6.75	45.5625	2.59808	8.21584
6.26	39.1876	2.50200	7.91202	6.76	45.6976	2.60000	8.22192
6.27	39.3129	2.50400	7.91833	6.77	45.8329	2.60192	8.22800
6.28	39.4384	2.50599	7.92465	6.78	45.9684	2.60384	8.23408
6.29	39.5641	2.50799	7.93095	6.79	46.1041	2.60576	8.24015
6.30	39.6900	2.50998	7.93725	6.80	46.2400	2.60768	8.24621
6.31	39.8161	2.51197	7.94355	6.81	46.3761	2.60960	8.25227
6.32	39.9424	2.51396	7.94984	6.82	46.5124	2.61151	8.25833
6.33	40.0689	2.51595	7.95613	6.83	46.6489	2.61343	8.26438
6.34	40.1956	2.51794	7.96241	6.84	46.7856	2.61534	8.27043
6.35	40.3225	2.51992	7.96869	6.85	46.9225	2.61725	8.27647
6.36	40.4496	2.52190	7.97496	6.86	47.0596	2.61916	8.28251
6.37	40.5769	2.52389	7.98123	6.87	47.1969	2.62107	8.28855
6.38	40.7044	2.52587	7.98749	6.88	47.3344	2.62298	8.29458
6.39	40.8321	2.52784	7.99375	6.89	47.4721	2.62488	8.30060
6.40	40.9600	2.52982	8.00000	6.90	47.6100	2.62679	8.30662
6.41	41.0881	2.53180	8.00625	6.91	47.7481	2.62869	8.31264
6.42	41.2164	2.53377	8.01249	6.92	47.8864	2.63059	8.31865
6.43	41.3449	2.53574	8.01873	6.93	48.0249	2.63249	8.32466
6.44	41.4736	2.53772	8.02496	6.94	48.1636	2.63439	8.33067
6.45	41.6025	2.53969	8.03119	6.95	48.3025	2.63629	8.33667
6.46	41.7316	2.54165	8.03741	6.96	48.4416	2.63818	8.34266
6.47	41.8609	2.54362	8.04363	6.97	48.5809	2.64008	8.34865
6.48	41.9904	2.54558	8.04984	6.98	48.7204	2.64197	8.35464
6.49	42.1201	2.54755	8.05605	6.99	48.8601	2.64386	8.36062

n	n^2	$\sqrt{n}$	$\sqrt{10n}$	n	n^2	$\sqrt{n}$	$\sqrt{10n}$
7.00	49.0000	2.64575	8.36660	7.50	56.2500	2.73861	8.66025
7.01	49.1401	2.64764	8.37257	7.51	56.4001	2.74044	8.66603
7.02	49.2804	2.64953	8.37854	7.52	56.5504	2.74226	8.67179
7.03	49.4209	2.65141	8.38451	7.53	56.7009	2.74408	8.67756
7.04	49.5616	2.65330	8.39047	7.54	56.8516	2.74591	8.68332
7.05	49.7025	2.65518	8.39643	7.55	57.0025	2.74773	8.68907
7.06	49.8436	2.65707	8.40238	7.56	57.1536	2.74955	8.69483
7.07	49.9849	2.65895	8.40833	7.57	57.3049	2.75136	8.70057
7.08	50.1264	2.66083	8.41427	7.58	57.4564	2.75318	8.70632
7.09	50.2681	2.66271	8.42021	7.59	57.6081	2.75500	8.71206
7.10	50.4100	2.66458	8.42615	7.60	57.7600	2.75681	8.71780
7.11	50.5521	2.66646	8.43208	7.61	57.9121	2.75862	8.72353
7.12	50.6944	2.66833	8.43801	7.62	58.0644	2.76043	8.72926
7.13	50.8369	2.67021	8.44393	7.63	58.2169	2.76225	8.73499
7.14	50.9796	2.67208	8.44985	7.64	58.3696	2.76405	8.74071
7.15	51.1225	2.67395	8.45577	7.65	58.5225	2.76586	8.74643
7.16	51.2656	2.67582	8.46168	7.66	58.6756	2.76767	8.75214
7.17	51.4089	2.67769	8.46759	7.67	58.8289	2.76948	8.75785
7.18	51.5524	2.67955	8.47349	7.68	58.9824	2.77128	8.76356
7.19	51.6961	2.68142	8.47939	7.69	59.1361	2.77308	8.76926
7.20	51.8400	2.68328	8.48528	7.70	59.2900	2.77489	8.77496
7.21	51.9841	2.68514	8.49117	7.71	59.4441	2.77669	8.78066
7.22	52.1284	2.68701	8.49706	7.72	59.5984	2.77849	8.78635
7.23	52.2729	2.68887	8.50294	7.73	59.7529	2.78029	8.79204
7.24	52.4176	2.69072	8.50882	7.74	59.9076	2.78209	8.79773
7.25	52.5625	2.69258	8.51469	7.75	60.0625	2.78388	8.80341
7.26	52.7076	2.69444	8.52056	7.76	60.2176	2.78568	8.80909
7.27	52.8529	2.69629	8.52643	7.77	60.3729	2.78747	8.81476
7.28	52.9984	2.69815	8.53229	7.78	60.5284	2.78927	8.82043
7.29	53.1441	2.70000	8.53815	7.79	60.6841	2.79106	8.82610
7.30	53.2900	2.70185	8.54400	7.80	60.8400	2.79285	8.83176
7.31	53.4361	2.70370	8.54985	7.81	60.9961	2.79464	8.83742
7.32	53.5824	2.70555	8.55570	7.82	61.1524	2.79643	8.84308
7.33	53.7289	2.70740	8.56154	7.83	61.3089	2.79821	8.84873
7.34	53.8756	2.70924	8.56738	7.84	61.4656	2.80000	8.85438
7.35	54.0225	2.71109	8.57321	7.85	61.6225	2.80179	8.86002
7.36	54.1696	2.71293	8.57904	7.86	61.7796	2.80357	8.86566
7.37	54.3169	2.71477	8.58487	7.87	61.9369	2.80535	8.87130
7.38	54.4644	2.71662	8.59069	7.88	62.0944	2.80713	8.87694
7.39	54.6121	2.71846	8.59651	7.89	62.2521	2.80891	8.88257
7.40	54.7600	2.72029	8.60233	7.90	62.4100	2.81069	8.88819
7.41	54.9081	2.72213	8.60814	7.91	62.5681	2.81247	8.89382
7.42	55.0564	2.72397	8.61394	7.92	62.7264	2.81425	8.89944
7.43	55.2049	2.72580	8.61974	7.93	62.8849	2.81603	8.90505
7.44	55.3536	2.72764	8.62554	7.94	63.0436	2.81780	8.91067
7.45	55.5025	2.72947	8.63134	7.95	63.2025	2.81957	8.91628
7.46	55.6516	2.73130	8.63713	7.96	63.3616	2.82135	8.92188
7.47	55.8009	2.73313	8.64292	7.97	63.5209	2.82312	8.92749
7.48	55.9504	2.73496	8.64870	7.98	63.6804	2.82489	8.93308
7.49	56.1001	2.73679	8.65448	7.99	63.8401	2.82666	8.93868

n	n^2	$\sqrt{n}$	$\sqrt{10n}$	n	n^2	$\sqrt{n}$	$\sqrt{10n}$
8.00	64.0000	2.82843	8.94427	8.50	72.2500	2.91548	9.21954
8.01	64.1601	2.83019	8.94986	8.51	72.4201	2.91719	9.22497
8.02	64.3204	2.83196	8.95545	8.52	72.5904	2.91890	9.23038
8.03	64.4809	2.83373	8.96103	8.53	72.7609	2.92062	9.23580
8.04	64.6416	2.83549	8.96660	8.54	72.9316	2.92233	9.24121
8.05	64.8025	2.83725	8.97218	8.55	73.1025	2.92404	9.24662
8.06	64.9636	2.83901	8.97775	8.56	73.2736	2.92575	9.25203
8.07	65.1249	2.84077	8.98332	8.57	73.4449	2.92746	9.25743
8.08	65.2864	2.84253	8.98888	8.58	73.6164	2.92916	9.26283
8.09	65.4481	2.84429	8.99444	8.59	73.7881	2.93087	9.26823
8.10	65.6100	2.84605	9.00000	8.60	73.9600	2.93258	9.27362
8.11	65.7721	2.84781	9.00555	8.61	74.1321	2.93428	9.27901
8.12	65.9344	2.84956	9.01110	8.62	74.3044	2.93598	9.28440
8.13	66.0969	2.85132	9.01665	8.63	74.4769	2.93769	9.28978
8.14	66.2596	2.85307	9.02219	8.64	74.6496	2.93939	9.29516
8.15	66.4225	2.85482	9.02774	8.65	74.8225	2.94109	9.30054
8.16	66.5856	2.85657	9.03327	8.66	74.9956	2.94279	9.30591
8.17	66.7489	2.85832	9.03881	8.67	75.1689	2.94449	9.31128
8.18	66.9124	2.86007	9.04434	8.68	75.3424	2.94618	9.31665
8.19	67.0761	2.86182	9.04986	8.69	75.5161	2.94788	9.32202
8.20	67.2400	2.86356	9.05539	8.70	75.6900	2.94958	9.32738
8.21	67.4041	2.86531	9.06091	8.71	75.8641	2.95127	9.33274
8.22	67.5684	2.86705	9.06642	8.72	76.0384	2.95296	9.33809
8.23	67.7329	2.86880	9.07193	8.73	76.2129	2.95466	9.34345
8.24	67.8976	2.87054	9.07744	8.74	76.3876	2.95635	9.34880
8.25	68.0625	2.87228	9.08295	8.75	76.5625	2.95804	9.35414
8.26	68.2276	2.87402	9.08845	8.76	76.7376	2.95973	9.35949
8.27	68.3929	2.87576	9.09395	8.77	76.9129	2.96142	9.36483
8.28	68.5584	2.87750	9.09945	8.78	77.0884	2.96311	9.37017
8.29	68.7241	2.87924	9.10494	8.79	77.2641	2.96479	9.37550
8.30	68.8900	2.88097	9.11043	8.80	77.4400	2.96648	9.38083
8.31	69.0561	2.88271	9.11592	8.81	77.6161	2.96816	9.38616
8.32	69.2224	2.88444	9.12140	8.82	77.7924	2.96985	9.39149
8.33	69.3889	2.88617	9.12688	8.83	77.9689	2.97153	9.39681
8.34	69.5556	2.88791	9.13236	8.84	78.1456	2.97321	9.40213
8.35	69.7225	2.88964	9.13783	8.85	78.3225	2.97489	9.40744
8.36	69.8896	2.89137	9.14330	8.86	78.4996	2.97658	9.41276
8.37	70.0569	2.89310	9.14877	8.87	78.6769	2.97825	9.41807
8.38	70.2244	2.89482	9.15423	8.88	78.8544	2.97993	9.42338
8.39	70.3921	2.89655	9.15969	8.89	79.0321	2.98161	9.42868
8.40	70.5600	2.89828	9.16515	8.90	79.2100	2.98329	9.43398
8.41	70.7281	2.90000	9.17061	8.91	79.3881	2.98496	9.43928
8.42	70.8964	2.90172	9.17606	8.92	79.5664	2.98664	9.44458
8.43	71.0649	2.90345	9.18150	8.93	79.7449	2.98831	9.44987
8.44	71.2336	2.90517	9.18695	8.94	79.9236	2.98998	9.45516
8.45	71.4025	2.90689	9.19239	8.95	80.1025	2.99166	9.46044
8.46	71.5716	2.90861	9.19783	8.96	80.2816	2.99333	9.46573
8.47	71.7409	2.91033	9.20326	8.97	80.4609	2.99500	9.47101
8.48	71.9104	2.91204	9.20869	8.98	80.6404	2.99666	9.47629
8.49	72.0801	2.91376	9.21412	8.99	80.8201	2.99833	9.48156

n	n^2	$\sqrt{n}$	$\sqrt{10n}$	n	n^2	$\sqrt{n}$	$\sqrt{10n}$
9.00	81.0000	3.00000	9.48683	9.50	90.2500	3.08221	9.74679
9.01	81.1801	3.00167	9.49210	9.51	90.4401	3.08383	9.75192
9.02	81.3604	3.00333	9.49737	9.52	90.6304	3.08545	9.75705
9.03	81.5409	3.00500	9.50263	9.53	90.8209	3.08707	9.76217
9.04	81.7216	3.00666	9.50789	9.54	91.0116	3.08869	9.76729
9.05	81.9025	3.00832	9.51315	9.55	91.2025	3.09031	9.77241
9.06	82.0836	3.00998	9.51840	9.56	91.3936	3.09192	9.77753
9.07	82.2649	3.01164	9.52365	9.57	91.5849	3.09354	9.78264
9.08	82.4464	3.01330	9.52890	9.58	91.7764	3.09516	9.78775
9.09	82.6281	3.01496	9.53415	9.59	91.9681	3.09677	9.79285
9.10	82.8100	3.01662	9.53939	9.60	92.1600	3.09839	9.79796
9.11	82.9921	3.01828	9.54463	9.61	92.3521	3.10000	9.80306
9.12	83.1744	3.01993	9.54987	9.62	92.5444	3.10161	9.80816
9.13	83.3569	3.02159	9.55510	9.63	92.7369	3.10322	9.81326
9.14	83.5396	3.02324	9.56033	9.64	92.9296	3.10483	9.81835
9.15	83.7225	3.02490	9.56556	9.65	93.1225	3.10644	9.82344
9.16	83.9056	3.02655	9.57079	9.66	93.3156	3.10805	9.82853
9.17	84.0889	3.02820	9.57601	9.67	93.5089	3.10966	9.83362
9.18	84.2724	3.02985	9.58123	9.68	93.7024	3.11127	9.83870
9.19	84.4561	3.03150	9.58645	9.69	93.8961	3.11288	9.84378
9.20	84.6400	3.03315	9.59166	9.70	94.0900	3.11448	9.84886
9.21	84.8241	3.03480	9.59687	9.71	94.2841	3.11609	9.85393
9.22	85.0084	3.03645	9.60208	9.72	94.4784	3.11769	9.85901
9.23	85.1929	3.03809	9.60729	9.73	94.6729	3.11929	9.86408
9.24	85.3776	3.03974	9.61249	9.74	94.8676	3.12090	9.86914
9.25	85.5625	3.04138	9.61769	9.75	95.0625	3.12250	9.87421
9.26	85.7476	3.04302	9.62289	9.76	95.2576	3.12410	9.87927
9.27	85.9329	3.04467	9.62808	9.77	95.4529	3.12570	9.88433
9.28	86.1184	3.04631	9.63328	9.78	95.6484	3.12730	9.88939
9.29	86.3041	3.04795	9.63846	9.79	95.8441	3.12890	9.89444
9.30	86.4900	3.04959	9.64365	9.80	96.0400	3.13050	9.89949
9.31	86.6761	3.05123	9.64883	9.81	96.2361	3.13209	9.90454
9.32	86.8624	3.05287	9.65401	9.82	96.4324	3.13369	9.90959
9.33	87.0489	3.05450	9.65919	9.83	96.6289	3.13528	9.91464
9.34	87.2356	3.05614	9.66437	9.84	96.8256	3.13688	9.91968
9.35	87.4225	3.05778	9.66954	9.85	97.0225	3.13847	9.92472
9.36	87.6096	3.05941	9.67471	9.86	97.2196	3.14006	9.92975
9.37	87.7969	3.06105	9.67988	9.87	97.4169	3.14166	9.93479
9.38	87.9844	3.06268	9.68504	9.88	97.6144	3.14325	9.93982
9.39	88.1721	3.06431	9.69020	9.89	97.8121	3.14484	9.94485
9.40	88.3600	3.06594	9.69536	9.90	98.0100	3.14643	9.94987
9.41	88.5481	3.06757	9.70052	9.91	98.2081	3.14802	9.95490
9.42	88.7364	3.06920	9.70567	9.92	98.4064	3.14960	9.95992
9.43	88.9249	3.07083	9.71082	9.93	98.6049	3.15119	9.96494
9.44	89.1136	3.07246	9.71597	9.94	98.8036	3.15278	9.96995
9.45	89.3025	3.07409	9.72111	9.95	99.0025	3.15436	9.97497
9.46	89.4916	3.07571	9.72625	9.96	99.2016	3.15595	9.97998
9.47	89.6809	3.07734	9.73139	9.97	99.4009	3.15753	9.98499
9.48	89.8704	3.07896	9.73653	9.98	99.6004	3.15911	9.98999
9.49	90.0601	3.08058	9.74166	9.99	99.8001	3.16070	9.99500
				10.00	100.000	3.16228	10.0000

FORMULAS

Formula 1. Calculation of the Median

$$Mdn = \ell\ell + \left(\frac{.5N - \Sigma f_b}{f_w} \right) i$$

in which Σ = the sum of

f_b = frequency below the interval which contains the Mdn

f_w = frequency within the interval which contains the Mdn

Formula 2. Calculation of the Mean

$$\bar{X} = \frac{\Sigma f X}{N}$$

Formula 3. Calculation of the Percentile

Percentile in decimal form $\quad \dfrac{\left(\dfrac{X - \ell\ell}{i} \right) f_w + \Sigma f_b}{N}$

in which X = score value for which the percentile is to be computed
f_b = frequency below the i which contains the score
f_w = frequency within the i which contains the score

Multiply the decimal form of the percentile by 100 in order to determine the percentile.

Formula 4. Calculation of the Range

$$\text{Range} = H - L$$

in which H = highest score in frequency distribution
L = lowest score in frequency distribution

Formula 5. Calculation of the Semi-interquartile Range

$$Q = \frac{Q_3 - Q_1}{2}$$

Formula 6. Calculation of a Deviation Score

$$x = X - \bar{X}$$

Formula 7. Calculation of the Average Deviation

$$\text{A.D.} = \frac{\Sigma f|x|}{N}$$

in which $|x|$ = the absolute deviation of a raw score from the mean

---

Formula 8. Calculation of the Sample Variance

Deviation Score Method $\quad s'^2 = \dfrac{\Sigma f x^2}{N}$ (Formula 8a)

Raw Score Method $\quad s'^2 = \dfrac{\Sigma f X^2}{N} - \bar{X}^2$ (Formula 8b)

Formula 9. Calculation of the Sample Standard Deviation

$$s' = \sqrt{s'^2}$$

Formula 10. Calculation of a Relative Deviate

$$z = \frac{x}{s'}$$

Formula 11. Calculation of the Sum of Squared Deviations ("Sum of Squares") (Formulas 11a and 11b are Equivalent)*

Deviation Score Method $\Sigma x^2 = \Sigma(X - \bar{X})^2$ (Formula 11a)

Raw Score Method $\Sigma x^2 = \Sigma X^2 - \dfrac{(\Sigma X)^2}{N}$ (Formula 11b)

Formula 12. Estimate of the Population Variance from Sample Data (Formulas 12a and 12b are Equivalent)

Deviation Score Method $s^2 = \dfrac{\Sigma x^2}{N - 1}$ (Formula 12a)

Raw Score Method $s^2 = \dfrac{N\Sigma X^2 - (\Sigma X)^2}{N(N - 1)}$ (Formula 12b)

Formula 13. Estimate of the Standard Error of the Mean

$$s_{\bar{X}} = \frac{s}{\sqrt{N}}$$

*The symbol f is omitted in these and subsequent formulas. It is to be assumed that all frequencies in the distribution are used in the calculations.

Formula 14. Estimation of the Common Population Variance (Pooled Variance) from the Data in Two Samples (Formulas 14a and 14b are Equivalent)

$$s^2 = \frac{\Sigma x_1^2 + \Sigma x_2^2}{N_1 + N_2 - 2} \qquad \text{(Formula 14a)}$$

$$s^2 = \frac{(N_1 - 1)s_1^2 + (N_2 - 1)s_2^2}{N_1 + N_2 - 2} \qquad \text{(Formula 14b)}$$

Formula 15. Estimate of the Standard Error of the Difference between Means (Pooled Variance Method)

$$s_{\bar{X}_1 - \bar{X}_2} = \sqrt{\frac{s^2}{N_1} + \frac{s^2}{N_2}}$$

Formula 16. Calculation of the t Ratio for Independent Means

$$t = \frac{\bar{X}_1 - \bar{X}_2}{s_{\bar{X}_1 - \bar{X}_2}}$$

Degrees of Freedom: $N_1 + N_2 - 2$

Formula 17. Estimation of the Population Variance of Difference Scores

$$s_D^2 = \frac{N\Sigma D^2 - (\Sigma D)^2}{N(N - 1)}$$

in which $D = X_1 - X_2$ for each pair of scores

Formula 18. Estimation of the Population Standard Error of the Mean Difference Scores (Formulas 18a and 18b are Equivalent)

$$s_{\bar{D}} = \sqrt{\frac{s_D^2}{N}}$$ (Formula 18a)

$$s_{\bar{D}} = \sqrt{\frac{N\Sigma D^2 - (\Sigma D)^2}{N^2(N-1)}}$$ (Formula 18b)

in which N = number of pairs of scores

Formula 19. Calculation of the t ratio for Non-independent Means

$$t = \frac{\bar{X}_1 - \bar{X}_2}{s_{\bar{D}}}$$

Degrees of freedom: $N - 1$ pairs of scores

Formula 20. F Test. Formula for Computing the F Ratio in the Analysis of Variance

$$F = \frac{\text{Mean Square between groups}}{\text{Mean Square within groups}} = \frac{MS_b}{MS_w}$$

Formula 21. Composition of the Total Sum of Squares

Total sum of squares = sum of squares between groups + sum of squares within groups.

$$SS_t = SS_b + SS_w$$

Formulas 22 through 24. Calculation of Sum of Squares

Total Sum of Squares $\qquad SS_t = \Sigma X^2 - \dfrac{(\Sigma X)^2}{N_t}$ (Formula 22)

Sum of Squares within Groups $\qquad SS_w = SS_A + SS_B + SS_C$ (Formula 23)
$$\text{(within group)}$$

Sum of Squares between Groups $\qquad SS_b = SS_t - SS_w$ (Formula 24a)

$$SS_b = N_A(\bar{X}_A - \bar{X}_t)^2 + N_B(\bar{X}_B - \bar{X}_t)^2 + N_C(\bar{X}_C - \bar{X}_t)^2 \qquad \text{(Formula 24b)}$$

Formulas 25 through 27. Calculation of Degrees of Freedom for Analysis of Variance

Degrees of freedom

Total $\qquad df_t = N - 1$ (Formula 25)

Between groups $\qquad df_b = $ No. of groups $- 1$ (Formula 26)

Within groups $\qquad df_w = df_t - df_b$ (Formula 27)

Formulas 28 and 29. Calculation of Mean Squares (variance estimates)

$$MS_b = \dfrac{SS_b}{df_b} \qquad \text{(Formula 28)}$$

$$MS_w = \dfrac{SS_w}{df_w} \qquad \text{(Formula 29)}$$

Formula 30. Computational Formulas for Sums of Squares

Group A	Group B	Group C	Total
ΣX_A	ΣX_B	ΣX_C	ΣX_t
$\Sigma X_A^{\,2}$	$\Sigma X_B^{\,2}$	$\Sigma X_C^{\,2}$	$\Sigma X_t^{\,2}$
N_A	N_B	N_C	N_t

Step 1   Correction term $C = \dfrac{(\Sigma X_t)^2}{N_t}$

Step 2   Total sum of squares $SS_t = \Sigma X_t^{\,2} - C$

Step 3   Sum of squares between $SS_b = \dfrac{(\Sigma X_A)^2}{N_A} + \dfrac{(\Sigma X_B)^2}{N_B} + \dfrac{(\Sigma X_C)^2}{N_C} - C$
groups

Step 4   Sum of squares within $SS_w = SS_t - SS_b$
groups

Formula 31. F Test. Calculation of the F Ratio for Comparison of Two Variance Estimates

$$F = \frac{\text{larger } s^2}{\text{smaller } s^2}$$

Formula 32. Calculation of the Pearson Product-Moment Correlation Coefficient

$$r = \frac{N\Sigma XY - (\Sigma X)(\Sigma Y)}{\sqrt{[N\Sigma X^2 - (\Sigma X)^2]\,[N\Sigma Y^2 - (\Sigma Y)^2]}}$$

in which N = number of pairs of scores

Degrees of Freedom: $N - 2$

Formulas 33-35. Formulas for Calculation of the Regression of Y on X

Formula 33. $\quad\quad\quad \tilde{Y} = a + b_{yx}X$ (regression equation)

Formula 34. $\quad b_{yx} = \dfrac{\Sigma XY - \dfrac{(\Sigma X)(\Sigma Y)}{N}}{\Sigma X^2 - \dfrac{(\Sigma X)^2}{N}}$ (regression coefficient)

Formula 35. $\quad\quad\quad a = \bar{Y} - b_{yx}\bar{X}$

in which $\tilde{Y}$ is the predicted value of Y

Formulas 36-38. Formulas for Calculation of the Regression of X on Y

Formula 36. $\quad\quad\quad \tilde{X} = a + b_{xy}Y$ (regression equation)

Formula 37. $\quad b_{xy} = \dfrac{\Sigma XY - \dfrac{(\Sigma X)(\Sigma Y)}{N}}{\Sigma Y^2 - \dfrac{(\Sigma Y)^2}{N}}$ (regression coefficient)

Formula 38. $\quad\quad\quad a = \bar{X} - b_{xy}\bar{Y}$

where $\tilde{X}$ is the predicted value of X

Formula 39. Calculation of Spearman's Rank Order
Correlation Coefficient (rho)

$$\rho = 1 - \frac{6\Sigma D^2}{N(N^2 - 1)}$$

in which $\quad D$ = difference between a pair of ranks

$\quad\quad\quad\quad N$ = number of pairs of ranks

Formula 40. Calculation of the Chi Square when $df = 1$

$$\chi^2 = \sum \frac{(|O - E| - .5)^2}{E}$$

in which O = observed frequency

E = expected frequency

The subtraction of .5 from each $|O - E|$ represents the Yates' correction for continuity.

Formula 41. Calculation of the Chi Square when df is Larger than 1

$$\chi^2 = \sum \frac{(O - E)^2}{E}$$

Formula 42. Calculation of the Expected Frequency (E) of a Cell

$$E = \frac{(N_{row}) (N_{col})}{N_{total}}$$

Degrees of Freedom: (number of rows $-$ 1) (number of columns $-$ 1)

GLOSSARY OF SYMBOLS
AND ABBREVIATIONS

a	Intercept in the regression equation
$A.D.$	Average deviation
b_{xy}	Regression coefficient for variable X on variable Y
b_{yx}	Regression coefficient for variable Y on variable X
D	Difference between two scores or ranks
df	Degrees of freedom
E	Expected frequency (in chi-square test)
F	Test statistic for the ratio of two variances
f	Frequency
f_b	Frequency below a class interval
f_w	Frequency within a class interval
i	Number of values encompassed by a class interval
$\ell\ell$	Lower limits of a class interval
Mdn	Median
MS	Mean square (in analysis of variance)
N	Number of scores or ranks
O	Observed frequency (in chi-square test)
P	Probability
Q	Semi-interquartile range
Q_1	Quartile designation (1st quartile)
r	Pearson product-moment correlation coefficient
r^2	Coefficient of determination
s'	Sample standard deviation
s'^2	Sample variance
s	Estimate of population standard deviation
s^2	Estimate of population variance
$s_{\bar{X}}$	Estimate of the standard error of the mean
s_D^2	Estimate of the population variance of difference scores
$s_{\bar{X}_1-\bar{X}_2}$	Estimate of the standard error of the difference between means
SS_b	Sum of squares between groups (in analysis of variance)
SS_w	Sum of squares within groups (in analysis of variance)
SS_t	Sum of squares of total groups (in analysis of variance)
t	Student's t-test statistic
X	Score value
$\bar{X}$	Sample mean

$\tilde{X}$	Estimate value (in regression equation)
x	Deviation of a score from the mean
$|x|$	Absolute deviation score
$\tilde{Y}$	Estimated value (in regression equation)
α	Probability of making a Type I error
β	Probability of making a Type II error
Σ	The sum of
μ	Population mean
σ	Population standard deviation
$\sigma_{\bar{X}}$	Standard error of the mean
σ^2	Population variance
$\sigma_{\bar{X}_1 - \bar{X}_2}$	Standard error of the difference between means
χ^2	Chi-square test statistic
ρ	Rank-order correlation coefficient

INDEX